SOUNDINGS

Leaving Certificate Poetry
Exam Anthology

Edited by
AUGUSTINE MARTIN

Foreword to this edition by
JOSEPH O'CONNOR

Gill & Macmillan

Gill & Macmillan Ltd
Hume Avenue, Park West, Dublin 12
with associated companies throughout the world
www.gillmacmillan.ie

© Introduction and Notes, Augustine Martin, 1969
© Foreword, Joseph O'Connor, 2010

978 07171 4841 7

Print origination in Ireland by Browne & Nolan Ltd
Printed in the UK by MPG Books Ltd, Cornwall

The paper used in this book comes from the wood
pulp of managed forests. For every tree felled at least
one tree is planted, thereby renewing natural
resources.

A CIP catalogue record for this book is available
from the British Library.

5 4 3

CONTENTS

FOREWORD

In my memory I have a scrapbook of images of my teenage schooldays in Ireland. The strange word 'Zoso'—it had appeared on the sleeve of an album by Led Zeppelin—stencilled onto the flap of a hessian satchel. A yellowing copy of the 1916 Proclamation, framed on the classroom wall. The phrase 'Phil Lynott Rules OK' carved into an ancient, time-blackened desk, which had a hole once intended for an inkwell. A statue of the Virgin Mary in an alcove of the corridor, the blue of her sash chipped by some long forgotten mishap. The papery taste of the communion wafer, the aroma of chalk dust, the celestial loveliness of a girl called Julie Elder—a neighbour I adored but never had the courage to talk to. Sebastian Barry describes old age as a burning headland that you don't know how you got to. The same is true of youth.

Among that tarot-deck of images there is one that still evokes so much shimmering pleasure that I can reach across the years and touch it. Its awful cover like a hippy's batik T-shirt; its glories and grandiosities, its appalling typography, the smell of its pages when rain soaked your schoolbag, the confusions and consolations it pointed to. It was a book that changed my life, a passport, a pillow, a collection of signposts, a treasury. It was perhaps the only textbook you'd ever read for pleasure. It was a collection of poetry called *Soundings*.

It was compiled and edited by a great educator, the late Gus Martin of UCD. Its contents opened worlds you hadn't known were there: the fiery cathedral of John Donne's mind, the October orchards of Thomas Kinsella. You tramped the roads with Chaucer's pilgrims, heard nightingales with Keats, lost yourself in the imperial march of John Milton's rhythms as utterly as Lucifer lost Paradise. Led Zeppelin sang of the Stairway to Heaven, but poetry was a walk on the wild side.

I was young in the era of The Boomtown Rats and punk rock, but no lyric that was ever spat into a microphone by the glorious Johnny Rotten could ever compete with the strangeness of Emily Dickinson. 'I felt a Funeral, in my Brain,' she said. Every teenager on the cusp of adulthood knew what she meant. 'When night stirred at sea/And the fire brought a crowd in,/They say that her beauty/Was music in mouth.' Austin Clarke's longing for the planter's daughter voiced the inarticulate speech of the heart. Dylan Thomas gave us the drunkenness of words, their intoxicating power. Yeats revealed that they could do anything you wanted. And the anthology did more than anyone has ever done to establish Patrick Kavanagh as a poet of immense significance. His Canal Bank sonnets had some reverberating quality that made every teenager I knew truly love them. This hurt, old man seemed one of us, somehow. His everyday redemptions might be ours.

But there was a seriousness about *Soundings*, a sense of not talking down to its readers. There was none of that excruciating attempt to get hip with the kids which can sometimes spoil anthologies of poetry for young people. *Soundings* was old-school. It knew what was what. It offered what the introduction terms 'great poems by great poets' and no apology for its assumptions or certainties. You took it as you found it or you didn't take it at all. It didn't want to be granddad at the disco.

Looking back, we might quibble. And I do so now. Were the Fab Four of Yeats, Kavanagh, Kinsella and Clarke truly the only Irish poets who merited inclusion? To have had only one woman poet in a 288-page book was a serious error of missed opportunities. But, despite its manifest failings of omission or commission, it offered a notion that had value and dignity: that this little windswept country on the western shores of Europe, where the rain fell horizontally and we didn't do a lot of things excellently, had been home to Easter Island giants of the language; that we were citizens of a republic, not condemned to mediocrity, and that between the cheaply printed cover was part of an astonishing inheritance.

Inspiring, annoying, generous, loving, *Soundings* was the book that brought poetry into hundreds of thousands of lives. It was virtual reality, decades before the Internet. It took you to places unimagined by Twitter. Amid the ink-stains of our adolescence, the shocking sweetness of first kisses, the pimples and growth-spurts and uncertainties and aches, it saw to it that poetry would find a way of seeding itself. We owe it that, and I truly honour it for that. Love does not rejoice in the wrong.

Poetry has a slow detonation. Its fuse burns long. Poems I struggled with as a teenager have become friends I couldn't live without. It was Gus Martin's genius to know that loving poetry is a marriage. There are good days and tough ones, rows and reunions, frustrations when you don't understand. Yes, you have to work at it but how immense are the rewards. All of it is worth it for the joy of those moments when the world bursts into life like a fruit.

If *Soundings* in several senses belongs to its era, it still has much to say. These days, young people in school are likely to be invited to write poems themselves, to experience poetry as a living adventure rather than a sternly beautiful inheritance. And through the excellent work of the Arts Council and Poetry Ireland, Irish schoolchildren can have the experience of meeting and hearing a poet, of talking back to poetry's makers with the openness and wonderment people of my own age reserved for talking to poems. I envy them that—and yet, and yet. Every reader meets Yeats in 'Among School Children', John Donne in 'Batter my Heart'. You just have to believe they are there, as Gus Martin believed it. A poetry reading is often a wonderfully enriching experience but sometimes you lose so much by hearing a poem read aloud. You don't even know how long it will be. It would be sad to see the solitary reading of poetry disappear.

Seamus Heaney's haunting poem 'The Given Note' talks of a traditional Irish tune coasting out of the night 'on loud weather'. Teenage years are loud, full of bombardments and indignations, the gorgeous fireworks of our certainties. We found ourselves so strange that we sought out simplicities. We thought we knew everything. And in one sense we did. For in *Soundings* we had been given a gift that would last a whole lifetime: the idea that between reader and writer, in the unique intimacy of that space, miracles of pleasure can happen. How poorer we would have been, in our frightened island of the past, without the secrets whose freedoms it rumoured.

Joseph O'Connor
Dublin, 2010

INTRODUCTION

The Intermediate Certificate course was designed to lead the student into poetry by the easier, more familiar roads. It contained a good deal of comic verse, dashing poems of adventure, poems of school-time or childhood experience, poems arising directly from Irish life. There was also poetry by the greatest writers in the language—Chaucer, Shakespeare, Donne, Wordsworth, Keats, Yeats, Eliot—though these writers were represented mostly by their less difficult poems. It was, in other words, a course designed to entice the young reader into the world of poetry through the gateways of his own experience, and to make his early encounters with verse as pleasant, varied and amusing as possible. The anthology, for instance, showed quite clearly that poetry often applies itself to a great range of enterprises, from the description of motor-cycling to the celebration of God's glory, from the questioning of death to the praise of young love. It demonstrated, too, that even great poets like Eliot could turn aside from contemplation of the Christian mysteries to delight in that brilliantly delinquent cat, Macavity. It showed, on the other hand, that the poets tended to concern themselves, as they do in this collection, with the great themes that have always interested sensitive and questioning people— birth, love and death, innocence, sin, man in nature, man in society, man in his relation to God, the sources of human joy and sorrow. It demonstrated, in other words, that poetry is co-extensive with life ; that great poetry must be grounded in life ; that it must reflect and transfigure the facts of living into the permanence and radiance of art.

It can, therefore, be assumed that the student taking up this book has already been introduced to most kinds of poetry, most forms of verse, and is now ready for more testing adventures in literature. The present anthology offers greater challenges, and promises even greater rewards. Clearly it is designed on sterner principles than its Intermediate predecessor : by and large it contains only great poems by great poets. Even in its Anglo-Irish section it is austere and critical, including only those poems that seem certain to endure. Some of the greatest poems in this collection are the simplest, others are among the most difficult. The thought in Shakespeare's " Like as the Waves " comes easier on the first reading than Donne's " Batter my Heart ", but they seem to me, in their different ways, of equal excellence. Yeats's " The Circus Animals' Desertion " is certainly more complex than his " No Second Troy " but its complexity does not make it either greater or inferior. The first of Thomas Kinsella's poems is more mysterious, less clear-cut, than his second, but both are comparable in depth, insight and symmetry.

Some of the poems are immediately understandable and enjoyable, others present certain initial obstacles to the reader. Milton's sonnet on his blindness is as comprehensible to the modern reader as it was to his own contemporaries, but his " Lycidas " requires a certain minimum of annotation before the modern student can achieve a full response to it. It is written according to pastoral conventions which the seventeenth-century reader, with his wide classical learning, readily accepted, but which the modern reader finds less easy to understand. On the other hand, a modern poet like Yeats was so engrossed in philosophy, mysticism and the history of art and ideas that many of his allusions are not immediately recognisable even to the most learned reader. In such cases the Explorations and Glossaries attempt to provide the necessary help.

It is a pity, in one sense, that such help is necessary. It would certainly be disastrous if the notes were in any circumstances to distract attention from the poem. It would be calamitous if the student were to imagine that familiarity with the questions and answers provided in the Explorations and the Glossaries might act as some sort of substitute for thorough and honest reading of the poems themselves. For, let it be agreed from the outset, the study of poetry must be based upon the reading of poems. When the poet has written his poem he has begun a process which is completed only when the reader has read it and made it his own. No poem means quite the same thing to any two readers, or even to the same reader at different periods of his life. Nobody—teacher, classmate, critic or parent—can read a poem for you. He may be able to offer help, elucidation, gloss, he may urge you to go back and look at things in the poem you may not have properly understood, but ultimately the reader himself must lay hold on the poem and experience it in the intimacy of his own mind. Unless he does this, the whole effort of teaching is at worst a fraud, at best a waste of time. This is why the primary virtue demanded in both the teacher and student of poetry is intellectual honesty. The poem is there for the reader, for his enjoyment and his enrichment ; it is not there as something to be used to please teachers, examiners or inspectors. One of the functions of the English class is to sponsor, encourage and facilitate this unique contact between pupil and poem. And that is the purpose of the Explorations and Glossaries in this edition.

Here we might distinguish between the functions of each. The Glossaries are meant merely to provide information neces-sary for the full understanding of a poem—information which the student might not have at his finger-tips. For instance, it is hardly insulting to assume that the average reader might not immediately identify Milton's references to ' Rabba ', or 'Arnon ', Jonson's to ' Japhets lyne ' or Yeats's to ' golden-thighed Pythagoras '. To remove these obstacles from the reader's way is clearly to help him get on with the main business of reading and understanding the poem. Similarly, it was thought useful to explain unusual or archaic words that might not be explained in a pocket dictionary. In one or two cases where the poet's thought seemed especially problematical it was decided to provide an approximate paraphrase. This was only done in cases of extreme difficulty, as with Dylan Thomas's "A Refusal to Mourn ". In this poem, for instance, the syntax is elliptical and the thought difficult unless viewed in terms of Thomas's universal attitude to death. It has, therefore, been briefly sum-marised. But the Glossaries are largely meant as data which will save pupil and teacher the drudgery and difficulty of plough-ing through reference works and wasting time which might be better spent in the vital activity of reading and enjoying the poetry.

The Explorations are of a different order, and are intended to serve a different purpose. These are all directed at the poem ; designed to send the reader back to the poem in order to savour it more fully. They urge the reader to encounter the poem at different levels, to probe its central themes and concerns more strenuously, to examine the progress of the thought through the poem, to consider how the thought is sometimes modified by an image here, an ambiguity there, a shift of tone or emphasis in another place. Their progress is usually from the thematic to the technical : the early questions incline to ask what the poem is about, the later ones seek to discover how this theme has been rendered through word, phrase, line and stanza, through cadence and image.

The method is largely interrogative, because it would be wrong to make dogmatic statements about the theme, tone or atmosphere of a poem, where so much depends on personal response. The questions are designed not to impose the editor's interpretation on the reader, but to help the reader form his own. There may be several legitimate answers to any question, and at times these may appear even to contradict one another. It is worth stressing, therefore, that any opinion which is solidly grounded in the text is valid. In the class discussion that might arise out of any or all of these Explorations the student has a chance to clarify his own views and sharpen his insights. In some cases the questions may serve best as written exercises.

But one result of these Explorations, and one for which no apology is offered, ought to be to make the student realise that poems don't happen by accident or miracle, and that, unlike Topsy, they haven't 'just growed'. A poem is a work of art, an 'artifact', something made by a combination of vision and skill. To lift the bonnet of a beautiful car and examine the engine is not to decrease but to increase our appreciation and respect both for the car and the men who built it. When later we stand back and see it move off our admiration is all the more valuable for being better informed. A poet works with words. In poetry words are made work harder than in any other medium. In great poetry words are never wasted, they are often made to perform several feats, to convey different meanings and feelings at the same time.

The good reader becomes conscious of these many functions and possibilities. When John Donne, addressing himself to God, writes

> Take me to you, imprison me, for I,
> Except you enthrall me, never shall be free,
> Nor ever chaste, except you ravish me.

the alert reader knows that he is dealing in a series of very sophisticated paradoxes. He knows that the word ' enthrall ' has more than one possible meaning, that the word ' ravish ' has more than two, and that all these meanings are related to one another. In other words he knows that he is dealing with language working superbly and pushed to the limits of its performance. When, on the other hand, he reads a poem like Hopkins's " The Windhover "—which is written in honour of Christ, Our Lord—and is given this incomparable description of a falcon in flight, he is conscious of how the movement of the words and images so perfectly mimes the strenuous but graceful motion of the bird :

> I caught this morning morning's minion, kingdom of daylight's
>   dauphin, dapple-dawn-drawn Falcon, in his riding
> Of the rolling level underneath him steady air, and striding
> High there, how he rung upon the rein of a wimpling wing
> In his ecstasy !

The reader is alert to the heraldic and chivalric imagery in which the hawk is rendered and which is turned to such good account at the end of the poem where the bird is compared to Christ, the greatest of all princes and dauphins. One could go on giving examples, but this would be to anticipate the work of the Explorations which try to conduct, through questions, this sort of enquiry in terms of each individual poem. In so doing they try to treat each poem as a unique statement by a uniquely sensitive intelligence about some aspect of life's mystery, a statement which deserves as sensitive and intelligent a response from the reader as he can give.

It is hardly necessary, at this level, to go into great detail in defining literary terms, especially as the more important of these have already been defined at Intermediate level in the *Exploring English* series. However, one might recapitulate briefly on the main categories used. A *convention* is a method of presentation in a literary work which its contemporary readers or audiences accepted without question. In " Lycidas ", for instance, Milton adopts the pastoral convention of comparing himself and King to shepherds driving their flocks afield when, in fact, they were student-poets at Cambridge. He makes bold to pluck the berries of his talent from the laurels and the myrtles before they are ripe, and calls upon the Sisters of the sacred well to help him mourn. These invocations were conventional in the pastoral mode, and it is only to modern readers, unfamiliar with that mode that they need to be explained. Similar adjustments must be made by the reader in approaching the mock-heroic of Pope and the epic of Milton—such conventions are explained as they arise.

By *language* we mean the basic manner of handling words, whether they are abstract or concrete, long or short, latinate, Anglo-Saxon or Anglo-Irish in derivation, whether they are conceptual or imagistic. By *imagery* is meant any use of words that tends to present a meaningful picture to the mind's eye. There are three main kinds of images. There is the *symbol*, which occurs when something in the poem subsumes to itself meanings beyond itself. Hopkins's windhover is present in the poem, it is a real bird, but as the poem proceeds it becomes clear that it stands for more than itself. What it stands for is not spelt out as an equation, it is left for the reader to infer. This is the method of symbol. The *simile* is different. We find in the seventh stanza of " Thoughts in a Garden " that Marvell compares his soul to a bird—' There, like a bird, it sits and sings . . . ' There is no real bird present, the bird is imported to illustrate a certain aspect of the poet's soul ; it is formally compared to his soul. Such formal comparisons which use the words ' like ' or ' as ' are easily recognised as similes. *Metaphors* are less formal comparisons, they do not employ such words as ' like ' or ' as '. Most poetic language is metaphorical. It is the marvellous and daring exertion of the metaphors that gives these lines of Yeats such vividness :

> An aged man is but a paltry thing,
> A tattered coat upon a stick, unless
> Soul clap its hands and sing, and louder sing
> For every tatter in its mortal dress . . .

Finally, symbol, simile and metaphor can be gathered into the generic term, *image*—a useful term, especially when in doubt.

By *theme* is meant the central concern of the poem ; the thought or preoccupation which gives unity to all the details, the idea which everything in the poem—words, images, stanzas —strives to express. By *tone* is meant something very close to tone of voice in speech or conversation. It is difficult to understand a poem's full meaning until one has discovered the right tone of voice in which to speak it ; as in conversation, the tone is part of the meaning. There is a great difference between Hopkins's passionate salutation to the windhover and Pope's mock obeisance at the court of Queen Anne :

> Here thou, great Anna ! whom three realms obey,
> Dost sometimes counsel take—and sometimes Tea.

Pope's tone is *ironical*, it invites the reader into a conspiracy of understanding at the expense of the royal court. Indeed, in any passage it is the tone that indicates the writer's attitude to the object he is contemplating, whether human, animate or inanimate.

In the matter of prosody one feels even more strongly the rightness of the position taken up in *Exploring English 3*. Exhaustive discussion of the various kinds of metrical feet from anapaest to amphibrach is not only time-consuming but in certain respects baneful to the enjoyment of poetry. Consequently the information given here, while slightly more ample than in the earlier volume, is sparing and strictly functional. The basic foot in English is the *iambus*, an unstressed syllable followed by a stressed one. The dominant line in English poetry is the *iambic pentameter* or five-foot iambic line :

> | When I | consid | er eve | rything | that grows |

This is the metre in which Chaucer wrote " The Canterbury Tales ", in which Shakespeare and Marlowe wrote their plays, in which Milton wrote his epics, in which Dryden and Pope wrote their satires, in which Wordsworth wrote " Tintern Abbey ", and in which every sonneteer wrote his sonnets.

When succeeding lines of iambic pentameter are unrhymed they are called *blank verse*, and when they rhyme in pairs they are called *heroic couplets* :

> All humane things are subject to decay,
> And, when Fate summons, Monarchs must obey.

Other forms of this metre are simply described as seven-foot, six-foot, four-foot, three-foot and two-foot iambic lines. The iambus is a rising foot, the light beat is followed by a heavy one. A variation on this rising beat is the *anapaest*, which consists of two light beats followed by a heavy one. Examples of this occur frequently in blank verse to break the monotony of the regular iambus :

| Say first, | for Heav | en hides not | hing from | thy view. |

The *trochee* is a falling foot, a heavy beat followed by a light one —in other words it is the reverse of the iambus. Poems in which trochaic metre is predominant are rare in English. It is more often used as a variation on iambic patterns as in Tennyson's "The Lotos-Eaters" where there is a subtle and persistent blend of different rhythms :

| Hateful | is the | dark-blue | sky, |

| Vaulted | o'er the | dark-blue | sea. |

| Death | is the end | of life ; | ah ! why |

| Should life | all lab | our be? |

A variation on the falling trochaic beat is the *dactyl*. The best way to fix this metrical foot in the mind is to think of the Irish poet Oliver Gogarty who became a character of equally dactylic nomenclature, Malachi Mulligan, in Joyce's *Ulysses*. It is doubtful whether senior students need even this amount of prosodical information for full appreciative discussion of English poetry. Certainly it is hard to see that they need any more.

In the matter of poetic forms it is useful to distinguish two main divisions of non-dramatic poetry, the *narrative* and the *lyrical*. Narrative verse tells a story. Its greatest manifestation is in the *epic* of which "Paradise Lost" is the greatest example in English. Its most sophisticated is the *mock-heroic*, or *mock-epic*, of which Pope's "The Rape of the Lock" is a distinguished example. Lyrical verse is distinguished by its musical quality and by the personal nature of its thought. Its most exalted form is the *ode*—" Tintern Abbey " is an outstanding example—and its most rigorous is the *sonnet*. There are two kinds of sonnet, the Petrarchan which uses the rhyme scheme, *abba, abba, cd, cd, cd*, with the allowed variation in the last six lines of *cde, cde*. There is usually a shift of thought or mood between the first eight lines, the octet, and the last six, the sestet. The other kind is the Shakespearean which has the rhyme scheme *abab, cdcd, efef, gg*. The final couplet usually contains a summary or a reversal of the thought that has been developed through the first twelve lines. The predominant metre of the sonnet is, of course, iambic pentameter. Another species of poetry is *satire* which can combine lyrical, narrative and dramatic methods as in " The Rape of the Lock ". Satire is a form of literature which attacks persons, customs or institutions in order to show their weaknesses, evils or absurdities. The great period of satire in English literature was the Augustan age and among its greatest exponents were Dryden and Pope.

There was a temptation to give here a potted history of English literature, or at least to enumerate and describe briefly the chief movements from Chaucer to the present day—Elizabethan, Metaphysical, Augustan, Romantic, Victorian, Modern. But this might have led to the danger that students would then come to the individual poems determined to find in them the tendencies of their period as outlined in such a description. Therefore, it was thought better to approach the poems first as poems and, where it was considered helpful, to bring in information from the history of poetry or ideas and incorporate this either in the biographical note on the poet or in the annotation of the individual poem.

In other words, every attempt must be made to preserve the integrity of each poem for the response of the individual reader. Between the covers of this book there is a splendid body of poetry, some of the finest poems from one of the greatest literatures in the world. They are there for the student, they are there to be enjoyed. Some of them may be difficult on first or second reading, but all of them will richly repay the effort to come to grips with them. A Beethoven symphony comes less easily to the ear and the sensibility than a pop song, but once it has made its impact it endures. So too with a great poem : it enters the mind and haunts the memory with its rhythms, images and intuitions. In his essay, *On Prose and Verse*, that very original Irish poet, James Stephens, wrote :

> For the poet is not singular nor unique : if he has memories, they are shared by us ; and if he has poesy, so have we all. Unless delight is behind the writer of even a sad tale, his very sadness will be untrue ; for it is the function of the artist to transform all that is sad, all that is ugly, all that is ' real ' into the one quality which reconciles the diversities that trouble us ; into Pure Poetry.

One might add that, unless delight is behind the learning and teaching of poetry, behind the reflection, frustration and effort that is a necessary part of that teaching and learning, the entire exercise is in vain. On the other hand, when it is enthusiastically tackled it can be one of the most rewarding and exciting of all human pursuits.

AUGUSTINE MARTIN

The Canterbury Tales

THE PROLOGUE

Here biginneth the Book of the Tales of Caunterbury.

Whan that Aprille with his shoures sote
The droghte of Marche hath perced to the rote,
And bathed every veyne in swich licour,
Of which vertu engendred is the flour ;
Whan Zephirus eek with his swete breeth   5
Inspired hath in every holt and heeth
The tendre croppes, and the yonge sonne
Hath in the Ram his halfe cours y-ronne,
And smale fowles maken melodye,
That slepen al the night with open yë,   10
(So priketh hem nature in hir corages) :
Than longen folk to goon on pilgrimages
(And palmers for to seken straunge strondes)
To ferne halwes, couthe in sondry londes ;
And specially, from every shires ende   15
Of Engelond, to Caunterbury they wende,
The holy blisful martir for to seke,
That hem hath holpen, whan that they were seke.
    Bifel that, in that seson on a day,
In Southwerk at the Tabard as I lay   20
Redy to wenden on my pilgrimage
To Caunterbury with ful devout corage,
At night was come in-to that hostelrye
Wel nyne and twenty in a companye,
Of sondry folk, by aventure y-falle   25
In felawshipe, and pilgrims were they alle,
That toward Caunterbury wolden ryde ;
The chambres and the stables weren wyde,
And wel we weren esed atte beste.
And shortly, whan the sonne was to reste,   30
So hadde I spoken with hem everichon,
That I was of hir felawshipe anon,
And made forward erly for to ryse,
To take our wey, ther as I yow devyse.

But natheles, whyl I have tyme and space,   35
Er that I ferther in this tale pace,
Me thinketh it acordaunt to resoun,
To telle yow al the condicioun
Of ech of hem, so as it semed me,
And whiche they weren, and of what degree ;   40
And eek in what array that they were inne :
And at a knight than wol I first biginne.
   A KNIGHT ther was, and that a worthy man,
That fro the tyme that he first bigan
To ryden out, he loved chivalrye,   45
Trouthe and honour, fredom and curteisye.
Ful worthy was he in his lordes werre,
And therto hadde he riden (no man ferre)
As wel in Cristendom as hethenesse,
And ever honoured for his worthinesse.   50
   At Alisaundre he was, whan it was wonne ;
Ful ofte tyme he hadde the bord bigonne
Aboven alle naciouns in Pruce.
In Lettow hadde he reysed and in Ruce,
No Cristen man so ofte of his degree.   55
In Gernade at the sege eek hadde he be
Of Algezir, and riden in Belmarye.
At Lyeys was he, and at Satalye,
Whan they were wonne ; and in the Grete See
At many a noble aryve hadde he be.   60
At mortal batailles hadde he been fiftene,
And foughten for our feith at Tramissene
In listes thryes, and ay slayn his fo.
This ilke worthy knight had been also
Somtyme with the lord of Palatye,   65
Ageyn another hethen in Turkye :
And evermore he hadde a sovereyn prys.
And though that he were worthy, he was wys,
And of his port as meke as is a mayde.
He never yet no vileinye ne sayde   70
In al his lyf, un-to no maner wight.
He was a verray parfit gentil knight.
But for to tellen yow of his array,
His hors were gode, but he was nat gay.

Of fustian he wered a gipoun   75
Al bismotered with his habergeoun ;
For he was late y-come from his viage,
And wente for to doon his pilgrimage.
   With him ther was his sone, a yong SQUYER,
A lovyere, and a lusty bacheler,   80
With lokkes crulle, as they were leyd in presse.
Of twenty yeer of age he was, I gesse.
Of his stature he was of evene lengthe,
And wonderly deliver, and greet of strengthe.
And he had been somtyme in chivachye,   85
In Flaundres, in Artoys, and Picardye,
And born him wel, as of so litel space,
In hope to stonden in his lady grace.
Embrouded was he, as it were a mede
Al ful of fresshe floures, whyte and rede.   90
Singinge he was, or floytinge, al the day ;
He was as fresh as is the month of May.
Short was his goune, with sleves longe and wyde.
Wel coude he sitte on hors, and faire ryde.
He coude songes make and wel endyte,   95
Juste and eek daunce, and wel purtreye and wryte.
So hote he lovede, that by nightertale
He sleep namore than dooth a nightingale.
Curteys he was, lowly, and servisable,
And carf biforn his fader at the table.   100
   A YEMAN hadde he, and servaunts namo
At that tyme, for him liste ryde so ;
And he was clad in cote and hood of grene ;
A sheef of pecok-arwes brighte and kene
Under his belt he bar ful thriftily ;   105
(Wel coude he dresse his takel yemanly :
His arwes drouped noght with fetheres lowe),
And in his hand he bar a mighty bowe.
A not-heed hadde he, with a broun visage.
Of wode-craft wel coude he al the usage.   110
Upon his arm he bar a gay bracer,
And by his syde a swerd and a bokeler,
And on that other syde a gay daggere,
Harneised wel, and sharp as point of spere ;

A Cristofre on his brest of silver shene.   115
An horn he bar, the bawdrik was of grene ;
A forster was he, soothly, as I gesse.
   Ther was also a Nonne, a PRIORESSE,
That of hir smyling was ful simple and coy ;
Hir gretteste ooth was but by sëynt Loy ;   120
And she was cleped madame Eglentyne.
Ful wel she song the service divyne,
Entuned in hir nose ful semely ;
And Frensh she spak ful faire and fetisly,
After the scole of Stratford atte Bowe,   125
For Frensh of Paris was to hir unknowe.
At mete wel y-taught was she with-alle ;
She leet no morsel from hir lippes falle,
Ne wette hir fingres in hir sauce depe.
Wel coude she carie a morsel, and wel kepe,   130
That no drope ne fille up-on hir brest.
In curteisye was set ful muche hir lest.
Hir over lippe wyped she so clene,
That in her coppe was no ferthing sene
Of grece, whan she dronken hadde hir draughte.   135
Ful semely after hir mete she raughte,
And sikerly she was of greet disport,
And ful plesaunt, and amiable of port,
And peyned hir to countrefete chere
Of court, and been estatlich of manere,   140
And to ben holden digne of reverence.
But, for to speken of hir conscience,
She was so charitable and so pitous,
She wolde wepe, if that she sawe a mous
Caught in a trappe, if it were deed or bledde.   145
Of smale houndes had she, that she fedde
With rosted flesh, or milk and wastel-breed.
But sore weep she if oon of hem were deed,
Or if men smoot it with a yerde smerte :
And al was conscience and tendre herte.   150
Ful semely hir wimpel pinched was ;
Hir nose tretys ; hir eyen greye as glas ;
Hir mouth ful smal, and ther-to softe and reed ;
But sikerly she hadde a fair forheed ;

It was almost a spanne brood, I trowe ;   155
For, hardily, she was nat undergrowe.
Ful fetis was hir cloke, as I was war.
Of smal coral aboute hir arm she bar
A peire of bedes, gauded al with grene ;
And ther-on heng a broche of gold ful shene,   160
On which ther was first write a crowned A,
And after, *Amor vincit omnia.*
    Another NONNE with hir hadde she,
That was hir chapeleyne, and PREESTES THREE.

Explorations

Before attempting the following exercises it is essential that the student read the extract through often enough to understand—with the help of the glossary—the archaic words and the run of the metre. With regard to the metre, the reader may be puzzled as to when he ought to sound the final ' e ' in words and when to leave it silent. The readiest solution is to sound the ' e ' when it suits the metre and leave it silent when it does not. Indeed, a few careful, intelligent readings should dispose of all the obstacles to understanding and appreciation.

1. It is generally agreed that in ' The Canterbury Tales ' Chaucer portrayed some of his characters as ideal figures, and some as real and often very imperfect human beings. To what class would you assign each of the four in this extract ? Why ?

2. In the portrait of the Knight, the poet concentrates on all the qualities that we would look for in a knight. Does he do the same for the Prioresse ? What conclusions do you draw from the things he does not tell us about each ?

3. Are the things he tells us about the Prioresse important in a prioress—that she eats daintily, sings the divine service in the fashionable way, pities dead mice and is elegant in her habit ? What is Chaucer's purpose in mentioning them ?

4. Have you seen such people as the Prioresse in plays, films or novels, or have you ever met such a person in real life ? Has the Prioresse a serious defect of character ? If so, what is it ?

5. Have you met anyone like the Squire ? Identify the similarities and the differences.

6. The Knight, Squire and Yeoman are often referred to as the ' feudal group ' in the Prologue. Can you suggest why ? What sort

of picture of feudal society—structure, customs, dress and values—can you form by studying this group ? What further details are added by the portrait of the Prioresse ?

7. When we speak of tone in poetry we are usually thinking of the poet's attitude to the person or thing he is describing. Would you agree that Chaucer employs a different tone in describing each of his four characters here ? If so, indicate in a general way what the differences are.

8. There is a certain amount of irony in the portrait of the Squire. Quote the relevant lines. Comparing the portraits of the Squire and the Prioresse, in which is the irony more gentle ? Explain.

9. Is there irony in the motto on the Prioresse's brooch ? Is the entire portrait ironical ? Explain.

10. When Chaucer wishes to get subtle, ironic effects, he uses subtle, indirect means. When he wants simple, direct effects, he is extremely simple, both in language and method. Examine the portraits of the Knight, the Yeoman, and the Prioresse with this in mind.

11. Now re-read the opening of the poem. In what respects does it set the tone for the variety and humour that come after ? Consider the timing of line 12, its meaning, emphasis and tone.

12. Bearing in mind questions 1, 9 and 10 above, compose in verse or prose (a) a portrait of an ideal prioress, or (b) an imperfect knight or yeoman.

13. Write a note on Chaucer's use of significant detail in the extract.

14. Write a critical note on Chaucer's varying use of the adjective throughout the extract—start with those used in describing characters.

Glossary p. 205

Sonnet No. 15

When I consider everything that grows
Holds in perfection but a little moment,
That this huge stage presenteth nought but shows
Whereon the stars in secret influence comment :
When I perceive that men as plants increase,   5
Cheered and check'd e'en by the self-same sky,
Vaunt in their youthful sap, at height decrease,
And wear their brave state out of memory :
Then the conceit of this inconstant stay
Sets you most rich in youth before my sight,   10
Where wasteful Time debateth with decay,
To change your day of youth to sullied night ;
   And, all in war with Time for love of you,
   As he takes from you, I engraft you new.

Explorations

1. The poet is meditating upon the transience of youth and beauty, the manner in which man reaches his prime and then begins to decline towards death. He discusses the matter first in general and then in particular terms. Where does the poem alter its focus ? Explain.

2. Men are compared to plants in the first two lines and to actors in the second two lines. Show how both images are blended in the next quatrain. See whether the imagery is continued into the last section of the poem.

3. What view of life is contained in the poem—tragic, comic, cheerful, or despairing ? Is there a blend of these feelings ? Explain, referring to relevant details of phrase or imagery. Try reading the poem aloud.

4. Which looms larger in the poem, the thoughts about life and death, or the feeling of love and friendship ? In this respect compare the poem with *Sonnets 60, 73* or *116*.

5. The sonnet presents a closely knit sequence of thought. Comment on the economy and force with which the main and subsidiary themes are developed.

6. In terms of imagery, compare this sonnet with *Sonnet 23* on the one hand and with *Sonnet 60* or *73* on the other.

Glossary p. 208

Sonnet No. 23

As an unperfect actor on the stage,
Who with his fear is put besides his part,
Or some fierce thing replete with too much rage,
Whose strength's abundance weakens his own heart;
So I, for fear of trust, forget to say   5
The perfect ceremony of love's rite,
And in mine own love's strength seem to decay,
O'ercharg'd with burthen of mine own love's might.
O! let my books be then the eloquence
And dumb presagers of my speaking breast,   10
Who plead for love, and look for recompense,
More than that tongue that more hath more express'd.
    O ! learn to read what silent love hath writ :
    To hear with eyes belongs to love's fine wit.

Explorations

1. The poet wishes to explain and excuse his failure to express his love with ' perfect ceremony'. What two arguments does he put forward in his defence ?

2. In failing to speak out his love, the poet considers himself an incompetent and unworthy lover. Is his sense of failure complete ? In trusting to poems rather than speeches, does he offer his beloved a greater compliment ? Before answering, look at the last line of the poem.

3. Paradox is truth inherent in a contradiction. Explain the various paradoxes that occur in this sonnet. Do you find them effective ? Explain.

4. Would you agree that there is a blend of pride and humility in the poem ? Show how they are blended. Does it help to remember that the poet is no longer a young man ?

5. Trace the development of the thought and feeling in the sonnet. What significant changes of tone occur in the second part of the poem ?

6. Read *Sonnet 73* and compare it with this sonnet in tone and theme. Read also *Sonnet 15*.

Glossary p. 208

Sonnet No. 29

When in disgrace with fortune and men's eyes
I all alone beweep my outcast state,
And trouble deaf heaven with my bootless cries,
And look upon myself, and curse my fate :
Wishing me like to one more rich in hope,   5
Featur'd like him, like him with friends possess'd,
Desiring this man's art, and that man's scope,
With what I most enjoy contented least :
Yet in these thoughts myself almost despising,
Haply I think on thee,—and then my state,   10
Like to the lark at break of day arising
From sullen earth, sings hymns at heaven's gate ;
    For thy sweet love remember'd such wealth brings
    That then I scorn to change my state with kings.

Explorations

1. There is a clear division in this poem. Where does it occur ? Is it a change of thought or feeling or both ? Read the poem aloud.

2. Are the miseries described purely individual to the poet, or are they common to all sorts of people ? Take them one by one. Comment on the poetic skill with which they are listed.

3. Can it be that the poet's misery at the outset is connected with the fact that he is thinking only of himself ? Before answering, glance at the last few lines.

4. The poem's two moods are joined by a common image of heaven. Examine this image in detail and discuss.

5. A good sonnet should achieve a sense of completeness. Does this one ? Examine carefully the two movements, beginning perhaps with the first and last lines of the poem.

6. Has the poem anything in common with the structure of a Petrarchan sonnet ? (See Introduction.) Glance at some of the other sonnets in the sequence with this idea in mind, especially at *Sonnet 30* in which you may also find similarities of theme.

Glossary p. 209

Sonnet No. 30

When to the sessions of sweet silent thought
I summon up remembrance of things past,
I sigh the lack of many a thing I sought,
And with old woes new wail my dear time's waste :
Then can I drown an eye, unus'd to flow,   5
For precious friends hid in death's dateless night,
And weep afresh love's long since cancell'd woe,
And moan th' expense of many a vanish'd sight :
Then can I grieve at grievances foregone,
And heavily from woe to woe tell o'er   10
The sad account of fore-bemoaned moan,
Which I new pay as if not paid before.
    But if the while I think on thee, dear friend,
    All losses are restor'd and sorrows end.

Explorations

1.   The mood is one of gloomy meditation. Do the sound effects contribute much to this mood ? Read the poem aloud in the tone you think appropriate and then discuss the sound in detail.

2.   The poet uses the word ' sweet ' when referring to his meditation. Is this consistent with what follows ?

3.   The opening metaphor is clearly a legal one. Explain it. What other ideas or phrases in the poem are drawn from the world of law ? What is their effect ?

4.   There is a great deal of deliberate verbal intricacy in the poem, as, for instance, in line 4. What is the effect of this ? Is it always successful ? Go through the poem again and think the matter out. If you come to the conclusion that the intricacy is overdone, state your reasons for thinking so.

5.   Do you find the shift of thought in the last couplet satisfactory ? If the sonnet were read in isolation from the other sonnets in the sequence, might it be less so ?

Glossary p. 209

Sonnet No. 55

Not marble, nor the gilded monuments
Of princes, shall outlive this powerful rime ;
But you shall shine more bright in these contents
Than unswept stone, besmear'd with sluttish time.
When wasteful war shall statues overturn,   5
And broils root out the work of masonry,
Nor Mars his sword nor war's quick fire shall burn
The living record of your memory.
'Gainst death and all-oblivious enmity
Shall you pace forth ; your praise shall still find room,   10
Even in the eyes of all posterity
That wear this world out to the ending doom.
    So, till the judgment that yourself arise,
    You live in this, and dwell in lovers' eyes.

Explorations

1.   The poet mingles several themes in this sonnet : the immortality of his verse, its durability compared with stone or marble, his service in immortalising his beloved. Which is the dominating theme ? Does the poet, in your opinion, blend the themes into a satisfying unity ? Read the poem carefully and ponder before answering.

2.   Consider the poem's structure, how the themes are introduced, sustained and developed, as the quatrains follow one another. Begin, perhaps, by picking out the references to the beloved.

3.   Which emerges more strongly from the poem, the poet's love or his pride ? Explain.

4.   Would you agree that this poem is full of sounds which echo the thought and mood ? Give instances. Read it aloud several times with this in mind. Pay particular attention to the light vowels and heavy consonants, and to the pace generally.

5.   Which lines do you find most vivid and energetic ? Can you explain why ?

6.   Write a critical note on Shakespeare's use of the adjective in this sonnet.

7.   Compare the imagery of this sonnet with that of *Sonnets 64* and *65*. Now contrast the themes.

Glossary p. 209

Sonnet No. 60

Like as the waves make towards the pebbled shore,
So do our minutes hasten to their end ;
Each changing place with that which goes before,
In sequent toil all forwards do contend.
Nativity, once in the main of light,   5
Crawls to maturity, wherewith being crown'd,
Crooked eclipses 'gainst his glory fight,
And Time that gave doth now his gift confound.
Time doth transfix the flourish set on youth
And delves the parallels in beauty's brow,   10
Feeds on the rarities of nature's truth,
And nothing stands but for his scythe to mow :
   And yet to times in hope my verse shall stand,
   Praising thy worth, despite his cruel hand.

Explorations

1. The poem opens with a general statement, ends with a particularised one. Examine the structure of the poem and see how the poet moves from the first to the final position.

2. The thought in the first quatrain is restated and developed in the second. Examine and compare the two sets of images. Which quatrain do you find more vivid ? Is the imagery of the first quatrain re-echoed anywhere in the second ?

3. Would you agree that Time grows more threatening as the sonnet proceeds ? Trace this progress through the various shifts of imagery, and see whether you find it effective. What would you say is the purpose of this poetic strategy, especially in view of the final couplet ?

4. Which lines or images in the poem appeal to you most ? Try to analyse why.

5. How would you describe the poet's tone—sad, cheerful, bitter, resigned, defiant . . .? Where is this tone most evident ? Does the tone remain consistent throughout ?

Glossary p. 209

Sonnet No. 64

When I have seen by Time's fell hand defaced
The rich proud cost of outworn buried age ;
When sometime lofty towers I see down razed,
And brass eternal slave to mortal rage :
When I have seen the hungry ocean gain   5
Advantage on the kingdom of the shore,
And the firm soil win of the watery main,
Increasing store with loss, and loss with store :
When I have seen such interchange of state,
Or state itself confounded to decay ;   10
Ruin hath taught me thus to ruminate—
That Time will come and take my love away.
　　This thought is as a death, which cannot choose
　　But weep to have that which it fears to lose.

Explorations

1. The poet gives several images of decay and transience. Which of them strikes you most forcibly and why ?

2. What is the theme of the sonnet ? In how far is it a love poem ?

3. There is a change of tone in the sonnet. Where is it ? What does it entail in terms of thought and feeling ?

4. Looking back at the way the poet organised his thought, can you see him preparing for this change ? Can you see any movement from the impersonal to the personal ? Explain.

5. The dominating imagery is of war and conquest on one hand and of rule on the other. Trace this imagery carefully through the poem and show how it operates. Where does it leave off ? Why ?

6. The language of the first eleven lines is different from that of the last three. Explain the difference and its significance.

7. What view of life is contained in the poem—grave, gay, tragic, bitter ?

8. Read carefully *Sonnets 55* and *65* and be ready to contrast and compare them with this in theme, tone and structure.

Glossary p. 210

Sonnet No. 65

Since brass, nor stone, nor earth, nor boundless sea,
But sad mortality o'ersways their power,
How with this rage shall beauty hold a plea,
Whose action is no stronger than a flower ?
O ! how shall summer's honey breath hold out   5
Against the wrackful siege of batt'ring days,
When rocks impregnable are not so stout,
Nor gates of steel so strong, but Time decays ?
O fearful meditation ! where, alack,
Shall Time's best jewel from Time's chest lie hid ?   10
Or what strong hand can hold his swift foot back ?
Or who his spoil of beauty can forbid ?
    O ! none, unless this miracle have might,
    That in black ink my love may still shine bright.

Explorations

1. The idea of Time is conveyed, through the first eight lines,
in a set of related images. What other words does the poet use here
for the enemy, Time ? Show how the images work.

2. Where does the poet use contrast ? What is its effectiveness ?

3. There is an extremely subtle and complex image in lines 9 and
10. Before looking at the glossary, see to what extent you can work
it out on your own.

4. What does Shakespeare mean by ' miracle ' in the last couplet ?
Is the word justified ? Is it in any sense the climax of the thought ?
Explain. If you do not think it is, can you suggest an alternative
climax ?

5. Would you agree that there is an increasing sense of desperation
and alarm as the poem proceeds ? If so, point out how this is created
and sustained. Is it at any point arrested ? If so, what is the effect ?

6. Discuss the poet's use of questions in this sonnet.

7. There are obvious points of comparison between this sonnet
and *Sonnet 64*. Consider the poems under the following heads :
imagery, tone, structure. Are there any other points of comparison ?

Glossary p. 210

Sonnet No. 71

No longer mourn for me when I am dead
Than you shall hear the surly sullen bell
Give warning to the world that I am fled
From this vile world, with vilest worms to dwell :
Nay, if you read this line, remember not   5
The hand that writ it ; for I love you so,
That I in your sweet thoughts would be forgot,
If thinking on me then should make you woe.
O ! if, I say, you look upon this verse,
When I perhaps compounded am with clay,   10
Do not so much as my poor name rehearse,
But let your love even with my life decay ;
    Lest the wise world should look into your moan,
    And mock you with me after I am gone.

Explorations

1. The poet implores his beloved to forget him after he has died.
What reasons does he urge for this ? Read carefully.

2. Does the poet intend that his plea be taken in its literal sense ?
Or is he using a device or convention to make known the intensity
and selflessness of his love ? Pay particular attention to lines 11 to 14.

3. Are you made to shudder at the gloomier images ? Analyse
briefly your feelings towards them.

4. What contribution is made to the poem by the various sound
effects and repetitions ?

5. One critic has observed that the poem ' was written in a mood
of such deep depression that it achieves an effect of quite gay sarcasm.'
Would you agree with him either about the depth of the depression
or the gaiety of the sarcasm ? How would you describe the tone of
the sonnet ? Illustrate.

6. Would you be horrified if one were to call this a witty poem ?
Read and digest it for several days before answering.

Sonnet No. 73

That time of year thou mayst in me behold
When yellow leaves, or none, or few, do hang
Upon those boughs which shake against the cold,
Bare ruin'd choirs, where late the sweet birds sang.
In me thou see'st the twilight of such day   5
As after sunset fadeth in the west,
Which by and by black night doth take away,
Death's second self, that seals up all in rest.
In me thou see'st the glowing of such fire,
That on the ashes of his youth doth lie,   10
As the death-bed whereon it must expire
Consum'd with that which it was nourish'd by.
   This thou perceiv'st, which makes thy love more strong,
   To love that well which thou must leave ere long.

Explorations

1. In this poem there are three sets of metaphors expressing a common theme. What is the theme? Which metaphor strikes you as the most vivid? Which is the most apt? Explain.

2. Would you agree that the poem has some striking combinations of sound, vision and sense? Explain and illustrate.

3. What is the poet's predominant mood and tone as he faces the certainty of old age and death—bitterness, sorrow, anger, regret, resignation . . . ? Which lines convey his feelings best? Explain.

4. What is the main theme of this poem, love or death? Consider the presence of ' thou ' in the poem. Does the final couplet strengthen or weaken the poem's total effect?

5. This is regarded by many as one of Shakespeare's most profound and beautiful sonnets. Give your reasons for agreeing or disagreeing with this judgement.

6. *Sonnets 64* and *73* are both concerned with love, the passage of time, and the approach of death. But they are each written from different points of view. Identify the differences. Which poem is the more arresting?

7. Examine each quatrain in detail. Comment upon it, exploring all its aspects, especially language and imagery.

Glossary p. 210

Sonnet No. 86

Was it the proud full sail of his great verse,
Bound for the prize of all too precious you,
That did my ripe thoughts in my brain inhearse,
Making their tomb the womb wherein they grew?
Was it his spirit, by spirits taught to write   5
Above a mortal pitch, that struck me dead?
No, neither he, nor his compeers by night
Giving him aid, my verse astonished.
He, nor that affable familiar ghost
Which nightly gulls him with intelligence,   10
As victors of my silence cannot boast;
I was not sick of any fear from thence:
   But when your countenance fill'd up his line,
   Then lack'd I matter; that enfeebled mine.

Note

While critics agree about the greatness of this sonnet, they differ widely as to the spirit in which it ought to be read. Shakespeare is troubled because a rival poet—probably Chapman, whose great translations of Homer were at this time appearing—is competing with him for the friendship and maybe the patronage of the young man to whom the preceding sonnets are addressed.

One school of critics argues that Shakespeare's praise of his rival's poetry is ironical, that he is in fact mocking the other poet's talent and his claims to have been inspired by spirits in his work. This ironic interpretation depends heavily on the word 'gulls' in line 10. The word literally means 'fools' and, if taken so, it certainly conjures up the picture of a poet who is taking himself far too seriously for his modest talents.

The other school argues that the first eight lines are so splendid and forceful that they must be sincere. Such critics re-interpret 'gulls' to make it mean the common deception that the Muse practises on all poets—filling their imaginations with 'intelligence', knowledge that may be very beautiful in itself, but which is a hindrance rather than a help in the practical business of living.

This difference of opinion among critics provides an excellent opportunity to assess the importance of tone in reading a poem. It is hoped that each student will earn, by sensitive reading, the right to his own interpretation.

Explorations

1. Shakespeare, confronted by his rival's work, finds himself unable to write. Where, and in what images, does he refer to this inarticulacy? Do any of these images seem to you specially vivid? Explain.

2. Do any other images in the poem strike you as particularly appropriate? Consider also the sound effects.

3. The poet considers, but then dismisses, certain possible causes of his failure of inspiration. What are they?

4. The real reason is given in the final couplet. What is it? Is the timing of it effective? Discuss.

5. Having read the poem alertly and studied it, are you ready to give your opinion as to whether the praise is sincere or whether it is a device to mock his rival's talent? Give your reasons.

6. This appears to be a poem motivated by jealousy. How real is the pain expressed? Can you account for the generosity apparent in the first few lines?

Glossary p. 210

Sonnet No. 87

Farewell ! thou art too dear for my possessing,
And like enough thou know'st thy estimate :
The charter of thy worth gives thee releasing ;
My bonds in thee are all determinate.
For how do I hold thee but by thy granting ?   5
And for that riches where is my deserving ?
The cause of this fair gift in me is wanting,
And so my patent back again is swerving.
Thyself thou gav'st, thy own worth then not knowing,
Or me, to whom thou gav'st it, else mistaking ;   10
So thy great gift, upon misprision growing,
Comes home again, on better judgment making.
    Thus have I had thee, as a dream doth flatter,
    In sleep a king, but, waking, no such matter.

Explorations

1. The governing image here is a legal one ; the poet represents the end of a friendship as the termination of a legal contract. Identify all the legal terminology and then trace the imagery from line to line.

2. Is there a rigorous logic about the argument ? Summarise the reasoning step by step. Do you find it sound ?

3. Read the poem aloud. How would you describe the pace and sound ? Do they suit the theme ?

4. The surface tone suggests a great sense of unworthiness in the poet and admiration for the beloved. Are there any hints that the poet may have reservations ?

5. Would you describe this as a poem of great feeling ? Give your reasons, whatever your opinion, and illustrate them with reference to significant lines, phrases and images.

6. How, in fact, would you define the tone of the sonnet ? Explain and illustrate by pointing to a line or phrase that seems typical of this tone. What is the effect, in this respect, of the double rhymes (see Introduction) and of the final phrase ? Read *Sonnet 116* with this question in mind.

Glossary p. 211

Sonnet No. 116

Let me not to the marriage of true minds
Admit impediments. Love is not love
Which alters when it alteration finds,
Or bends with the remover to remove.
O, no ! it is an ever-fixed mark,   5
That looks on tempests and is never shaken ;
It is the star to every wand'ring bark,
Whose worth's unknown, although his height be taken.
Love's not Time's fool, though rosy lips and cheeks
Within his bending sickle's compass come ;   10
Love alters not with his brief hours and weeks,
But bears it out even to the edge of doom.
  If this be error, and upon me proved,
  I never writ, nor no man ever loved.

Explorations

1. Would you agree that the poet's feeling rises steadily as the poem proceeds ? Read it again carefully, preferably aloud, then mark the various stages of intensity.

2. Would you agree that there is both strength and tenderness in the sonnet ? Can you indicate examples of each ?

3. What is the central theme of the poem ? What do you think was the occasion of it ? *Sonnets 86* and *87* may help you to get it in perspective.

4. What is the effect of the language, sound and pace of the twelfth line ? Is this the climax of the thought ? Explain.

5. Much of the poem's grace and clarity comes from the poet's use of antithesis, the balance of one idea against another, often its opposite : ' Whose worth's unknown, although his height be taken.' Where else in the poem is this device to be found ? What sort of satisfaction does it give the reader ?

6. Is the poet's view of love and time the same as that expressed in the earlier sonnets ? If not, where does the difference lie—in theme, tone, image ? You might look especially at *Sonnets 15, 55, 64, 65* or *71.*

Glossary p. 211

Sonnet No. 130

My mistress' eyes are nothing like the sun ;
Coral is far more red than her lips' red :
If snow be white, why then her breasts are dun ;
If hairs be wires, black wires grow on her head.
I have seen roses damask'd, red and white,   5
But no such roses see I in her cheeks ;
And in some perfumes is there more delight
Than in the breath that from my mistress reeks.
I love to hear her speak, yet well I know
That music hath a far more pleasing sound :   10
I grant I never saw a goddess go,—
My mistress, when she walks, treads on the ground.
    And yet, by heaven, I think my love as rare
    As any she belied with false compare.

Explorations

1. From the outset let us be clear that Shakespeare is mocking a conventional form of love poetry in which extravagant praise is lavished by the poet on the lady he is praising ; attributing to her, eyes that shine like the sun, lips like coral, cheeks like the rose, and so on. Consequently, the poem is about two things, the girl and the poetic convention. Now having read the poem once or twice, do you think he is being altogether sincere in the final couplet ? Why ?

2. In the three quatrains is he (a) mocking the girl, (b) soberly stating her real but limited attractiveness, or (c) combining both of these ? Go carefully through the poem and put an interpretation on every descriptive phrase within these terms of reference. Be careful that you do not spoil the delicate balance of tone by putting a false modern meaning on the word ' reeks ' which merely means ' exhales'.

3. Would you say he is fond of her ? Explain and illustrate.

4. How would you describe the tone of the poem ? Point out a phrase or two that seem to embody the tone especially well. Read the poem aloud so as to illustrate your opinion.

5. Do you think this poem witty or humorous ? Do you find it disconcerting ? Give reasons for your answer.

Glossary p. 211

Sonnet No. 146

Poor soul, the centre of my sinful earth,
Rebuke these rebel powers that thee array !
Why dost thou pine within and suffer dearth,
Painting thy outward walls so costly gay ?
Why so large cost, having so short a lease,   5
Dost thou upon thy fading mansion spend ?
Shall worms, inheritors of this excess,
Eat up thy charge ? Is this thy body's end ?
Then, soul, live thou upon thy servant's loss,
And let that pine to aggravate thy store ;   10
Buy terms divine in selling hours of dross :
Within be fed, without be rich no more.
   So shalt thou feed on Death, that feeds on men,
   And Death once dead, there's no more dying then.

Explorations

1. The first two quatrains ask the sort of questions that the final six lines attempt to answer. What is the central concern of the questions ? In general terms, what is the answer ?

2. To what is the body compared in the course of the first eight lines ? Is it an effective metaphor ? Trace its development. Does it remind you of any biblical statement on similar themes ?

3. Analyse the argument of the first three quatrains, then sort out the apparent contradictions of the final couplet and relate them to the rest of the poem.

4. To whom do you think this poem is addressed ? Work out all the implications of the first line. How would you describe the tone of the poem ?

5. This poem has sometimes been rated as evidence that Shakespeare held a specifically Christian view of life. Examine the evidence.

6. Sonnets 60, 73 and 146 are concerned with the passing of youth and beauty and the approach of death. Compare and contrast the central ideas in these poems and the images used to convey them.

Glossary p. 212

A Hymne to God the Father

Heare mee, O God !
  A broken heart
  Is my best part :
Use still thy rod,
  That I may prove   5
  Therein, thy Love.

If thou hadst not
  Beene sterne to mee,
  But left me free,
I had forgot   10
  My selfe and thee.

For, sin's so sweet,
  As minds ill bent
  Rarely repent,
Untill they meet   15
  Their punishment.

Who more can crave
  Then thou hast done :
  That gav'st a Sonne,
To free a slave ?   20
  First made of nought ;
  With all since bought.

Sinne, Death, and Hell,
  His glorious Name
  Quite overcame,   25
Yet I rebell,
  And slight the same.

But, I'le come in,
  Before my losse,
  Me farther tosse,
As sure to win   30
  Under his Crosse.

Explorations

1. Paraphrase in your own words the thought here as it moves from stanza to stanza. Is there any obvious logic in the progress of the thought?

2. Examine the stanza arrangement. Can you suggest a reason why the first and fourth stanzas differ in length from the others? Does the second long stanza mark a change in the direction of the thought?

3. In what sense do the first and last stanzas act as a frame? Does such similarity help to give a sense of completeness? Explain.

4. How would you describe Jonson's manner in stating his theme—simple, complex, direct, subtle, obvious . . .? How does it compare with Donne's statement of a similar theme in his poem of the same name? Read both poems carefully before answering.

5. Consider the poet's attitude to God. How does the tone of the poem reveal this attitude? In how far is it a personal prayer to God and in how far a general reflection on sin and salvation?

Glossary p. 212

An Ode. To himselfe

Where do'st thou carelesse lie
    Buried in ease and sloth ?
Knowledge, that sleepes, doth die ;
And this Securitie,
    It is the common Moath,   5
That eats on wits, and Arts, and oft destroyes
    them both.

Are all th'Aonian springs
    Dri'd up ? lyes Thespia wast ?
Doth Clarius Harp want strings,
That not a Nymph now sings !   10
    Or droop they as disgrac't,
To see their Seats and Bowers by chattring
    Pies defac't ?

If hence thy silence be,
    As 'tis too just a cause ;
Let this thought quicken thee,   15
Minds that are great and free,
    Should not on fortune pause,
'Tis crowne enough to vertue still, her owne
    applause.

What though the greedie Frie
    Be taken with false Baytes   20
Of worded Balladrie,
And thinke it Poesie ?
    They die with their conceits,
And only pitious scorne, upon their folly
    waites.

Then take in hand thy Lyre,   25
    Strike in thy proper straine,
With Japhets lyne, aspire
Sols Chariot for new fire,
    To give the world againe :
Who aided him, will thee, the issue of Joves
    braine.   30

And since our Daintie age
Cannot endure reproofe,
Make not thy selfe a Page,
To that strumpet the Stage,
But sing high and aloofe,   35
Safe from the wolves black jaw, and the dull
Asses hoofe.

Explorations

1. This is one of two odes that Jonson wrote in disgust about the theatre of his day where vulgar and second-rate drama was more appreciated than his own great comedies. In the first stanza he questions himself harshly about his own idleness. In the second, he suggests two reasons for this ' sloth '. What are they ?

2. In the third stanza he admits that these form ' too just a cause ' for his ' sloth ', but goes on to argue that he ought still persist in his writing. What arguments does he put forward in support of this ?

3. In stanza four, he compares the theatre-goers to ' greedie Frie '. Work out the rest of the imagery in this stanza. How would you describe the tone here—angry, bitter, proud, contemptuous . . . ?

4. Read the notes in the glossary on Japhet, Sol and Jove and explain the thought of stanza five in detail.

5. The final stanza brings the thought to a conclusion. Jonson was a satirist, and he suggests that satire is going out of fashion. In lines 33 to 35 he implies that there are two courses of action and he chooses one of them. What are the courses open to him ? What does he mean by ' the wolves black jaw, and the dull Asses hoofe ' ?

6. Consider the tone of the poem as a whole. To whom do you think was Jonson really addressing it—to himself or to a wider audience ?

7. What sort of man would you say Jonson was ? What is his attitude to the playgoers of his time ? What is his attitude towards his vocation as a writer ? What has it in common with Shakespeare's in *Sonnet 55* ? In what respects do they differ ?

8. Comment on the structure of the stanzas. Work out the metre and rhyme scheme of the first stanza. How, for instance, does the long concluding line affect the pace of the thought ? Now consider the whole poem with this in mind.

Glossary p. 212

Song : *from* The Silent Woman

Still to be neat, still to be drest,
As, you were going to a feast ;
Still to be pou'dred, still perfum'd :
Lady, it is to be presum'd,
Though arts hid causes are not found, 5
All is not sweet, all is not sound.

Give me a looke, give me a face,
That makes simplicitie a grace ;
Robes loosely flowing, haire as free :
Such sweet neglect more taketh me, 10
Then all th'adulteries of art.
They strike mine eyes, but not my heart.

Explorations

1. There are two references to ' art ' in the poem. What is meant by the word ? What concrete examples of it are given in the poem ?

2. What quality does the poet oppose to art ? What illustrations of this quality does he give ?

3. What exactly does he mean by this ' simplicitie ' ? Is it something the lady must study ? Or is it something altogether natural ? How can she make ' simplicitie a grace ' ?

4. What does the poet mean by line 6 ? Can you suggest two possible meanings for the word ' adulteries ' in line 11 ? Are the meanings in any way related ? In what way are they opposed to the word ' sound ' in line 6 ? Are there any suggestions in the poem that artificiality might reflect on character ?

5. Now define as accurately as you can Jonson's idea of how the perfect woman ought to care for her appearance and face the world. Be precise.

The Good-Morrow

I wonder, by my troth, what thou and I
Did, till we loved ? were we not wean'd till then ?
But suck'd on country pleasures, childishly ?
Or snorted we in the Seven Sleepers' den ?
'Twas so ; but this, all pleasures fancies be ;   5
If ever any beauty I did see,
Which I desired, and got, 'twas but a dream of thee.

And now good-morrow to our waking souls,
Which watch not one another out of fear ;
For love all love of other sights controls,   10
And makes one little room an everywhere.
Let sea-discoverers to new worlds have gone ;
Let maps to other, worlds on worlds have shown ;
Let us possess one world ; each hath one, and is one.

My face in thine eye, thine in mine appears,   15
And true plain hearts do in the faces rest ;
Where can we find two better hemispheres
Without sharp north, without declining west ?
Whatever dies, was not mix'd equally ;
If our two loves be one, or thou and I   20
Love so alike that none can slacken, none can die.

Explorations

1. In the last line of the first stanza the poet declares that any previous beauty that he may have desired or known was but ' a dream ' of his beloved. Examine how this idea has been prepared for in the previous lines.

2. The first line of the second stanza imagines the lovers waking up from this dream to a new reality. The last line shows them in possession of a new world. What is this world ? How is it distinguished from the world of explorers and astronomers ? How is it distinguished from the world of childish pleasures ? Examine the intervening imagery carefully, particularly line 11. Now turn to the last stanza to see this imagery worked to its conclusion. Explain the logic of it.

3. The lovers are reflected in each other's eyes. The eyes themselves are now their world : they are ' better hemispheres ' than the

world itself. In what respect? Because they are more shapely, boundless, beautiful? Or because they contain each other?

4. Try to sum up the philosophy of love that is contained in the poem. In the poet's view, what is the effect of perfect love on its possessors? Would you agree that there is warmth and zest in this poem? If so, where is it evident?

5. Now glance over the imagery from start to finish and note its complexity and its consistency.

6. In terms of structure, can you trace any clear progress of thought as the poem moves through the three stanzas? Explain.

7. Read *The Anniversary* and compare it with this poem in terms of imagery, tone and structure.

8. Much metaphysical poetry is ironic in tone. Is this so in this instance? Explain with quotations.

Glossary p. 213

The Anniversary

All kings, and all their favourites,
    All glory of honours, beauties, wits,
The sun itself, which makes time, as they pass,
Is elder by a year now than it was
When thou and I first one another saw.   5
All other things to their destruction draw,
    Only our love hath no decay;
This no to-morrow hath, nor yesterday;
Running it never runs from us away,
But truly keeps his first, last, everlasting day.   10

Two graves must hide thine and my corse;
    If one might, death were no divorce.
Alas! as well as other princes, we
—Who prince enough in one another be—
Must leave at last in death these eyes and ears,   15
Oft fed with true oaths, and with sweet salt tears;
    But souls where nothing dwells but love
—All other thoughts being inmates—then shall prove
This or a love increasèd there above,
When bodies to their graves, souls from their graves   20
    remove.

And then we shall be throughly blest ;
But now no more than all the rest.
Here upon earth we're kings, and none but we
Can be such kings, nor of such subjects be.
Who is so safe as we ? where none can do   25
Treason to us, except one of us two.
True and false fears let us refrain,
Let us love nobly, and live, and add again
Years and years unto years, till we attain
To write threescore ; this is the second of our reign.   30

Explorations

1. What, according to the poet, in the first stanza of his love poem, is the general effect of time ? In what way are he and his lover exempt from that effect ?

2. In what way is the position stated in stanza one modified in stanza two where the poet speaks of death, separate burial and eternity ? Does the thought of death, especially in the first five lines of the stanza, sadden him ? Does the tone alter in the final lines of the stanza ? If so, why ?

3. In the first four lines of the last stanza the poet seems to place the joy of heaven—which will be shared by everyone there—beneath his earthly love which is confined solely to him and his beloved. Show how this thought is worked out in the images.

4. Each lover is both prince and subject at the same time. Is this a contradiction ? Trace this complex image through the three stanzas and examine the logic with which it is worked out.

5. Examine the structure of the thought as it moves to its conclusion through the three stanzas.

6. Is there passion as well as logic in the poem ? If so, where is it evident ?

7. Compare the poem with *The Good-Morrow* in terms of tone and theme.

8. Read carefully Shakespeare's *Sonnet 71* and be ready to discuss it in relation to *The Anniversary* in terms of theme, tone and imagery.

Glossary p. 213

A Hymn to God the Father

Wilt Thou forgive that sin where I begun,
  Which was my sin, though it were done before ?
Wilt Thou forgive that sin, through which I run,
  And do run still, though still I do deplore ?
    When Thou hast done, Thou hast not done,   5
      For I have more.

Wilt Thou forgive that sin which I have won
  Others to sin, and made my sin their door ?
Wilt Thou forgive that sin which I did shun
  A year or two, but wallowed in a score ?   10
    When Thou hast done, Thou hast not done.
      For I have more.

I have a sin of fear, that when I have spun
  My last thread, I shall perish on the shore ;
But swear by Thyself, that at my death Thy Son   15
  Shall shine as he shines now, and heretofore :
    And, having done that, Thou hast done :
      I fear no more.

Explorations

1. The thought, especially in the first two stanzas, presents no great difficulty. Do you find anything unusual in the way it is expressed ? Look at the sounds, the repetitions, the sentence lengths, the punctuation. Compare the structure of these two stanzas.

2. What is the central theme of each of these two stanzas ? What does the second add to the thought of the first ?

3. What is the poet's last sin ? What ' shore ' is he referring to ?

4. Would you agree that there is a pun on the poet's name in line 17 ? Does it furnish a suitable climax to the poet's thought ? Look back at the earlier stanzas.

5. There is an even richer pun in lines 15 and 16. Explain it.

6. The Metaphysicals are frequently referred to as ' witty '. Does the present poem deserve the adjective ? Is the wit appropriate to the theme ? Why ? Describe the tone of the poem, taking as many adjectives as you wish to do so.

7. What relationship does the poet seem to have with his Maker ? Compare it to that implied in Jonson's poem on the same theme.

Glossary p. 213

At the Round Earth's Imagined Corners

At the round earth's imagined corners blow
Your trumpets, angels, and arise, arise
From death, you numberless infinities
Of souls, and to your scattered bodies go ;
All whom the flood did, and fire shall o'erthrow,   5
All whom war, death, age, agues, tyrannies,
Despair, law, chance hath slain, and you, whose eyes
Shall behold God, and never taste death's woe.

But let them sleep, Lord, and me mourn a space ;
For, if above all these my sins abound,   10
'Tis late to ask abundance of Thy grace,
When we are there. Here on this lowly ground,
Teach me how to repent, for that's as good
As if Thou hadst seal'd my pardon with Thy blood.

Explorations

1. Would you agree that there is a marvellously vivid picture of
the Last Judgement in the opening eight lines ? If so, how is it
achieved ? Examine the individual images and the manner in which
they are arranged. In all these, be minute and explicit.

2. Read the poem aloud as you think it should be read. Look
at the movement of the lines, where they stop and where they over-
flow. Consider the repetitions and the tone of voice in which they are
delivered. What does the sound contribute to the sense ?

3. What is the central thought of the sestet ? How is this thought
helped by the previous eight lines ?

4. There is a change of tone and of scope in the sestet. Explain
what kind of change. Again, what do imagery, syntax and sound
contribute to creating this new effect ? Is the contrast deliberate ?
Why ?

5. What sort of relationship between man and God is suggested
by the poem as a whole ? Is it similar to that contained in Donne's
two other sonnets ? Explain. In what respects does it differ from his
A Hymn to God the Father ?

Batter my Heart

Batter my heart, three-person'd God ; for you
As yet but knock ; breathe, shine, and seek to mend ;
That I may rise, and stand, o'erthrow me, and bend
Your force, to break, blow, burn, and make me new.
I, like an usurp'd town, to another due,⠀⠀⠀⠀⠀⠀⠀⠀⠀5
Labour to admit you, but O, to no end.
Reason, your viceroy in me, me should defend,
But is captived, and proves weak or untrue.
Yet dearly I love you, and would be loved fain,
But am betroth'd unto your enemy ;⠀⠀⠀⠀⠀⠀⠀⠀10
Divorce me, untie, or break that knot again,
Take me to you, imprison me, for I,
Except you enthrall me, never shall be free,
Nor ever chaste, except you ravish me.

Explorations

1.⠀In this very complex poem the poet uses a number of images. He compares himself, for instance, to a town and to a woman. Consider these images and show how they apply.

2.⠀Who or what is God's 'enemy' ? Where else is it referred to ?

3.⠀God is presented as prince, conqueror, lover. Do you agree ? Explain and illustrate.

4.⠀Do you agree that this is a poem of great violence ? In what words and phrases is this evident ? Consider the verbs in particular. Is this violence effective in conveying the poet's passionate appeal to God ?

5.⠀There is a daring paradox in the last line. The word ' ravish ' can mean enrapture, rape, or carry off. All these meanings are to some extent present. When taken in conjunction with ' chaste ', which meaning is uppermost ? Explain the paradox in the previous line. Is there a possible ambiguity in the word ' enthrall ' ? Explain.

6.⠀The New Testament is full of paradoxes, such as ' He that findeth his life shall lose it ; and he that loseth his life for my sake shall find it '. In the Anglican *Book of Common Prayer* there is a reference to the author of peace ' whose service is perfect freedom '. Would it be fair to say that the present poem is built on a system of such paradoxes ?

7.⠀Is there a change of theme, tone and imagery between the octet and the sestet ? Glance again at question 1 above.

8.⠀Is this a great religious poem ?

Glossary p. 213

O, My Black Soul

O, my black soul, now thou art summoned
By sickness, Death's herald and champion ;
Thou'rt like a pilgrim, which abroad hath done
Treason, and durst not turn to whence he's fled ;
Or like a thief, which till death's doom be read,   5
Wisheth himself deliver'd from prison,
But damn'd and haled to execution,
Wisheth that still he might be imprisoned.
Yet grace, if thou repent, thou canst not lack ;
But who shall give thee that grace to begin ?   10
O, make thyself with holy mourning black,
And red with blushing, as thou art with sin ;
Or wash thee in Christ's blood, which hath this might,
That being red, it dyes red souls to white.

Explorations

1. In the first quatrain the sinful soul is compared to a pilgrim who has ' done treason'. Is this a suitable simile ? Explain.

2. In the second quatrain the soul is compared to a thief who faces first imprisonment and then death. How does this quatrain advance the thought ? How does the imagery accord with that of the first quatrain ?

3. In what way does the theme change in the movement from the octet to the sestet ? Is there a change of tone ?

4. Work out the rôle played by colour in this poem. Examine and discuss its symbolism in detail.

5. What is the problem of grace posed by lines 9 and 10 ? Is it satisfactorily dealt with in the last four lines ? Explain.

6. Compare this poem with *Batter my Heart* in theme and the use of imagery. Which poem do you prefer ? Why ?

Glossary p. 213

The Collar

I struck the board, and cry'd, No more.
                    I will abroad.
        What ? shall I ever sigh and pine ?
My lines and life are free ; free as the rode,
        Loose as the winde, as large as store.   5
                Shall I be still in suit ?
        Have I no harvest but a thorn
        To let me bloud, and not restore
        What I have lost with cordiall fruit ?
                        Sure there was wine   10
Before my sighs did drie it : there was corn
                Before my tears did drown it.
        Is the yeare onely lost to me ?
                Have I no bayes to crown it ?
No flowers, no garlands gay ? all blasted ?   15
                All wasted ?
        Not so, my heart : but there is fruit,
                        And thou hast hands.
        Recover all thy sigh-blown age
On double pleasures : leave thy cold dispute   20
Of what is fit, and not. Forsake thy cage,
                Thy rope of sands,
Which pettie thoughts have made, and made to thee
        Good cable, to enforce and draw,
                        And be thy law,   25
        While thou didst wink and wouldst not see.
                        Away ; take heed :
                        I will abroad.
Call in thy deaths head there : tie up thy fears.
                He that forbears   30
                To suit and serve his need,
                        Deserves his load.
But as I rav'd and grew more fierce and wilde
                At every word,
Me thoughts I heard one calling, *Child* !   35
        And I reply'd, *My Lord*.

Explorations

1. The collar was a common symbol for religious and moral restraint. What other images in this poem are concerned with freedom and restraint ? Can you trace how the images are linked ?

2. The first sixteen lines of the poem are largely concerned with questions. What have these questions in common ? In what spirit are they asked ? Give some examples.

3. In how far are the questions answered in the next sixteen lines ? Are these true answers ? If not, is there anything in phrase or image that suggests falseness ? Explain, being specific.

4. Is there anything in the tone and movement of the final lines to suggest that they contain the true answer ? Read over carefully before answering.

5. The poet, up to the end of the poem, is in rebellion against his condition. What are the things he resents ? What things does he feel himself deprived of ?

6. Paraphrase the thought in the poem and then show how the thought is related to the structure.

7. Herbert was a classical scholar as well as being an Anglican divine. Is there any evidence of this in the imagery he uses ?

8. Herbert is noted for the conversational directness of his language. Is there any evidence of it here ? Explain and illustrate.

9. The poet is also noted as one of the first English poets to use free verse, that is to alter line-length and metre as his subject demanded. Can you suggest any reason why free verse suits this subject ?

Glossary p. 214

Love

Love bade me welcome : yet my soul drew back,
Guiltie of dust and sinne.
But quick-ey'd Love, observing me grow slack
From my first entrance in,
Drew nearer to me, sweetly questioning,   5
If I lack'd any thing.

A guest, I answer'd, worthy to be here :
Love said, You shall be he.
I the unkinde, ungratefull ? Ah my deare,
I cannot look on thee.   10
Love took my hand, and smiling did reply,
Who made the eyes but I ?

Truth Lord, but I have marr'd them : let my shame
Go where it doth deserve.
And know you not, sayes Love, who bore the blame ?   15
My deare, then I will serve.
You must sit down, sayes Love, and taste my meat :
So I did sit and eat.

Explorations

1. Herbert creates a dramatic situation in order to convey his insight on Love. What is the situation he imagines ?

2. What qualities are revealed in the words and actions of Love ? Is it human or divine love he is speaking of, or is it both ?

3. What obstacles must Love, as host, overcome in the poet, as guest ?

4. Paraphrase the whole encounter in your own words. Does it lose or gain by being thus summarised ? Explain.

5. What is the moral or message of this parable ?

6. What is the tone of the dialogue ? Read it aloud so as to bring out what you regard as its dominant mood.

7. There are certain examples of Herbert's conversational language in *The Collar*. Are there other, and maybe rather different, examples of it here ? Explain.

Life

I made a posie, while the day ran by :
Here will I smell my remnant out, and tie
                    My life within this band.
But Time did becken to the flowers, and they
By noon most cunningly did steal away,   5
                    And wither'd in my hand.

My hand was next to them, and then my heart :
I took, without more thinking, in good part
                    Times gentle admonition :
Who did so sweetly deaths sad taste convey,   10
Making my minde to smell my fatall day ;
                    Yet sugring the suspicion.

Farewell deare flowers, sweetly your time ye spent,
Fit, while ye liv'd, for smell or ornament,
                    And after death for cures.   15
I follow straight without complaints or grief,
Since if my sent be good, I care not if
                    It be as short as yours.

Explorations

1. The poet uses the dying flowers to express a certain attitude to
death and Time. What is this attitude ? Read the poem carefully.

2. He says in stanza two that he took ' Times gentle admonition '
in ' good part '. What was the admonition ?

3. Does the phrase ' Times gentle admonition ' give us the key to
the poem's tone ? What is its tone ? Point out other phrases in which
it is evident. Is the tone consistent ?

4. There is a beautifully worked image in the final stanza. Explain
its application fully. Would you agree that it gives a fine sense of com-
pleteness to the poem ? Glance back over the other stanzas.

5. The poem appeals to several of the senses. How does this
sensuousness compare with that of Marvell in *Thoughts in a Garden* or
that of Keats in *Ode to a Nightingale* ?

6. How does the poem compare in tone with *Love* and with *The
Collar* ?

Glossary p. 214

Vertue

Sweet day, so cool, so calm, so bright,
The bridall of the earth and skie :
The dew shall weep thy fall to night ;
           For thou must die.

Sweet rose, whose hue angrie and brave   5
Bids the rash gazer wipe his eye :
Thy root is ever in its grave,
           And thou must die.

Sweet spring, full of sweet dayes and roses,
A box where sweets compacted lie ;   10
My musick shows ye have your closes,
           And all must die.

Onely a sweet and vertuous soul,
Like season'd timber, never gives ;
But though the whole world turn to coal,   15
           Then chiefly lives.

Explorations

1. As the poet writes about them what have the day, the rose and the spring in common ? In what way does the ' vertuous soul ' differ from them ?

2. In what sense is the day the marriage of earth and sky ? Trace this image.

3. Can you suggest why the ' rash gazer ' should wipe his eye on seeing the rose ? Is he dazzled by its beauty, cowed by its anger, sad that its beauty might fade . . . ? Again trace the image to the end of the stanza.

4. In what way does stanza three advance the thought and imagery of stanzas one and two ? Consider it carefully. What does ' all ' in line 12 refer to ?

5. How does the soul differ from the day, the rose and the spring ? Has the poet concluded his poem successfully ? Explain.

6. Read *Life* and be ready to compare the two poems in terms of theme. Now consider in each case the poet's method of expressing it.

Glossary p. 214

The Retreate

Happy those early dayes ! when I
Shin'd in my Angell-infancy.
Before I understood this place
Appointed for my second race,
Or taught my soul to fancy ought   5
But a white, Celestiall thought,
When yet I had not walkt above
A mile, or two, from my first love,
And looking back (at that short space,)
Could see a glimpse of his bright-face ;   10
When on some gilded Cloud, or flowre
My gazing soul would dwell an houre,
And in those weaker glories spy
Some shadows of eternity ;
Before I taught my tongue to wound   15
My Conscience with a sinfull sound,
Or had the black art to dispence
A sev'rall sinne to ev'ry sence,
But felt through all this fleshly dresse
Bright shootes of everlastingnesse.   20
    O how I long to travell back
And tread again that ancient track !
That I might once more reach that plaine,
Where first I left my glorious traine,
From whence th' Inlightned spirit sees   25
That shady City of Palme trees ;
But (ah !) my soul with too much stay
Is drunk, and staggers in the way.
Some men a forward motion love,
But I by backward steps would move,   30
And when this dust falls to the urn
In that state I came return.

Explorations

1. The poem may be divided into three movements : (1) the poet looks back and praises ' those early dayes ' ; (2) he wishes he could return to them ; (3) he accepts that he cannot do so this side of death. Point out these three stages of the thought.

2. The ' early dayes ' were, above all, days of innocence. What phrases and images does the poet employ to convey this quality ? What other qualities has this early time ?

3. As the poet travels from this early world into adulthood he becomes more divided within himself. Where is this idea suggested ? What is the cause of this discord ? Look for the answer in the text.

4. The poet's comparison of the soul to a drunken man is surely a daring one. Does it succeed ? Are there any other unusual or striking images or phrases in the poem ? Explain.

5. There is imagery of light and dark in the poem. Trace it and suggest its purpose.

6. Examine the poem's punctuation. Do you find anything curious about it ? Do you find it particularly suitable to the mood and pace of the poem ? Read aloud. Give your answer in some detail.

7. In what senses could this be called a ' metaphysical ' poem ?

8. Read *O, My Black Soul* for comparison of mood and theme.

Glossary p. 214

The Showre

'Twas so, I saw thy birth : That drowsie Lake
From her faint bosome breath'd thee, the disease
Of her sick waters, and Infectious Ease.
      But, now at Even
      Too grosse for heaven,   5
Thou fall'st in teares, and weep'st for thy mistake.

Ah ! it is so with me ; oft have I prest
Heaven with a lazie breath, but fruitles this
Peirc'd not ; Love only can with quick accesse
      Unlock the way,   10
      When all else stray
The smoke, and Exhalations of the brest.

Yet, if as thou doest melt, and with thy traine
Of drops make soft the Earth, my eyes could weep
O're my hard heart, that's bound up, and asleep,   15
      Perhaps at last
      (Some such showres past,)
My God would give a Sun-shine after raine.

Explorations

1.   The first stanza presents the shower as a diseased breath of the sick lake which rises towards heaven but is rejected and falls weeping for its mistake. What was its mistake—the sickness, the ' Infectious Ease ', the ascent, the presumption of that ascent ? It may help you to read stanza two again.

2.   In the second stanza the poet speaks of his own attempt to gain access to God. What is the cause of his failure ? What has his ' lazie breath ' in common with the breath of the lake ? What virtue would have given him access ?

3.   In the final stanza the poet draws a lesson of hope from the action of the shower. What is that lesson ? How is the poet to apply it to himself? How is it linked with the notion of Love as mentioned in stanza two ?

4.   This is a typical ' metaphysical ' poem. The imagery is far-fetched and it is elaborately and logically worked out. It also exhibits the metaphysical poet's constant concern with the relationships between God and man. Read Donne's sonnet *Batter my Heart* and compare the two poems with these qualities in mind.

5.   Consider the structure of the poem ; how the thought is introduced, developed and resolved through the three stanzas. Note how the two elements in the poem, poet and shower, are first mentioned apart from each other, are brought closer together, and finally fused as the thought is resolved.

Glossary p. 214

Man

Weighing the stedfastness and state
Of some mean things which here below reside,
Where birds like watchful Clocks the noiseless date
    And Intercourse of times divide,
Where Bees at night get home and hive, and flowrs   5
        Early, aswel as late,
Rise with the Sun, and set in the same bowrs ;

I would (said I) my God would give
The staidness of these things to man ! for these
To his divine appointments ever cleave,   10
    And no new business breaks their peace ;
The birds nor sow, nor reap, yet sup and dine,
        The flowres without clothes live,
Yet Solomon was never drest so fine.

Man hath stil either toyes, or Care,   15
He hath no root, nor to one place is ty'd,
But ever restless and Irregular
    About this Earth doth run and ride,
He knows he hath a home, but scarce knows where,
        He sayes it is so far   20
That he hath quite forgot how to go there.

He knocks at all doors, strays and roams,
Nay hath not so much wit as some stones have
Which in the darkest nights point to their homes,
    By some hid sense their Maker gave ;   25
Man is the shuttle, to whose winding quest
        And passage through these looms
God order'd motion, but ordain'd no rest.

Explorations

1. Having read the poem very carefully and grasped its general sense you will probably note that the first two stanzas are formed of a single sentence. (Disregard the exclamation mark.) Can you suggest a reason why ? Where are the subject and verb situated in the sentence ? Is the placing in any way significant ? Would you agree that this first sentence presents the first movement of the poet's thought ? Explain.

2. The focus of the thought changes in the third stanza. In what way ? Trace the thought briefly to the end of the poem.

3. Examine the images in the first two stanzas by means of which the poet illustrates the stability of nature. Do you find them apt, graceful, vivid ? Explain. What is the effect of the biblical reference coming where it does ?

4. Is it true that the final lines sum up the poem's thought satisfactorily ? What, therefore, is man's greatest failing ? When answering consider the two references to ' home '. What home has the poet in mind ?

5. The images in the first half of the poem are drawn from nature. Is there a change in the second half ? Does this change reflect a change of thought or emphasis ? Do you find the images in the second half of the poem more original, vivid, moving or apt than those in the first half ? Explain.

6. You will have observed that each of the last two stanzas is formed of a single sentence. Now review the structure of the poem as a whole.

7. Would you describe this as a metaphysical poem ? Why ?

Glossary p. 215

Peace

My Soul, there is a Countrie
 Far beyond the stars,
Where stands a winged Centrie
 All skilfull in the wars,
There above noise, and danger   5
 Sweet peace sits crown'd with smiles,
And one born in a Manger
 Commands the Beauteous files,
He is thy gracious friend,
 And (O my Soul awake !)   10
Did in pure love descend
 To die here for thy sake,
If thou canst get but thither,
 There growes the flowre of peace,
The Rose that cannot wither,   15
 Thy fortresse, and thy ease ;
Leave then thy foolish ranges ;
 For none can thee secure,
But one, who never changes,
 Thy God, thy life, thy Cure.   20

Explorations

1. Though this is clearly a simple poem the imagery is worth considering, especially for some interesting ambiguities. These might be probed through the following questions :

How many references are there to war-like things in the poem ?
What kinds of peace are represented in the picture of heaven ?
How are the two sets of images related ?
Do they blend satisfactorily for the general benefit of the poem ?

2. Read the poem aloud at the pace and rhythm you think appropriate. How do the metre and punctuation contribute to its movement ?

3. Read *Man* by the same poet and see whether it illumines the poet's idea of peace.

4. Read *A Hymne to God the Father* and compare it to *Peace* both as a poem and as a prayer. Might *Peace* also be the words of a hymn ?

Glossary p. 215

Thoughts in a Garden

How vainly men themselves amaze
To win the palm, the oak, or bays,
And their uncessant labours see
Crown'd from some single herb or tree,
Whose short and narrow-vergèd shade   5
Does prudently their toils upbraid ;
While all the flowers and trees do close
To weave the garlands of repose !

Fair Quiet, have I found thee here,
And Innocence thy sister dear ?   10
Mistaken long, I sought you then
In busy companies of men :
Your sacred plants, if here below,
Only among the plants will grow :
Society is all but rude   15
To this delicious solitude.

No white nor red was ever seen
So amorous as this lovely green.
Fond lovers, cruel as their flame,
Cut in these trees their mistress' name :   20
Little, alas ! they know or heed
How far these beauties hers exceed !
Fair trees ! wheres'e'er your barks I wound,
No name shall but your own be found.

When we have run our passions' heat,   25
Love hither makes his best retreat :
The gods, that mortal beauty chase,
Still in a tree did end their race ;
Apollo hunted Daphne so
Only that she might laurel grow ;   30
And Pan did after Syrinx speed
Not as a nymph, but for a reed.

What wondrous life in this I lead !
Ripe apples drop about my head ;
The luscious clusters of the vine   35
Upon my mouth do crush their wine ;

The nectarine and curious peach
Into my hands themselves do reach ;
Stumbling on melons, as I pass,
Ensnared with flowers, I fall on grass.   40

Meanwhile the mind from pleasure less
Withdraws into its happiness ;
The mind, that Ocean where each kind
Does straight its own resemblance find ;
Yet it creates, transcending these,   45
Far other worlds, and other seas ;
Annihilating all that's made
To a green thought in a green shade.

Here at the fountain's sliding foot,
Or at some fruit-tree's mossy root,   50
Casting the body's vest aside,
My soul into the boughs does glide ;
There, like a bird, it sits and sings,
Then whets and combs its silver wings,
And, till prepared for longer flight,   55
Waves in its plumes the various light.

Such was that happy Garden-state
While man there walk'd without a mate :
After a place so pure and sweet,
What other help could yet be meet !   60
But 'twas beyond a mortal's share
To wander solitary there :
Two paradises 'twere in one,
To live in Paradise alone.

How well the skilful gard'ner drew   65
Of flowers and herbs this dial new !
Where, from above, the milder sun
Does through a fragrant zodiac run :
And, as it works, th' industrious bee
Computes its time as well as we.   70
How could such sweet and wholesome hours
Be reckon'd, but with herbs and flowers !

Explorations

1. Though on the surface it appears such a simple, direct, witty and graceful poem, *Thoughts in a Garden*, is very subtle and complex in the metaphysical manner. An appreciation of this complexity will increase the reader's pleasure, and it is a poem that will repay the most strenuous reading. The first stanza might be taken as an example of Marvell's poetic method :— He wishes to exalt the repose of the garden above all other human conditions ; he therefore points out the irony by which men toil for rewards as short-lived as garlands cut from trees, when a world of trees and flowers can be enjoyed without any exertion in the solitude of the garden. Furthermore, the shade afforded by the garland when it is worn is so meagre compared to that of a grove of trees that it serves to upbraid the wearer with his folly. Whether there is a pun on the word ' upbraid ' may be left open—but it is possible that the poet had in mind the toil of the victor in braiding his hair before donning the garland.

2. The second stanza presents the virtues of the garden. What are they ? Explain the plant image.

3. White or red are traditional colours of human love. Marvell declares the ' lovely green ' of his trees a superior sort of love. Note how he develops the conceit in the next two stanzas. How would you describe the tone of his reproach to the ' Fond lovers '—take for instance the word ' cruel '.

4. How serious is Marvell when he suggests in stanza four that Apollo and Pan pursued the nymphs in the hope of finding them turned into plants ? What is the tone of this stanza ?

5. The poet has been writing about love. Now in stanza five he describes the garden as if it were a human lover wooing him. Trace the imagery with care, considering in particular its appeal to the different senses.

6. What contrasting aspect of the garden's excellence appears in stanza six ? What meaning or meanings can you offer for the last two lines ? At this stage what qualities, spiritual and physical, has the word ' green ' gathered to itself?

7. Marvell now compares the contemplative soul to a bird. Is it an apt comparison ? Consider it thoroughly—from several angles. What might be meant by ' longer flight ' ? Perhaps the next stanza may give a clue to one interpretation.

8. How serious is Marvell's tone in stanza eight when he suggests that Eve actually diminished the pleasure of Eden ? Are we per-

pared already by the earlier stanzas for this sort of assertion about woman, solitude, the garden ? Explain and comment.

9. In the final stanza the poet returns from eternity to the world of time—time measured by a sun-dial of herbs and flowers. Is this a suitable symbol—together with that of the bee—with which to end this intricate meditation on time, eternity, nature and solitude ? Why ? What is the general mood of this final stanza—cool, passionate, temperate ? How is it established ? Be specific.

10. Read the poem over carefully and find your way into its developing thought and changing mood. There is room for endless exploration here.

11. Read Keats's *Ode to a Nightingale* and compare it with this poem in terms of sensuousness, or Yeats's *Sailing to Byzantium* for certain similarities of theme.

Glossary p. 215

Lycidas

In this Monody the Author bewails a learned Friend, unfortunatly drown'd in his Passage from *Chester* on the *Irish* Seas, 1637. And by occasion foretels the ruine of our corrupted Clergy then in their height.

Yet once more, O ye Laurels, and once more
Ye Myrtles brown, with Ivy never-sear,
I com to pluck your Berries harsh and crude,
And with forc'd fingers rude,
Shatter your leaves before the mellowing year.   5
Bitter constraint, and sad occasion dear,
Compels me to disturb your season due :
For *Lycidas* is dead, dead ere his prime
Young *Lycidas*, and hath not left his peer :
Who would not sing for *Lycidas* ? he knew   10
Himself to sing, and build the lofty rhyme.
He must not flote upon his watry bear
Unwept, and welter to the parching wind,
Without the meed of som melodious tear.
    Begin then, Sisters of the sacred well,   15
That from beneath the seat of *Jove* doth spring,
Begin, and somwhat loudly sweep the string.
Hence with denial vain, and coy excuse,
So may som gentle Muse
With lucky words favour my destin'd Urn,   20
And as he passes turn,
And bid fair peace be to my sable shrowd.
For we were nurst upon the self-same hill,
Fed the same flock, by fountain, shade, and rill.
    Together both, ere the high Lawns appear'd   25
Under the opening eye-lids of the morn,
We drove a field, and both together heard
What time the Gray-fly winds her sultry horn,
Batt'ning our flocks with the fresh dews of night,
Oft till the Star that rose, at Ev'ning, bright   30
Toward Heav'ns descent had slop'd his westering wheel.
Mean while the Rural ditties were not mute,
Temper'd to th'Oaten Flute ;
Rough *Satyrs* danc'd, and *Fauns* with clov'n heel,

From the glad sound would not be absent long,   35
And old *Damætas* lov'd to hear our song.
   But O the heavy change, now thou art gon,
Now thou art gon, and never must return !
Thee Shepherd, thee the Woods, and desert Caves,
With wilde Thyme and the gadding Vine o'regrown,   40
And all their echoes mourn.
The Willows, and the Hazle Copses green,
Shall now no more be seen,
Fanning their joyous Leaves to thy soft layes.
As killing as the Canker to the Rose,   45
Or Taint-worm to the weanling Herds that graze,
Or Frost to Flowers, that their gay wardrop wear,
When first the White thorn blows ;
Such, *Lycidas*, thy loss to Shepherds ear.
   Where were ye Nymphs when the remorseless deep   50
Clos'd o're the head of your lov'd *Lycidas* ?
For neither were ye playing on the steep,
Where your old *Bards*, the famous *Druids* ly,
Nor on the shaggy top of *Mona* high,
Nor yet where *Deva* spreads her wisard stream :   55
Ay me, I fondly dream !
Had ye bin there—for what could that have don ?
What could the Muse her self that *Orpheus* bore,
The Muse her self, for her inchanting son
Whom Universal nature did lament,   60
When by the rout that made the hideous roar,
His goary visage down the stream was sent,
Down the swift *Hebrus* to the *Lesbian* shore.
   Alas ! What boots it with uncessant care
To tend the homely slighted Shepherds trade,   65
And strictly meditate the thankles Muse,
Were it not better don as others use,
To sport with *Amaryllis* in the shade,
Or with the tangles of *Neæra's* hair ?
Fame is the spur that the clear spirit doth raise   70
(That last infirmity of Noble mind)
To scorn delights, and live laborious dayes ;
But the fair Guerdon when we hope to find,
And think to burst out into sudden blaze,

Comes the blind *Fury* with th'abhorred shears,   75
And slits the thin spun life. But not the praise,
Phœbus repli'd, and touch'd my trembling ears ;
Fame is no plant that grows on mortal soil,
Nor in the glistering foil
Set off to th'world, nor in broad rumour lies,   80
But lives and spreds aloft by those pure eyes,
And perfet witnes of all judging *Jove* ;
As he pronounces lastly on each deed,
Of so much fame in Heav'n expect thy meed.

   O Fountain *Arethuse*, and thou honour'd floud,   85
Smooth-sliding *Mincius*, crown'd with vocall reeds,
That strain I heard was of a higher mood :
But now my Oate proceeds,
And listens to the Herald of the Sea
That came in *Neptune's* plea,   90
He ask'd the Waves, and ask'd the Fellon winds,
What hard mishap hath doom'd this gentle swain ?
And question'd every gust of rugged wings
That blows from off each beaked Promontory,
They knew not of his story,   95
And sage *Hippotades* their answer brings,
That not a blast was from his dungeon stray'd,
The Ayr was calm, and on the level brine,
Sleek *Panope* with all her sisters play'd.
It was that fatall and perfidious Bark   100
Built in th'eclipse, and rigg'd with curses dark,
That sunk so low that sacred head of thine.

   Next *Camus*, reverend Sire, went footing slow,
His Mantle hairy, and his Bonnet sedge,
Inwrought with figures dim, and on the edge   105
Like to that sanguine flower inscrib'd with woe.
Ah ; Who hath reft (quoth he) my dearest pledge ?
Last came, and last did go,
The Pilot of the *Galilean* lake,
Two massy Keyes he bore of metals twain,   110
(The Golden opes, the Iron shuts amain)
He shook his Miter'd locks, and stern bespake,
How well could I have spar'd for thee, young swain,
Anow of such as for their bellies sake,

Creep and intrude, and climb into the fold ?   115
Of other care they little reck'ning make,
Then how to scramble at the shearers feast,
And shove away the worthy bidden guest.
Blind mouthes ! that scarce themselves know how to hold
A Sheep-hook, or have learn'd ought els the least   120
That to the faithfull Herdmans art belongs !
What recks it them ? What need they ? They are sped ;
And when they list, their lean and flashy songs
Grate on their scrannel Pipes of wretched straw,
The hungry Sheep look up, and are not fed,   125
But swoln with wind, and the rank mist they draw,
Rot inwardly, and foul contagion spread :
Besides what the grim Woolf with privy paw
Daily devours apace, and nothing sed,
But that two-handed engine at the door,   130
Stands ready to smite once, and smite no more.
   Return *Alpheus*, the dread voice is past,
That shrunk thy streams ; Return *Sicilian* Muse,
And call the Vales, and bid them hither cast
Their Bels, and Flourets of a thousand hues.   135
Ye valleys low where the milde whispers use,
Of shades and wanton winds, and gushing brooks
On whose fresh lap the swart Star sparely looks,
Throw hither all your quaint enameld eyes,
That on the green terf suck the honied showres,   140
And purple all the ground with vernal flowres.
Bring the rathe Primrose that forsaken dies.
The tufted Crow-toe, and pale Gessamine,
The white Pink, and the Pansie freakt with jeat,
The glowing Violet.   145
The Musk-rose, and the well attir'd Woodbine.
With Cowslips wan that hang the pensive hed,
And every flower that sad embroidery wears :
Bid *Amaranthus* all his beauty shed,
And Daffadillies fill their cups with tears,   150
To strew the Laureat Herse where *Lycid* lies.
For so to interpose a little ease,
Let our frail thoughts dally with false surmise.
Ay me ! Whilst thee the shores, and sounding Seas

Wash far away, where ere thy bones are hurld, 155
Whether beyond the stormy *Hebrides*,
Where thou perhaps under the whelming tide
Visit'st the bottom of the monstrous world ;
Or whether thou to our moist vows deny'd,
Sleep'st by the fable of *Bellerus* old, 160
Where the great vision of the guarded Mount
Looks toward *Namancos* and *Bayona's* hold ;
Look homeward Angel now, and melt with ruth.
And, O ye *Dolphins*, waft the haples youth.

Weep no more, woful Shepherds, weep no more, 165
For *Lycidas* your sorrow is not dead,
Sunk though he be beneath the watry floar,
So sinks the day-star in the Ocean bed,
And yet anon repàìrs his drooping head,
And tricks his beams, and with new spangled Ore, 170
Flames in the forehead of the morning sky :
So *Lycidas* sunk low, but mounted high,
Through the dear might of him that walk'd the waves,
Where other groves, and other streams along,
With *Nectar* pure his oozy Lock's he laves, 175
And hears the unexpressive nuptiall Song,
In the blest Kingdoms meek of joy and love.
There entertain him all the Saints above,
In solemn troops, and sweet Societies
That sing, and singing in their glory move, 180
And wipe the tears for ever from his eyes.
Now *Lycidas* the Shepherds weep no more ;
Hence forth thou art the Genius of the shore,
In thy large recompense, and shalt be good
To all that wander in that perilous flood. 185

Thus sang the uncouth Swain to th'Okes and rills,
While the still morn went out with Sandals gray,
He touch'd the tender stops of various Quills,
With eager thought warbling his *Dorick* lay :
And now the Sun had stretch'd out all the hills, 190
And now was dropt into the Western bay ;
At last he rose, and twitch'd his Mantle blew :
To-morrow to fresh Woods, and Pastures new.

Explorations

From the start it is useful to consider the part played by what we call ' literary convention ' in this poem. A convention can be described as any ' unrealistic ' device used by a writer which he can reasonably expect will be accepted by his reader or audience. It is unrealistic, for instance, that an actor should talk aloud to himself and yet be heard at the back of the gallery while remaining inaudible to his fellow-actors on the stage, but for many centuries this has been a useful ' convention ' for playwrights who wish us to know what is going on in a character's mind. Similarly, Milton uses the convention of the pastoral elegy to mourn his friend, John King, who has been drowned. In pastoral convention a poet may be referred to as a shepherd, his work at Cambridge may be dealt with in terms of a shepherd's work, the classical deities may be called upon to mourn him or to account for his death, his funeral bier may be seen as bedecked with flowers even though we know that his body has not in fact been recovered. But in this poem Milton goes beyond the pure pastoral convention : the word for shepherd ' pastor ' is also used for clergymen, and the poet takes the opportunity of mourning King both as a potential writer and clergyman.

1. Read the poem through without comment, then go back over it and identify the conventions used, suggesting in every case the meaning and purpose.

2. Leaving aside the matter of their friendship, why do you think that Milton at this stage of his life should feel constrained to write a poem on King's death ? In answering, read the opening passage of the poem down to line 15.

3. What further, but related, reason is given in the passage immediately following, down to line 24 ?

4. What further reason is suggested in the passage which follows that one in turn ?

5. In the long nature passage from lines 26 to 49 is the poet painting a real or an ideal landscape ? Point out particular phrases, details or references that seem to bear out your opinion. Can you relate this treatment of nature to the poem's general purpose ?

6. In lines 50 to 63 Milton asks the nymphs why they did not guard the life of Lycidas. What special claim might the dead man have had on them for protection ? Look in particular at the reference to the Muse of Poetry and her son.

7.   From lines 64 to 75 Milton considers the serious poet's laborious work, his quest for fame, his temptations to more frivolous work, and the irony of sudden death. Show clearly how the thought moves.

8.   How does the poet resolve his dilemma in the lines that immediately follow ?

9.   The passage that follows lines 64 to 84 is frequently referred to as the poem's first digression. Read it carefully and then say whether you think it an actual digression or a logical progression of the poem's thought. It may help to glance back at the opening passage.

10.   Read the passage where the Herald of the Sea questions the water deities about the death of Lycidas. Now look back over the poem, at the references to the sea in particular, and try to decide whether the sea is represented as friendly, hostile or neutral to the young poet. Bear this consideration in mind for future reference.

11.   What main charges are laid at the door of the corrupt clergy in the passage where St. Peter enters ? Are they vividly expressed ? Where in particular ? How would you describe the tone of the passage ? Why do you think St. Peter is mentioned in his rôle as ' Pilot of the Galilean lake ' ?

12.   This passage is often seen as the poem's second digression. Would you agree that it is digressive ? Explain. Has it anything in common with the previous digression ?

13.   Passing over the conventional ' flower-passage ', look carefully at lines 154 to 164 which dwell on the corpse of Lycidas being borne by the sea. Read it aloud for its movement, sound and energy. Would you agree that the feeling of grief and desolation reaches its most poignant in these lines ? Explain.

14.   In what way does the entire feeling of the poem change in the passage that follows ? Is it true that in the passage, lines 165 to 186, all the perplexities and sorrows dwelt on earlier are resolved—the fate of young poets, priests, shepherds who are cut off in youth ? Ponder and explain.

15.   Trace, one by one, the pagan and the Christian images and ideas in this passage. Could it be argued that the pagan and Christian elements in the poem are reconciled in its imagery ? Note particularly how they have been blended in the passage representing St. Peter.

16.   Why does Milton end the poem with a passage returning to the pastoral shepherd motif ? What does he mean by it ? In what sense is he an ' uncouth Swain ' ? Glance back at the opening passage and comment on the way the poem has been framed.

17. Having considered the poem in terms of the questions above now re-read it in order to get its full unity back into focus, and to prepare yourself for such considerations as these :

(a) What part does sea imagery play in the poem ? Begin, perhaps, with lines 167 to 168, and then go back to the beginning. Having dealt with the sea imagery look now at the images of rivers and streams. Can they be distinguished from the sea images in tone, feeling or meaning ?

(b) What part does the vegetation imagery play in the poem ? Does the landscape with its plants, grasses and flowers reflect feelings of joy or sadness ? Is it hostile or friendly ?

(c) Has the poem a satisfactory unity ? Is it a satisfactory contemplation of the central themes ? Are the various other related themes dealt with satisfactorily ? Explain with quotations.

(d) Which passages do you like best ? Read each of them aloud for sound as well as sense. In what way does each of them advance the theme and the contemplation ?

(e) Do you consider that the conventions are skilfully used ? What are the various effects created by the poet's use of proper names ?

(f) *Lycidas* is regarded as a great poem. How did you respond to it ?

18. Take one passage from the poem and write a critical analysis of it, showing what part is played in it by its language, imagery, sound effects, and, finally, what part it plays in the poem as a whole.

Glossary p. 215

How soon hath Time

How soon hath Time the suttle theef of youth,
   Stoln on his wing my three and twentith yeer !
   My hasting dayes flie on with full career,
   But my late spring no bud or blossom shew'th.
Perhaps my semblance might deceive the truth,   5
   That I to manhood am arriv'd so near,
   And inward ripenes doth much less appear,
   That som more timely-happy spirits indu'th.
Yet be it less or more, or soon or slow,
   It shall be still in strictest measure eev'n   10
   To that same lot, however mean, or high,
Toward which Time leads me, and the will of Heav'n ;
   All is, if I have grace to use it so,
   As ever in my great task Masters eye.

Explorations

1. The first eight lines of this sonnet pose a problem which is resolved in the sestet. What is the problem and what is its solution ?

2. Examine the imagery in the first quatrain. How is it continued into the second ? In what way does the imagery develop and expand the thought ?

3. Compare the poet's attitude to Time in line 1 with his attitude towards it in line 12. Does the development of the thought in between justify the reversal of attitude ?

4. How would you describe the sonnet's tone—light, solemn, gloomy, pensive, resigned ? Read the poem aloud. Is the tone supported by the movement of the lines ? Explain. Is there a change of pace and feeling at any stage in the poem ? Explain.

5. In all respects but one this is a strict Petrarchan sonnet. In what respect ? Is the poem's general regularity of form reflected in its thought, punctuation, metre, imagery ? Take these one by one.

6. Is the poem Christian in its thought ? Explain. In defining his attitude does Milton use any phrases which are especially telling ? Compare this poem with Milton's sonnet on his blindness, referring in particular to the religious viewpoint of the poet.

7. Read Donne's sonnet *Batter my Heart* and contrast it with this in terms of theme, tone and subtlety of thought and imagery.

Glossary p. 218

When I Consider

When I consider how my light is spent,
　E're half my days, in this dark world and wide,
　And that one Talent which is death to hide,
　Lodg'd with me useless, though my Soul more bent
To serve therewith my Maker, and present　　　　5
　My true account, least he returning chide,
　Doth God exact day-labour, light deny'd,
　I fondly ask ; But patience to prevent
That murmur, soon replies, God doth not need
　Either man's work or his own gifts, who best　　10
　Bear his milde yoak, they serve him best, his State
Is Kingly.　Thousands at his bidding speed
　And post o're Land and Ocean without rest :
　They also serve who only stand and waite.

Explorations

1.　Take the line ' Doth God exact day-labour, light deny'd ' and work out its possible meanings. See whether you can connect it with the parable of the Talents alluded to in lines 3 and 4.

2.　Why was the loss of sight so particularly grievous to Milton ? Why should it prompt him to question God's will and providence ? In what tone does Milton pose his query ? Comment on ' fondly '.

3.　What sort of answer to his dilemma does the poet find within the poem ?

4.　Trace the imagery of light and darkness in the first eight lines. Do you judge that it is subtly and suggestively used ? Explain.

5.　In rhyme scheme this sonnet is altogether regular. Is it similarly strict in the division of octet from sestet, or in the arrangement of thought within quatrains ? Is the movement of the thought reflected in the movement of the lines ? Examine it closely and be specific. In all these respects compare it to the sonnet *How soon hath Time*.

6.　What is the feeling in the last line ? Consider the mood of the poem as a whole.

7.　What relationship between God and man is finally described in the poem ? How does it compare to that suggested in Donne's *A Hymn to God the Father* or in Herbert's *The Collar* ?

Glossary p. 218

Avenge O Lord

Avenge O Lord thy slaughter'd Saints, whose bones
  Lie scatter'd on the Alpine mountains cold,
  Ev'n them who kept thy truth so pure of old,
  When all our Fathers worship't Stocks and Stones,
Forget not : in thy book record their groanes   5
  Who were thy Sheep and in their antient Fold
  Slayn by the bloody *Piemontese* that roll'd
  Mother with Infant down the Rocks. Their moans
The Vales redoubl'd to the Hills, and they
  To Heav'n. Their martyr'd blood and ashes sow   10
  O're all th'*Italian* fields where still doth sway
The triple Tyrant : that from these may grow
  A hunder'd-fold, who having learnt thy way
  Early may fly the *Babylonian* wo.

Explorations

1. Would you agree that this sonnet has a rapid forward motion from beginning to end ? How is this motion reflected in the movement of the lines, in the punctuation and in the sonnet structure ?

2. How would you describe the tone of the sonnet—angry, sad, vengeful, bitter . . . ? Does the tone change or intensify as the thought progresses ?

3. There is both resentment and praise in the poem. Show where each is evidenced. Towards whom is each directed ? On what grounds is each feeling based ?

4. Would you agree that the poem for its size shows a tremendous sweep of thought, of historical and religious allusion ? How is this achieved ? Explain, referring to the historical context in which the poem was written.

5. There is a saying that ' the blood of martyrs is the seed of the Church '. Show how this image is deployed in the present poem.

6. Is the poem a passionate utterance ? If so, where and how is this passion manifested ?

Glossary p. 219

Paradise Lost, Book I

Of Man's first disobedience, and the fruit
Of that forbidden Tree, whose mortal taste
Brought death into the world, and all our woe,
With loss of Eden, till one greater Man
Restore us, and regain the blissful seat,   5
Sing, Heavenly Muse, that on the secret top
Of Oreb, or of Sinai, didst inspire
That shepherd, who first taught the chosen seed,
In the beginning how the Heavens and Earth
Rose out of Chaos : or, if Sion hill   10
Delight thee more, and Siloa's brook that flowed
Fast by the oracle of God, I thence
Invoke thy aid to my adventurous song,
That with no middle flight intends to soar
Above the Aonian mount, while it pursues   15
Things unattempted yet in prose or rhyme.
And chiefly thou, O Spirit, that dost prefer
Before all temples the upright heart and pure,
Instruct me, for thou know'st ; thou from the first
Wast present, and, with mighty wings outspread,   20
Dove-like sat'st brooding on the vast Abyss,
And mad'st it pregnant : what in me is dark
Illumine, what is low raise and support ;
That to the height of this great argument
I may assert Eternal Providence,   25
And justify the ways of God to men.
  Say first, for Heaven hides nothing from thy view,
Nor the deep tract of Hell, say first what cause
Moved our grand parents, in that happy state,
Favoured of Heaven so highly, to fall off   30
From their Creator, and transgress His Will
For one restraint, lords of the world besides.
Who first seduced them to that foul revolt ?
The infernal Serpent ; he it was, whose guile,
Stirred up with envy and revenge, deceived   35
The Mother of Mankind, what time his pride
Had cast him out from Heaven, with all his host

Of rebel Angels, by whose aid, aspiring
To set himself in glory above his peers,
He trusted to have equalled the Most High,   40
If he opposed ; and with ambitious aim
Against the throne and monarchy of God
Raised impious war in Heaven and battle proud,
With vain attempt. Him the Almighty Power
Hurled headlong flaming from the ethereal sky,   45
With hideous ruin and combustion, down
To bottomless perdition ; there to dwell
In adamantine chains and penal fire,
Who durst defy the Omnipotent to arms.
Nine times the space that measures day and night   50
To mortal men, he with his horrid crew
Lay vanquished, rolling in the fiery gulf,
Confounded though immortal. But his doom
Reserved him to more wrath ; for now the thought
Both of lost happiness and lasting pain   55
Torments him ; round he throws his baleful eyes,
That witnessed huge affliction and dismay,
Mixed with obdúrate pride and steadfast hate.
At once, as far as Angel's ken, he views
The dismal situation waste and wild,   60
A dungeon horrible, on all sides round,
As one great furnace flamed ; yet from those flames
No light, but rather darkness visible
Served only to discover sights of woe,
Regions of sorrow, doleful shades, where peace   65
And rest can never dwell, hope never comes
That comes to all ; but torture without end
Still urges, and a fiery deluge, fed
With ever-burning sulphur unconsumed.
Such place Eternal Justice had prepared   70
For those rebellious ; here their prison ordained
In utter darkness, and their portion set,
As far removed from God and light of Heaven
As from the centre thrice to the utmost pole.
Oh how unlike the place from whence they fell !   75
There the companions of his fall, o'erwhelmed
With floods and whirlwinds of tempestuous fire,

He soon discerns ; and, weltering by his side,
One next himself in power, and next in crime,
Long after known in Palestine, and named   80
Beëlzebub. To whom the Arch-Enemy,
And thence in Heaven called Satan, with bold words
Breaking the horrid silence, thus began :
    " If thou beest he—but Oh how fallen ! how changed
From him, who in the happy realms of light,   85
Clothed with transcendent brightness, didst outshine
Myriads, though bright ! If he, whom mutual league,
United thoughts and counsels, equal hope
And hazard in the glorious enterprise,
Joined with me once, now misery hath joined   90
In equal ruin : into what pit thou seest
From what height fallen, so much the stronger proved
He with his thunder : and till then who knew
The force of those dire arms ? Yet not for those,
Nor what the potent victor in his rage   95
Can else inflict, do I repent, or change,
Though changed in outward lustre, that fixed mind,
And high disdain from sense of injured merit,
That with the Mightiest raised me to contend,
And to the fierce contention brought along   100
Innumerable force of Spirits armed,
That durst dislike his reign, and, me preferring,
His utmost power with adverse power opposed
In dubious battle on the plains of Heaven,
And shook his throne. What though the field be lost ?   105
All is not lost ; the unconquerable will,
And study of revenge, immortal hate,
And courage never to submit or yield :
And what is else not to be overcome ?
That glory never shall his wrath or might   110
Extort from me. To bow and sue for grace
With suppliant knee, and deify his power
Who, from the terror of this arm, so late
Doubted his empire—that were low indeed ;
That were an ignominy and shame beneath   115
This downfall ; since by fate the strength of gods
And this empyreal substance cannot fail ;

Since, through experience of this great event,
In arms not worse, in foresight much advanced,
We may with more successful hope resolve   120
To wage by force or guile eternal war,
Irreconcilable to our grand foe,
Who now triumphs, and in the excess of joy
Sole reigning holds the tyranny of Heaven."
   So spake the apostate Angel, though in pain,   125
Vaunting aloud, but racked with deep despair ;
And him thus answered soon his bold compeer :
   " O Prince, O Chief of many thronèd Powers,
That led the embattled Seraphim to war
Under thy conduct, and, in dreadful deeds   130
Fearless, endangered Heaven's perpetual King,
And put to proof his high supremacy,
Whether upheld by strength, or chance, or fate !
Too well I see and rue the dire event,
That with sad overthrow and foul defeat   135
Hath lost us Heaven, and all this mighty host
In horrible destruction laid thus low,
As far as gods and Heavenly essences
Can perish : for the mind and spirit remains
Invincible, and vigour soon returns,   140
Though all our glory extinct, and happy state
Here swallowed up in endless misery.
But what if he our conqueror (whom I now
Of force believe almighty, since no less
Than such could have o'erpowered such force as ours)   145
Have left us this our spirit and strength entire,
Strongly to suffer and support our pains,
That we may so suffice his vengeful ire ;
Or do him mightier service, as his thralls
By right of war, whate'er his business be,   150
Here in the heart of Hell to work in fire,
Or do his errands in the gloomy deep ?
What can it then avail, though yet we feel
Strength undiminished, or eternal being
To undergo eternal punishment ? "   155
Whereto with speedy words the Arch-Fiend replied :
" Fallen Cherub, to be weak is miserable,

Doing or suffering : but of this be sure,
To do aught good never will be our task,
But ever to do ill our sole delight,   160
As being the contrary to his high will
Whom we resist. If then his providence
Out of our evil seek to bring forth good,
Our labour must be to pervert that end,
And out of good still to find means of evil ;   165
Which oft times may succeed, so as perhaps
Shall grieve him, if I fail not, and disturb
His inmost counsels from their destined aim.
But see ! the angry Victor hath recalled
His ministers of vengeance and pursuit   170
Back to the gates of Heaven ; the sulphurous hail,
Shot after us in storm, o'erblown hath laid
The fiery surge, that from the precipice
Of Heaven received us falling ; and the thunder,
Winged with red lightning and impetuous rage,   175
Perhaps hath spent his shafts, and ceases now
To bellow through the vast and boundless deep.
Let us not slip the occasion, whether scorn,
Or satiate fury yield it from our foe.
Seest thou yon dreary plain, forlorn and wild,   180
The seat of desolation, void of light,
Save what the glimmering of these livid flames
Casts pale and dreadful ? Thither let us tend
From off the tossing of these fiery waves ;
There rest, if any rest can harbour there ;   185
And, re-assembling our afflicted powers,
Consult how we may henceforth most offend
Our enemy, our own loss how repair,
How overcome this dire calamity,
What reinforcement we may gain from hope,   190
If not, what resolution from despair."
    Thus Satan, talking to his nearest mate,
With head uplift above the wave, and eyes
That sparkling blazed ; his other parts besides,
Prone on the flood, extended long and large,   195
Lay floating many a rood, in bulk as huge
As whom the fables name of monstrous size,

Titanian, or Earth-born, that warred on Jove,
Briareos or Typhon, whom the den
By ancient Tarsus held, or that sea-beast   200
Leviathan, which God of all his works
Created hugest that swim the ocean-stream.
Him, haply, slumbering on the Norway foam,
The pilot of some small night-foundered skiff
Deeming some island, oft, as seamen tell,   205
With fixèd anchor in his scaly rind,
Moors by his side under the lee, while night
Invests the sea, and wishèd morn delays :
So stretched out huge in length the Arch-Fiend lay,
Chained on the burning lake ; nor ever thence   210
Had risen or heaved his head, but that the will
And high permission of all-ruling Heaven
Left him at large to his own dark designs,
That with reiterated crimes he might
Heap on himself damnation, while he sought   215
Evil to others, and enraged might see
How all his malice served but to bring forth
Infinite goodness, grace and mercy shewn
On Man by him seduced, but on himself
Treble confusion, wrath and vengeance poured.   220
Forthwith upright he rears from off the pool
His mighty stature ; on each hand the flames
Driven backward slope their pointing spires, and, rolled
In billows, leave i' the midst a horrid vale.
Then with expanded wings he steers his flight   225
Aloft, incumbent on the dusky air,
That felt unusual weight ; till on dry land
He lights—if it were land that ever burned
With solid, as the lake with liquid fire,
And such appeared in hue, as when the force   230
Of subterranean wind transports a hill
Torn from Pelorus, or the shattered side
Of thundering Ætna, whose combustible
And fuelled entrails thence conceiving fire,
Sublimed with mineral fury, aid the winds,   235
And leave a singèd bottom all involved
With stench and smoke : such resting found the sole

Of unblest feet. Him followed his next mate,
Both glorying to have scaped the Stygian flood
As gods, and by their own recovered strength,   240
Not by the sufferance of supernal power.
   " Is this the region, this the soil, the clime,"
Said then the lost Archangel, " this the seat
That we must change for Heaven ? this mournful gloom
For that celestial light ? Be it so, since he   245
Who now is sovran can dispose and bid
What shall be right: farthest from him is best,
Whom reason hath equalled, force hath made supreme
Above his equals. Farewell, happy fields,
Where joy for ever dwells ! Hail, horrors ! hail,   250
Infernal world ! and thou, profoundest Hell,
Receive thy new possessor, one who brings
A mind not to be changed by place or time.
The mind is its own place, and in itself
Can make a Heaven of Hell, a Hell of Heaven.   255
What matter where, if I be still the same,
And what I should be, all but less than he
Whom thunder hath made greater ? Here at least
We shall be free ; the Almighty hath not built
Here for his envy, will not drive us hence :   260
Here we may reign secure, and in my choice
To reign is worth ambition, though in Hell :
Better to reign in Hell, than serve in Heaven.
But wherefore let we then our faithful friends,
The associates and co-partners of our loss,   265
Lie thus astonished on the oblivious pool,
And call them not to share with us their part
In this unhappy mansion, or once more
With rallied arms to try what may be yet
Regained in Heaven, or what more lost in Hell ? "   270
   So Satan spake ; and him Beëlzebub
Thus answered : " Leader of those armies bright
Which but the Omnipotent none could have foiled,
If once they hear that voice, their liveliest pledge
Of hope in fears and dangers—heard so oft   275
In worst extremes, and on the perilous edge
Of battle when it raged, in all assaults

Their surest signal—they will soon resume
New courage and revive, though now they lie
Grovelling and prostrate on yon lake of fire,   280
As we erewhile, astounded and amazed—
No wonder, fallen such a pernicious height ! "
   He scarce had ceased when the superior Fiend
Was moving towards the shore ; his ponderous shield,
Ethereal temper, massy, large, and round,   285
Behind him cast. The broad circumference
Hung on his shoulders like the moon, whose orb
Through optic glass the Tuscan artist views
At evening from the top of Fesolè
Or in Valdarno, to descry new lands,   290
Rivers, or mountains, in her spotty globe.
His spear—to equal which the tallest pine
Hewn on Norwegian hills, to be the mast
Of some great ammiral, were but a wand—
He walked with, to support uneasy steps   295
Over the burning marle, not like those steps
On Heaven's azure ; and the torrid clime
Smote on him sore besides, vaulted with fire.
Nathless he so endured, till on the beach
Of that inflamèd sea he stood, and called   300
His legions, Angel forms, who lay entranced,
Thick as autumnal leaves that strow the brooks
In Vallombrosa, where the Etrurian shades
High over-arched embower ; or scattered sedge
Afloat, when with fierce winds Orion armed   305
Hath vexed the Red Sea coast, whose waves o'er threw
Busiris and his Memphian chivalry,
While with perfidious hatred they pursued
The sojourners of Goshen, who beheld
From the safe shore their floating carcases   310
And broken chariot-wheels : so thick bestrown,
Abject and lost, lay these, covering the flood,
Under amazement of their hideous change.
He called so loud that all the hollow deep
Of Hell resounded : " Princes, Potentates,   315
Warriors, the flower of Heaven, once yours, now lost,
If such astonishment as this can seize

Eternal Spirits : or have ye chosen this place
After the toil of battle to repose
Your wearied virtue, for the ease you find   320
To slumber here, as in the vales of Heaven ?
Or in this abject posture have ye sworn
To adore the Conqueror, who now beholds
Cherub and Seraph rolling in the flood
With scattered arms and ensigns, till anon   325
His swift pursuers from Heaven-gates discern
The advantage, and descending tread us down
Thus drooping, or with linkèd thunderbolts
Transfix us to the bottom of this gulf?
Awake, arise, or be for ever fallen ! "   330
    They heard, and were abashed, and up they sprung
Upon the wing, as when men wont to watch
On duty, sleeping found by whom they dread,
Rouse and bestir themselves ere well awake.
Nor did they not perceive the evil plight   335
In which they were, or the fierce pains not feel ;
Yet to their General's voice they soon obeyed
Innumerable. As when the potent rod
Of Amram's son, in Egypt's evil day,
Waved round the coast, up called a pitchy cloud   340
Of locusts, warping on the eastern wind,
That o'er the realm of impious Pharaoh hung
Like night, and darkened all the land of Nile :
So numberless were those bad Angels seen
Hovering on wing under the cope of Hell,   345
'Twixt upper, nether, and surrounding fires ;
Till, as a signal given, the uplifted spear
Of their great Sultan waving to direct
Their course, in even balance down they light
On the firm brimstone, and fill all the plain :   350
A multitude, like which the populous North
Poured never from her frozen loins, to pass
Rhene or the Danaw, when her barbarous sons
Came like a deluge on the South, and spread
Beneath Gibraltar to the Libyan sands.   355
Forthwith, from every squadron and each band,
The heads and leaders thither haste where stood

Their great Commander ; godlike shapes, and forms
Excelling human, princely dignities,
And powers that erst in Heaven sat on thrones ;   360
Though of their names in Heavenly records now
Be no memorial, blotted out and rased
By their rebellion, from the Books of Life.
Nor had they yet among the sons of Eve
Got them new names, till, wandering o'er the Earth,   365
Through God's high sufferance for the trial of Man,
By falsities and lies the greatest part
Of Mankind they corrupted to forsake
God their Creator, and the invisible
Glory of him that made them, to transform   370
Oft to the image of a brute, adorned
With gay religions full of pomp and gold,
And devils to adore for deities.
Then were they known to men by various names,
And various idols through the heathen world.   375
Say, Muse, their names then known, who first, who last,
Roused from the slumber on that fiery couch,
At their great Emperor's call, as next in worth
Came singly where he stood on the bare strand,
While the promiscuous crowd stood yet aloof.   380
The chief were those who, from the pit of Hell
Roaming to seek their prey on Earth, durst fix
Their seats long after next the seat of God,
Their altars by his altar, gods adored
Among the nations round, and durst abide   385
Jehovah thundering out of Sion, throned
Between the Cherubim ; yea, often placed
Within his sanctuary itself their shrines,
Abominations ; and with cursed things
His holy rites and solemn feasts profaned,   390
And with their darkness durst affront his light.
First, Moloch, horrid king, besmeared with blood
Of human sacrifice, and parents' tears,
Though, for the noise of drums and timbrels loud,
Their children's cries unheard, that passed through fire   395
To his grim idol. Him the Ammonite
Worshipped in Rabba and her watery plain,

In Argob and in Basan, to the stream
Of utmost Arnon. Nor content with such
Audacious neighbourhood, the wisest heart   400
Of Solomon he led by fraud to build
His temple right against the temple of God
On that opprobrious hill, and made his grove
The pleasant valley of Hinnom, Tophet thence
And black Gehenna called, the type of Hell.   405
Next Chemos, the óbscene dread of Moab's sons,
From Aroer to Nebo, and the wild
Of southmost Abarim ; in Hesebon
And Horonaim, Seon's realm, beyond
The flowery dale of Sibma clad with vines,   410
And Elealè to the Asphaltic pool.
Peor his other name, when he enticed
Israel in Sittim, on their march from Nile,
To do him wanton rites, which cost them woe.
Yet thence his lustful orgies he enlarged   415
Even to that hill of scandal, by the grove
Of Moloch homicide, lust hard by hate ;
Till good Josiah drove them thence to Hell.
With these came they who, from the bordering flood
Of old Euphrates to the brook that parts   420
Egypt from Syrian ground, had general names
Of Baalim and Ashtaroth—those male,
These feminine. For Spirits, when they please,
Can either sex assume, or both ; so soft
And uncompounded is their essence pure,   425
Not tied or manacled with joint or limb,
Nor founded on the brittle strength of bones,
Like cumbrous flesh ; but, in what shape they choose,
Dilated or condensed, bright or obscure,
Can execute their aery purposes,   430
And works of love or enmity fulfil.
For those the race of Israel oft forsook
Their living Strength, and unfrequented left
His righteous altar, bowing lowly down
To bestial gods ; for which their heads as low   435
Bowed down in battle, sunk before the spear
Of despicable foes. With these in troop

Came Astoreth, whom the Phœnicians called
Astarte, Queen of Heaven, with crescent horns ;
To whose bright image nightly by the moon   440
Sidonian virgins paid their vows and songs ;
In Sion also not unsung, where stood
Her temple on the offensive mountain, built
By that uxorious king whose heart, though large,
Beguiled by fair idolatresses, fell   445
To idols foul. Thammuz came next behind,
Whose annual wound in Lebanon allured
The Syrian damsels to lament his fate
In amorous ditties all a summer's day,
While smooth Adonis from his native rock   450
Ran purple to the sea, supposed with blood
Of Thammuz yearly wounded : the love-tale
Infected Sion's daughters with like heat,
Whose wanton passions in the sacred porch
Ezekiel saw, when, by the vision led,   455
His eye surveyed the dark idolatries
Of alienated Judah. Next came one
Who mourned in earnest, when the captive ark
Maimed his brute image, head and hands lopt off
In his own temple, on the grunsel-edge,   460
Where he fell flat, and shamed his worshippers :
Dagon his name, sea-monster, upward man
And downward fish ; yet had his temple high
Reared in Azotus, dreaded through the coast
Of Palestine, in Gath and Ascalon,   465
And Accaron and Gaza's frontier bounds.
Him followed Rimmon, whose delightful seat
Was fair Damascus, on the fertile banks
Of Abbana and Pharphar, lucid streams.
He also against the house of God was bold :   470
A leper once he lost and gained a king,
Ahaz, his sottish conqueror, whom he drew
God's altar to disparage and displace
For one of Syrian mode, whereon to burn
His odious offerings, and adore the gods   475
Whom he had vanquished. After these appeared
A crew who, under names of old renown,

Osiris, Isis, Orus, and their train,
With monstrous shapes and sorceries abused
Fanatic Egypt and her priests, to seek   480
Their wandering gods disguised in brutish forms
Rather than human. Nor did Israel scape
The infection, when their borrowed gold composed
The calf in Oreb ; and the rebel king
Doubled that sin in Bethel and in Dan,   485
Likening his Maker to the grazèd ox—
Jehovah, who, in one night, when he passed
From Egypt marching, equalled with one stroke
Both her first-bórn and all her bleating gods.
Belial came last, than whom a Spirit more lewd   490
Fell not from Heaven, or more gross to love
Vice for itself. To him no temple stood
Or altar smoked ; yet who more oft than he
In temples and at altars, when the priest
Turns atheist, as did Eli's sons, who filled   495
With lust and violence the house of God.
In courts and palaces he also reigns
And in luxurious cities, where the noise
Of riot ascends above their loftiest towers,
And injury and outrage ; and when night   500
Darkens the streets, then wander forth the sons
Of Belial, flown with insolence and wine.
Witness the streets of Sodom, and that night
In Gibeah, when the hospitable doors
Exposed their matrons, to prevent worse rape.   505
These were the prime in order and in might ;
The rest were long to tell, though far renowned,
The Ionian gods—of Javan's issue held
Gods, yet confessed later than Heaven and Earth,
Their boasted parents : Titan, Heaven's first-born,   510
With his enormous brood, and birthright seized
By younger Saturn ; he from mightier Jove,
His own and Rhea's son, like measure found ;
So Jove usurping reigned. These, first in Crete
And Ida known, thence on the snowy top   515
Of cold Olympus ruled the middle air,
Their highest Heaven ; or on the Delphian cliff,

Or in Dodona, and through all the bounds
Of Doric land ; or who with Saturn old
Fled over Adria to the Hesperian fields,   520
And o'er the Celtic roamed the utmost Isles.
All these and more came flocking ; but with looks
Downcast and damp, yet such wherein appeared
Obscure some glimpse of joy, to have found their Chief
Not in despair, to have found themselves not lost   525
In loss itself ; which on his countenance cast
Like doubtful hue. But he, his wonted pride
Soon recollecting, with high words, that bore
Semblance of worth, not substance, gently raised
Their fainted courage, and dispelled their fears.   530
Then straight commands that, at the warlike sound
Of trumpets loud and clarions, be upreared
His mighty standard. That proud honour claimed
Azazel as his right, a Cherub tall :
Who forthwith from the glittering staff unfurled   535
The imperial ensign, which, full high advanced,
Shone like a meteor streaming to the wind,
With gems and golden lustre rich emblazed,
Seraphic arms and trophies ; all the while
Sonorous metal blowing martial sounds :   540
At which the universal host up-sent
A shout that tore Hell's concave, and beyond
Frighted the reign of Chaos and old Night.
All in a moment through the gloom were seen
Ten thousand banners rise into the air,   545
With orient colours waving ; with them rose
A forest huge of spears ; and thronging helms
Appeared, and serried shields in thick array
Of depth immeasurable. Anon they move
In perfect phalanx to the Dorian mood   550
Of flutes and soft recorders ; such as raised
To height of noblest temper heroes old
Arming to battle, and instead of rage
Deliberate valour breathed, firm and unmoved
With dread of death to flight or foul retreat ;   555
Nor wanting power to mitigate and swage,
With solemn touches, troubled thoughts, and chase

Anguish and doubt and fear and sorrow and pain
From mortal or immortal minds. Thus they,
Breathing united force with fixèd thought,   560
Moved on in silence to soft pipes that charmed
Their painful steps o'er the burnt soil ; and now
Advanced in view they stand, a horrid front
Of dreadful length and dazzling arms, in guise
Of warriors old, with ordered spear and shield,   565
Awaiting what command their mighty Chief
Had to impose. He through the armèd files
Darts his experienced eye, and soon traverse
The whole battalion views—their order due,
Their visages and stature as of gods ;   570
Their number last he sums. And now his heart
Distends with pride, and hardening in his strength,
Glories ; for never, since created Man,
Met such embodied force as, named with these,
Could merit more than that small infantry   575
Warred on by cranes : though all the giant brood
Of Phlegra with the heroic race were joined
That fought at Thebes and Ilium, on each side
Mixed with auxiliar gods ; and what resounds
In fable or romance of Uther's son,   580
Begirt with British and Armoric knights ;
And all who since, baptized or infidel,
Jousted in Aspramont, or Montalban,
Damasco, or Marocco, or Trebisond ;
Or whom Biserta sent from Afric shore   585
When Charlemain with all his peerage fell
By Fontarabbia. Thus far these beyond
Compare of mortal prowess, yet observed
Their dread Commander. He, above the rest
In shape and gesture proudly eminent,   590
Stood like a tower ; his form had yet not lost
All her original brightness, nor appeared
Less than Archangel ruined, and the excess
Of glory obscured : as when the sun new-risen
Looks through the horizontal misty air   595
Shorn of his beams, or from behind the moon,
In dim eclipse, disastrous twilight sheds

On half the nations, and with fear of change
Perplexes monarchs. Darkened so, yet shone
Above them all the Archangel ; but his face   600
Deep scars of thunder had intrenched, and care
Sat on his faded cheek, but under brows
Of dauntless courage, and considerate pride
Waiting revenge. Cruel his eye, but cast
Signs of remorse and passion, to behold   605
The fellows of his crime, the followers rather
(Far other once beheld in bliss), condemned
For ever now to have their lot in pain ;
Millions of Spirits for his fault amerc'd
Of Heaven, and from eternal splendours flung   610
For his revolt ; yet faithful how they stood,
Their glory withered : as, when Heaven's fire
Hath scathed the forest oaks or mountain pines,
With singèd top their stately growth, though bare,
Stands on the blasted heath. He now prepared   615
To speak ; whereat their doubled ranks they bend
From wing to wing, and half enclose him round
With all his peers : attention held them mute.
Thrice he assayed, and thrice, in spite of scorn,
Tears, such as Angels weep, burst forth : at last   620
Words interwove with sighs found out their way :
   " O myriads of immortal Spirits ! O powers
Matchless, but with the Almighty !—and that strife
Was not inglorious, though the event was dire,
As this place testifies, and this dire change,   625
Hateful to utter. But what power of mind,
Foreseeing or presaging, from the depth
Of knowledge past or present, could have feared
How such united force of gods, how such
As stood like these, could ever know repulse ?   630
For who can yet believe, though after loss,
That all these puissant legions, whose exile
Hath emptied Heaven, shall fail to re-ascend,
Self-raised, and re-possess their native seat ?
For me, be witness all the host of Heaven,   635
If counsels different, or danger shunned
By me, have lost our hopes. But he who reigns

Monarch in Heaven, till then as one secure
Sat on his throne, upheld by old repute,
Consent or custom, and his regal state   640
Put forth at full, but still his strength concealed,
Which tempted our attempt, and wrought our fall.
Henceforth his might we know, and know our own,
So as not either to provoke, or dread
New war provoked ; our better part remains   645
To work in close design, by fraud or guile,
What force effected not ; that he no less
At length from us may find, who overcomes
By force hath overcome but half his foe.
Space may produce new worlds ; whereof so rife   650
There went a fame in Heaven that he ere long
Intended to create, and therein plant
A generation, whom his choice regard
Should favour equal to the Sons of Heaven.
Thither, if but to pry, shall be perhaps   655
Our first eruption, thither or elsewhere ;
For this infernal pit shall never hold
Celestial Spirits in bondage, nor the Abyss
Long under darkness cover. But these thoughts
Full counsel must mature. Peace is despaired,   660
For who can think submission ? War, then, war
Open or understood, must be resolved."
    He spake ; and, to confirm his words, out-flew
Millions of flaming swords, drawn from the thighs
Of mighty Cherubim ; the sudden blaze   665
Far round illumined Hell. Highly they raged
Against the Highest, and fierce with graspèd arms
Clashed on their sounding shields the din of war,
Hurling defiance toward the vault of Heaven.
    There stood a hill not far, whose grisly top   670
Belched fire and rolling smoke ; the rest entire
Shone with a glossy scurf, undoubted sign
That in his womb was hid metallic ore,
The work of sulphur. Thither, winged with speed,
A numerous brigade hastened. As when bands   675
Of pioneers, with spade and pickaxe armed,
Forerun the royal camp, to trench a field,

Soundings—4

Or cast a rampart. Mammon led them on,
Mammon, the least erected Spirit that fell
From Heaven, for even in Heaven his looks and thoughts   680
Were always downward bent, admiring more
The riches of Heaven's pavement, trodden gold,
Than aught divine or holy else enjoyed
In vision beatific. By him first
Men also, and by his suggestion taught,   685
Ransacked the centre, and with impious hands
Rifled the bowels of their mother Earth
For treasures better hid. Soon had his crew
Opened into the hill a spacious wound,
And digged out ribs of gold. Let none admire   690
That riches grow in Hell ; that soil may best
Deserve the precious bane. And here let those
Who boast in mortal things, and wondering tell
Of Babel, and the works of Memphian kings,
Learn how their greatest monuments of fame,   695
And strength, and art, are easily outdone
By Spirits reprobate, and in an hour
What in an age they, with incessant toil
And hands innumerable, scarce perform.
Nigh on the plain, in many cells prepared,   700
That underneath had veins of liquid fire
Sluiced from the lake, a second multitude
With wondrous art founded the massy ore,
Severing each kind, and scummed the bullion dross.
A third as soon had formed within the ground   705
A various mould, and from the boiling cells
By strange conveyance filled each hollow nook :
As in an organ, from one blast of wind,
To many a row of pipes the sound-board breathes.
Anon out of the earth a fabric huge   710
Rose like an exhalation, with the sound
Of dulcet symphonies and voices sweet,
Built like a temple, where pilasters round
Were set, and Doric pillars overlaid
With golden architrave ; nor did there want   715
Cornice or frieze, with bossy sculptures graven ;
The roof was fretted gold. Not Babylon,

Nor great Alcairo, such magnificence
Equalled in all their glories, to enshrine
Belus or Sérapis their gods, or seat   720
Their kings, when Egypt with Assyria strove
In wealth and luxury. The ascending pile
Stood fixed her stately height, and straight the doors,
Opening their brazen folds, discover, wide
Within, her ample spaces o'er the smooth   725
And level pavement : from the archèd roof,
Pendent by subtle magic, many a row
Of starry lamps and blazing cressets, fed
With naphtha and asphaltus, yielded light
As from a sky. The hasty multitude   730
Admiring entered, and the work some praise,
And some the architect : his hand was known
In Heaven by many a towered structure high,
Where sceptred Angels held their residence,
And sat as princes, whom the súpreme King   735
Exalted to such power, and gave to rule,
Each in his Hierarchy, the Orders bright.
Nor was his name unheard or unadored
In ancient Greece ; and in Ausonian land
Men called him Mulciber ; and how he fell   740
From Heaven, they fabled, thrown by angry Jove
Sheer o'er the crystal battlements : from morn
To noon he fell, from noon to dewy eve,
A summer's day ; and with the setting sun
Dropt from the zenith, like a falling star,   745
On Lemnos, the Ægæan isle. Thus they relate,
Erring ; for he with this rebellious rout
Fell long before ; nor aught availed him now
To have built in Heaven high towers ; nor did he scape
By all his engines, but was headlong sent   750
With his industrious crew to build in Hell.
Meanwhile the wingèd haralds, by command
Of sovran power, with awful ceremony
And trumpet's sound, throughout the host proclaim
A solemn council forthwith to be held   755
At Pandemonium, the high capital
Of Satan and his peers. Their summons called

From every band and squarèd regiment
By place or choice the worthiest ; they anon
With hundreds and with thousands trooping came   760
Attended. All accéss was thronged, the gates
And porches wide, but chief the spacious hall
(Though like a covered field, where champions bold
Wont ride in armed, and at the Soldan's chair
Defied the best of Panim chivalry   765
To mortal combat, or career with lance)
Thick swarmed, both on the ground and in the air,
Brushed with the hiss of rustling wings. As bees
In spring-time, when the sun with Taurus rides,
Pour forth their populous youth about the hive   770
In clusters ; they among fresh dews and flowers
Fly to and fro, or on the smoothèd plank,
The suburb of their straw-built citadel,
New rubbed with balm, expatiate and confer
Their state-affairs. So thick the aery crowd   775
Swarmed and were straitened ; till, the signal given,
Behold a wonder ! they but now who seemed
In bigness to surpass Earth's giant sons,
Now less than smallest dwarfs, in narrow room
Throng numberless, like that pygmean race   780
Beyond the Indian mount ; or faery elves,
Whose midnight revels, by a forest side
Or fountain, some belated peasant sees,
Or dreams he sees, while overhead the moon
Sits arbitress, and nearer to the Earth   785
Wheels her pale course ; they, on their mirth and dance
Intent, with jocund music charm his ear ;
At once with joy and fear his heart rebounds.
Thus incorporeal Spirits to smallest forms
Reduced their shapes immense, and were at large,   790
Though without number still, amidst the hall
Of that infernal court. But far within,
And in their own dimensions like themselves,
The great Seraphic Lords and Cherubim
In close recess and secret conclave sat,   795
A thousand demi-gods on golden seats,
Frequent and full. After short silence then,
And summons read, the great consult began.

Explorations

For the sake of convenience, the first set of Explorations examines Book I section by section. The general Explorations deal with it finally as a coherent unit in Milton's epic.

Section A
Lines 1–26

1. Milton indicates in the first 26 lines the purpose and theme of the epic. What is the nature and scope of the theme?

2. Describe the tone of the opening passage. Does it accord with the theme? Consider, for instance, the effect of the allusions and proper names.

3. In defending his use of unrhymed or blank verse, Milton mentions among its virtues ' fit quantity (or number) of syllables and the sense variously drawn out from one verse into another, not a jingling sound of like endings, a fault avoided by the learned ancients both in poetry and all good oratory.' Having read the opening verse paragraph aloud, examine these features, saying how each contributes to the movement of the thought. Do not neglect to count the syllables in chosen lines.

Section B
Lines 27–83

1. What events are dealt with between lines 27 and 49? In carrying out his very ambitious design Milton had to sweep through great periods of time and convey mighty events, often in short passages of poetry. How does he achieve this?

2. How vividly, in your opinion, is the actual fall of Satan's armies conveyed? What phrases or images strike you especially? Read the lines aloud and comment in detail on the effectiveness of the sound.

3. For Milton hell was vast, dark, fiery, everlasting, altogether unearthly. How does he manage to convey each of these qualities? Does he blend them all into a convincing mental picture? If so, can you suggest some of the means by which he does it? Consider language, sound, imagery, metre and punctuation. Pay especial attention to the adjectives he uses.

4. Do you agree that in the passage from lines 50 to 83 Milton conveys both mental and physical suffering? If so, point out examples of each, and comment on any feature that strikes you as especially vivid.

5. What do we learn of Satan's character in this passage? What are the chief causes of his pain? Which, do you think, is the greatest?

Section C
Lines 84–191

1. Satan argues that ' All is not lost '. Is this true ? Is he speaking in sincerity, self-delusion or actual deceitfulness ? Examine the ring of the language here. Think also about the reality of Satan's predicament.

2. When Satan has completed his speech to Beëlzebub, Milton remarks that he has been ' Vaunting aloud, but racked with deep despair '. Read Satan's speech through—preferably aloud—and then discuss where the despair is to be discerned beneath the boasting.

3. What features can you now add to your character study of Satan ? Is there any sense in which he has your sympathy ? Explain.

4. Examine how Satan uses antithesis—the balance of opposite ideas—in his speech, e.g., ' equal hope/And hazard '. Can you suggest a psychological reason why Satan should speak in this way ? Glance back at question 2 above.

5. Satan's first speech is clearly one of great force and resonance. What qualities of sound or image produce these effects ? What parts of the speech do you find particularly exciting ? Why ?

6. What is the gist of Beëlzebub's speech ? How does it differ in tone or emphasis from Satan's ? Be particular. Which of the two shows the more realistic grasp of their situation ? Why ?

7. What do we learn about God from Beëlzebub's speech ? What do we learn about the revolt in heaven ? Do we learn anything not already revealed by Satan ?

8. How does Beëlzebub's speech compare with Satan's in terms of resonance, force and majesty ? Is their difference in status somehow reflected in the poetry attributed to each ? If so, point out some features of phrase, image or movement that might reflect this difference.

9. The first twelve lines of Satan's reply to Beëlzebub set out his basic philosophy. Summarise this briefly. Is it based on a just assessment of his situation ? Outline the policy with which he intends to oppose the providence of God.

10. Milton cannot permit his poem to develop into a mere debate. He must retain our interest by keeping up the sense of action. How does he achieve this here ?

11. What further details are added to our picture of hell in the concluding lines of Satan's second speech ? How do you feel about Satan and his predicament at this stage ?

12. What is the effect of the antithesis in the last two lines ? Glance at question 4 above.

13. What impression have you formed by now of the war between God and Satan ? Look back at the various references to it. What sort of problems did the poet have to face in dealing with such a war ? How well do you think he overcame them ?

Section D

Lines 192–282

1. How does Milton convey a sense of Satan's hugeness ? Read aloud, and at the proper pace, the lines that describe him, and see how the sound and movement of the words, the combinations of vowels and consonants, contribute to the picture. What is the effect of the proper names of the creatures to which he is compared ?

2. How successful is the epic simile in lines 203 to 208 ? Give reasons for your opinion.

3. Note as Milton proceeds how he keeps extending his range of reference to reinforce the greatness and universality of his theme. To the monsters of Greek mythology he adds biblical allusions and legends from the colder world of the North Sea. It is well to be alert for this function of his images and mythological and legendary references.

4. Why does Milton find it necessary to point out, towards the end of the paragraph, that Satan could rise from the lake only by God's permission ? Is he, perhaps, trying to keep in check our sympathy and admiration for Satan ? Be alert for similar comments in the spaces of the narrative as the poem proceeds.

5. What further physical details do lines 221 to 241 add to our picture of Satan ? What details does it add to our vision of hell ? Which details in each case do you find more vivid and why ?

6. Satan, in his speech, gives a more final expression to the principles he now intends to live by. What are these principles and where have they previously been expressed or hinted at ?

7. Satan's powers of reasoning might appear to have been damaged by his fall from grace. Is there any evidence of this in the speech ? Be specific. Can you suggest other reasons for Satan's attitude to his predicament ?

8. Is this a persuasive speech ? Is it a convincing one ? Argue your case, whether your answer be positive or negative.

9. What is Beëlzebub's attitude to Satan ? In what way does his attitude affect our opinion of Satan ? What use does Milton make of Beëlzebub in the poem so far ?

Section E
Lines 283–363

1. The poet now turns from debate to description and narrative. What further details may we now add to our portrait of Satan? What details given here strike you as especially vivid? What is the effect of the similes and of the allusions? Glance back at question 3 in Section D.

2. Is Satan at his most tragic in passages such as this? What qualities in him strike you most forcibly—his majesty, his endurance, his courage, his desperation?

3. Would you agree that there is great energy in the language in this long passage? Explain, pointing out particular instances of it in line or phrase.

4. The poet first compares the swarming devils to the locusts of Egypt, then to Viking pirates. Which simile is the more apt, vivid, accurate? Why, in your opinion, does he use two such contrasting similes to express the same thing?

Section F
Lines 364–521

1. The poet now calls on the Muse to name the chief devils who became known as idols in the world. Why is the invocation made at this point in the poem—to remind us of his opening invocation (see line 4), to give a point of rest, to move the poem into a new phase . . . ?

2. In this long passage Milton—as is the custom with the epic—enumerates the ' prime in order and in might ' among the defeated host. For what reasons does he identify them by earthly names? In answering, note the range and scope of Milton's allusions—biblical, classical, geographical.

3. The entire paragraph enumerates the sort of sins to which these devils urged the human race down through history. Were these, by and large, sins of the flesh or of the spirit? Examine the language used by Milton in describing these sins, beginning perhaps with those ascribed to Belial and his followers.

4. The East has been traditionally regarded as a place of luxury and vice. Does Milton make use of this prejudice in the roll-call of the devils? If so, how?

5. The passage from line 381 to 521 sweeps powerfully through biblical history. Does this in any way help the general pattern of the poem? Why does Milton refer to classical and other mythologies? Explain their relevance in the overall design.

Section G
Lines 522-621

1. Satan raises the spirits of his broken army ' with high words ' that bore ' Semblance of worth, not substance '. What does Milton mean by this phrase ? Can you point out any examples of this thinking in his earlier speeches ?

2. Reconsider, at this point, your portrait of Satan. What new dimensions have been added to his personality to evoke our sympathy ? Note the human touches.

3. Milton, in this passage, calls forth all the resources of his language—rhythm, sound and image—to present the terror and majesty of the infernal army. Do you find it impressive ? What lines, phrases, sentences and images strike you especially ? Read selected passages aloud for their sound effects and discuss how these effects are managed.

4. What are the effects of the comparisons ? Why are so many of them human ? Comment on the effect of the proper names in this instance.

5. What is the effect of the epic simile in lines 594 to 599 ? What aspect of Satan does it catch ?

Section H
Lines 622-669

1. What kinds of hope does Satan hold out to his followers in these lines ? Is he being honest ? Is it a well-judged piece of rhetoric ? Explain, bearing in mind, Satan's position as leader of a routed army.

2. Was the speech good enough to justify the enthusiasm displayed in this short passage ? Do the defiant angels strike you as objects of awe or of pity ? Explain.

3. Was the angels' response the one we expected after line 645 ? In answering, consider lines 661 to 662.

Section I
Lines 670-798

1. Here Milton describes the building of Pandemonium. Examine the blend of metre and punctuation in the paragraph in order to see how the forward thrust and momentum are conveyed.

2. How does this vision of Pandemonium compare with the desolate picture of hell presented earlier ? What does it tell us of Satan's achievement and his potential as the prince of hell ? With what purpose was Pandemonium built ? With what sort of expectations does Book 1 end ?

3. Is there a sense in which Mammon and Mulciber are recreating their heaven in hell ? Is this also true of Satan ?

4. How evocative is the epic simile ? How does it compare with those referred to in question 4 in Section E. Explain. Is it a satisfactory image for the mustering of the devils ? Discuss.

5. Can you suggest why Milton, after the warlike magnificence of the earlier descriptions of Satan's followers, should now compare them to bees, pygmies and elves ?

6. What touches in the passage do you find especially striking ? Explain. Would you agree that the flourish in the final lines is at once an end and a beginning ?

General Explorations

1. Certain critics have argued that while Milton appears to be on God's side he is secretly ' of the Devil's party '. Can you find anything in his portrayal of Satan or God to support this view ? You might debate this opinion in class.

2. Irony occurs when the writer and reader are in a conspiracy of understanding at the expense of a character. Would you agree that Satan's actions and speeches in Book 1 are all seen in the light of irony ? If so, what is the basic cause of this irony ? Where is such irony most in evidence ?

3. C. S. Lewis has remarked that ' What we see in Satan is the horrible co-existence of a subtle and incessant intellectual activity with an incapacity to understand anything . . . He says " Evil be thou my good " (which includes " Nonsense be thou my sense ") and his prayer is granted '. On the other hand, Shelley argued that ' Milton's Devil as a moral being is as far superior to his God as one who perseveres in some purpose which he has conceived to be excellent in spite of adversity and torture is to one who in the cold security of undoubted triumph inflicts the most horrible revenge upon his enemy, not from any mistaken notion of inducing him to repent of a perseverance in enmity, but with the alleged design of exasperating him to deserve new torments.' After careful exploration of the poem, do you favour either of these views ? Explain, illustrate and discuss.

4. In what sense does the theme of *Paradise Lost* as stated in the first paragraph of the poem represent ' Things unattempted yet in prose or rhyme ' ? Answer with general reference to what you already know of epic, dramatic and religious literature.

5. What means in general does Milton use to give great historical, geographical and theological scope and dimension to his epic ? In your opinion, does his treatment rise to the magnificence of his theme in every respect ? Be specific in your answer, illustrating the points you make.

6. Consider again Milton's basic problem. He is dealing in this Book with a pre-temporal and unfurnished universe, yet he must find names, illustrations, narrative patterns and allusions to make it real. Examine, for a start, the passage following line 361 to see how Milton copes with the problem. Then review Book 1 with this consideration in mind.

7. Many critics have argued that Milton used a latinised form of English. Dr. Johnson asserted, for instance, that he ' formed his style by a perverse and pedantic principle. He was desirous to use English words with a foreign idiom.' A modern critic such as T. S. Eliot agreed with him. On the other hand, his Oxford editor, John Butt, disagreed totally : ' To correct this conventional impressionistic opinion one has only to open the poem anywhere and read . . . for all his learning and all the wealth of association and suggestion in his resonant language, Milton is much more accessible to the common reader than much of the poetry of our own time '. When you have studied the poem carefully give your own opinion on this topic and support it with reference and illustration.

8. Milton's use of the unrhymed iambic pentameter has been described as ' the most accomplished, magnificent and wide-ranging of all types of blank verse '. Choose a favourite speech in Shakespeare and compare it with one of Milton's finer paragraphs under the headings indicated in the quotation above. Choose similarly a paragraph from the *Tintern Abbey* ode and make similar comparisons. Examine all three for their sound, their punctuation and for the way in which the grammatical unit (the sentence) is related to the metrical units— the line and the verse paragraph.

Glossary p. 219

from Mac Flecknoe

All humane things are subject to decay,
And, when Fate summons, Monarchs must obey :
This *Fleckno* found, who, like *Augustus*, young
Was call'd to Empire and had govern'd long :
In Prose and Verse was own'd, without dispute   5
Through all the realms of Non-sense, absolute.
This aged Prince now flourishing in Peace,
And blest with issue of a large increase,
Worn out with business, did at length debate
To settle the Succession of the State ;   10
And pond'ring which of all his Sons was fit
To Reign, and wage immortal War with Wit,
Cry'd, 'tis resolv'd ; for Nature pleads that He
Should onely rule, who most resembles me :
Sh—— alone my perfect image bears,   15
Mature in dullness from his tender years ;
Sh—— alone of all my Sons is he
Who stands confirm'd in full stupidity.
The rest to some faint meaning make pretence,
But *Sh*—— never deviates into sense.   20
Some Beams of Wit on other souls may fall,
Strike through and make a lucid intervall ;
But *Sh*——'s genuine night admits no ray,
His rising Fogs prevail upon the Day :
Besides, his goodly Fabrick fills the eye   25
And seems design'd for thoughtless Majesty :
Thoughtless as Monarch Oakes that shade the plain,
And, spread in solemn state, supinely reign.
Heywood and *Shirley* were but Types of thee,
Thou last great Prophet of Tautology :   30
Even I, a dunce of more renown than they,
Was sent before but to prepare thy way :
And coarsely clad in *Norwich* Drugget came
To teach the Nations in thy greater name.
My warbling Lute, the Lute I whilom strung,   35
When to King *John of Portugal* I sung,

Was but the prelude to that glorious day,
When thou on silver *Thames* did'st cut thy way,
With well tim'd oars before the Royal Barge,
Swelled with the Pride of thy Celestial charge.   40

Explorations

1.   The method of the satire here is the same as that which Pope
uses in *The Rape of the Lock*, the mock-heroic. The characters are foolish
and the events trivial, but by treating them in a language and tone
appropriate to heroic characters and epic events the poet makes them
look doubly ridiculous.   The first jolt comes, for instance, in line 6,
where we have been expecting some word like ' wisdom ' and instead
get ' Non-sense '.   Read the extract through and see where similar
jolts or anti-climaxes occur.   Which of them strike you as especially
amusing ? Why ?

2.   What sorts of adjustments or substitutions would be required to
turn it into an altogether serious poem ?   You might take this as a
written or oral exercise.

3.   What special talents has Shadwell for the throne of Non-sense ?
Is he represented as an evil man or merely a foolish man ? Argue
your point.   Compile a list of the various qualities Dryden attributes
to Shadwell.

4.   The language and imagery is sometimes political and sometimes
biblical.   Where ?   Consider lines 1 to 10 and lines 30 to 40.   What sort
of effect is Dryden aiming at in each case ?

5.   The metrical form employed is the heroic couplet.   It has two
obvious virtues : on the one hand, it works almost like the stanza, in as
far as it often contains a completed thought within the two lines ; on
the other hand, it provides a sense of continuity as does blank verse.
Can you find instances of each of these virtues in the present extract ?
Explain the effect in each case you cite.

6.   One of the delights of the heroic couplet is what is called
antithesis, that is the balance, and often the contrast, of ideas between
the two lines, or between the two halves of the same line.   The first four
lines show examples of each.   Examine and explain these.   In what way
is the pattern repeated or varied elsewhere in the extract ? Take a look
at similar examples in *Absalom and Achitophel* and *The Rape of the Lock*
where the device is used more extensively and variously.

Glossary p. 226

from Absalom and Achitophel

Of these the false *Achitophel* was first,
A Name to all succeeding Ages curst.
For close Designs and crooked Counsels fit,
Sagacious, Bold, and Turbulent of wit,
Restless, unfixt in Principles and Place,   5
In Pow'r unpleased, impatient of Disgrace ;
A fiery Soul, which working out its way,
Fretted the Pigmy Body to decay :
And o'r informed the Tenement of Clay.
A daring Pilot in extremity ;   10
Pleas'd with the Danger, when the Waves went high
He sought the Storms ; but, for a Calm unfit,
Would Steer too nigh the Sands to boast his Wit.
Great Wits are sure to Madness near alli'd
And thin Partitions do their Bounds divide ;   15
Else, why should he, with Wealth and Honour blest,
Refuse his Age the needful hours of Rest ?
Punish a Body which he could not please,
Bankrupt of Life, yet Prodigal of Ease ?
And all to leave what with his Toil he won   20
To that unfeather'd two-legg'd thing, a Son :
Got, while his Soul did huddled Notions trie ;
And born a shapeless Lump, like Anarchy.
In Friendship false, implacable in Hate,
Resolv'd to Ruine or to Rule the State ;   25
To Compass this the Triple Bond he broke ;
The Pillars of the Publick Safety shook,
And fitted *Israel* for a Foreign Yoke ;
Then, seiz'd with Fear, yet still affecting Fame,
Usurp'd a Patriot's All-attoning Name.   30
So easie still it proves in Factious Times
With publick Zeal to cancel private Crimes :
How safe is Treason and how sacred ill,
Where none can sin against the Peoples Will,
Where Crouds can wink ; and no offence be known,   35
Since in anothers guilt they find their own.
Yet, Fame deserv'd, no Enemy can grudge ;

The Statesman we abhor, but praise the Judge.
In *Israels* courts ne'er sat an *Abbethdin*
With more discerning Eyes or Hands more clean,   40
Unbrib'd, unsought, the Wretched to redress ;
Swift of Dispatch and easie of Access.
Oh, had he been content to serve the Crown
With Vertues onely proper to the Gown,
Or had the rankness of the Soil been freed   45
From Cockle that opprest the Noble Seed,
David for him his tuneful Harp had strung,
And Heav'n had wanted one Immortal Song.
But wild Ambition loves to slide, not stand,
And Fortunes Ice prefers to Vertues Land.   50

Explorations

1. In the first line of the extract Dryden describes Achitophel as ' false '. In how far do the lines which follow bear out this description ? Compile a list of the attributes of Achitophel—physical, intellectual and moral.

2. What lines in the portrait do you think the most vivid, cruel, witty, damaging ? Explain your point of view in each case.

3. How would you describe Dryden's tone in the extract—bitter, angry, resentful, mocking, arrogant, vengeful ? Does it change at any point ? Give quotations to support your opinion.

4. How sincere is the poet in his praise of Achitophel in the second part of the extract ? Argue your point. Does this passage of praise modify or increase the satire of the rest ? Explain.

5. In one of his essays Dryden remarked that a satirist was not justified in transgressing the law of charity. Are there any parts of the present extract which seem to do so ?

6. At several stages in the extract Dryden pauses in his abuse of Achitophel in order to make general statements about man and life. In what way—if any—are they related to what goes before and after them ? What impression of himself is Dryden trying to give by including these remarks ?

7. The heroic couplet becomes a very limited and monotonous form if the poet does not vary it. What sort of variations does Dryden

introduce into this extract ? In each case try to suggest the purpose of the variation.

8.   Examine the use of antithesis—see question 6 on *Mac Flecknoe*—beginning with such a perfectly balanced and contrasted line as :

Bankrupt of Life, yet Prodigal of Ease

and moving on to other more various forms of it.

9.   What does alliteration contribute to the emphasis and rhythm of the thought ? Where, for instance, does Dryden alliterate on the stressed words ? Why ? Where do you find alliteration and antithesis combined ? With what effect ?

10.   Read Dryden's satire on Shadwell in *Mac Flecknoe* and compare it with the present extract in tone, movement and general intention.

Glossary p. 226

Excerpts from The Rape of the Lock
CANTO I

And now, unveil'd, the Toilet stands display'd,
Each silver Vase in mystic order laid.
First, rob'd in white, the Nymph intent adores,
With head uncover d, the Cosmetic pow'rs.
A heav'nly Image in the glass appears,   125
To that she bends, to that her eyes she rears ;
Th' inferior Priestess, at her altar's side,
Trembling, begins the sacred rites of Pride.
Unnumber'd treasures ope at once, and here
The various off'rings of the world appear ;   130
From each she nicely culls with curious toil,
And decks the Goddess with the glitt'ring spoil.
This casket India's glowing gems unlocks,
And all Arabia breathes from yonder box.
The Tortoise here and Elephant unite,   135
Transform'd to combs, the speckled, and the white.
Here files of pins extend their shining rows,
Puffs, Powders, Patches, Bibles, Billet-doux,
Now awful Beauty puts on all its arms ;
The fair each moment rises in her charms,   140
Repairs her smiles, awakens ev'ry grace,
And calls forth all the wonders of her face ;
Sees by degrees a purer blush arise,
And keener lightnings quicken in her eyes.
The busy Sylphs surround their darling care,   145
These set the head, and those divide the hair,
Some fold the sleeve, whilst others plait the gown ;
And Betty's prais'd for labours not her own.

Explorations

1.   The form, like that of Dryden's *Mac Flecknoe*, is mock-heroic. Here
Pope describes a society beauty at her dressing-table as if she were a
priestess offering homage to the gods before battle.   What images or
phrases help to give this commonplace scene a sense of the heroic and
of the marvellous ?   Which ones do you find most vivid or amusing ?
Explain.

2. An early critic of Pope thought he saw ' a small inaccuracy ' in the opening lines of this extract. ' He first makes his Heroine the chief Priestess, then the Goddess herself.' Did the critic miss Pope's point ? Who *is* Belinda worshipping ? What are ' the sacred rites of Pride ' ? What sort of satire is intended ?

3. Is there some sort of satire of Belinda and her world intended in line 138 ? Explain.

4. Does Pope altogether disapprove of Belinda ? How would you describe the tone of the passage—mocking, affectionate, severe . . . ? Can it be described in a single word ? Point to some lines or phrases in which this tone is especially revealed.

Glossary p. 227

Canto II

But now secure the painted vessel glides,
The sun-beams trembling on the floating tides :
While melting music steals upon the sky,
And soften'd sounds along the waters die ;   50
Smooth flow the waves, the Zephyrs gently play,
Belinda smil'd, and all the world was gay.
All but the Sylph—with careful thoughts opprest,
Th' impending woe sat heavy on his breast.
He summons strait his Denizens of air ;   55
The lucid squadrons round the sails repair ;
Soft o'er the shrouds aërial whispers breathe,
That seem'd but Zephyrs to the train beneath.
Some to the sun their insect-wings unfold,
Waft on the breeze, or sink in clouds of gold ;   60
Transparent forms, too fine for mortal sight,
Their fluid bodies half dissolv'd in light.
Loose to the wind their airy garments flew,
Thin glitt'ring textures of the filmy dew,
Dipt in the richest tincture of the skies,   65
Where light disports in ever-mingling dyes,
While ev'ry beam new transient colours flings,
Colours that change whene'er they wave their wings.

Explorations

1. In this extract the poet has to face the challenge of representing in language and imagery the action of the Sylphs—' Transparent forms, too fine for mortal sight '. How well do you think he succeeds ? Read

the passage aloud, having prepared it carefully. What words, phrases and images are especially evocative of this airy, insubstantial world ? Where is the poet particularly successful in combining them ?

2.   What images of light are to be found in the passage ? What part do they play ?

3.   Are the Sylphs beneficent or malign ? How is this conveyed ?

4.   What part do the sound effects play in creating the general effect ? Consider in detail the vowel and consonant variations. Again read the passage aloud.

5.   There is only one reference to Belinda : what does it tell us about her ? Can you guess why her guardian Sylph suddenly becomes anxious about her ? (See note on Sylph in glossary.)

Glossary p. 227

CANTO III

Close by those meads, for ever crown'd with flow'rs,
Where Thames with pride surveys his rising tow'rs,
There stands a structure of majestic frame,
Which from the neighb'ring Hampton takes its name.
Here Britain's statesmen oft the fall foredoom   5
Of foreign Tyrants, and of Nymphs at home ;
Here thou, great ANNA ! whom three realms obey,
Dost sometimes counsel take—and sometimes Tea.
    Hither the heroes and the nymphs resort,
To taste awhile the pleasures of a Court ;   10
In various talk th' instructive hours they past,
Who gave the ball, or paid the visit last ;
One speaks the glory of the British Queen,
And one describes a charming Indian screen ;
A third interprets motions, looks, and eyes ;   15
At ev'ry word a reputation dies.
Snuff, or the fan, supply each pause of chat,
With singing, laughing, ogling, *and all that.*
    Mean while, declining from the noon of day,
The sun obliquely shoots his burning ray ;   20
The hungry Judges soon the sentence sign,
And wretches hang that jury-men may dine ;
The merchant from th' Exchange returns in peace,
And the long labours of the Toilet cease.

For lo ! the board with cups and spoons is crown'd, 105
The berries crackle, and the mill turns round ;
On shining Altars of Japan they raise
The silver lamp ; the fiery spirits blaze :
From silver spouts the grateful liquors glide,
While China's earth receives the smoaking tide :   110
At once they gratify their scent and taste,
And frequent cups prolong the rich repaste.
Strait hover round the Fair her airy band ;
Some, as she sipp'd, the fuming liquor fann'd,
Some o'er her lap their careful plumes display'd,   115
Trembling, and conscious of the rich brocade.
Coffee (which makes the politician wise,
And see thro' all things with his half-shut eyes)
Sent up in vapours to the Baron's brain
New stratagems, the radiant Lock to gain.   120
Ah cease, rash youth ! desist ere 'tis too late,
Fear the just Gods, and think of Scylla's Fate !
Chang'd to a bird, and sent to flit in air,
She dearly pays for Nisus' injur'd hair !
But when to mischief mortals bend their will,   125
How soon they find fit instruments of ill !
Just then, Clarissa drew with tempting grace
A two-edg'd weapon from her shining case :
So Ladies in Romance assist their Knight,
Present the spear, and arm him for the fight.   130
He takes the gift with rev'rence, and extends
The little engine on his fingers' ends ;
This just behind Belinda's neck he spread,
As o'er the fragrant steams she bends her head.
Swift to the Lock a thousand Sprites repair,   135
A thousand wings, by turns, blow back the hair ;
And thrice they twitch'd the diamond in her ear ;
Thrice she look'd back, and thrice the foe drew near.
Just in that instant, anxious Ariel sought
The close recesses of the Virgin's thought ;   140
As on the nosegay in her breast reclin'd,
He watch'd th' Ideas rising in her mind,
Sudden he view'd, in spite of all her art,
An earthly Lover lurking at her heart.

Amaz'd, confus'd, he found his pow'r expir'd, 145
Resign'd to fate, and with a sigh retir'd.
 The Peer now spreads the glitt'ring Forfex wide,
T' inclose the Lock ; now joins it, to divide.
Ev'n then, before the fatal engine clos'd,
A wretched Sylph too fondly interpos'd ; 150
Fate urg'd the sheers, and cut the Sylph in twain,
(But airy substance soon unites again)
The meeting points the sacred hair dissever
From the fair head, for ever, and for ever !
 Then flash'd the living lightning from her eyes, 155
And screams of horror rend th' affrighted skies.
Not louder shrieks to pitying heav'n are cast,
When husbands, or when lap-dogs breathe their last ;
Or when rich China vessels, fall'n from high,
In glitt'ring dust, and painted fragments lie ! 160

Explorations

1. In lines 5 to 9 there is a perfect example of antithesis. Show how the first couplet is closely parallelled in the second ; also compare line 6 with line 8 in terms of structure and meaning. What does the poet convey by his two witty anti-climaxes ? Glance back at line 138 in Canto I. Where else in the passage do we find similar effects ? Discuss each in detail.

2. How serious is Pope in referring to the ' instructive hours ' which the visitors pass at Hampton Court ? What part does irony play in the entire passage ?

3. Line 24 is a deliberate parody of epic poetry, e.g., 'And the long labours of the Toilet cease'. Where else in the passage that follows is the behaviour of the characters placed in comic contrast with the behaviour of epic heroes ? What effects in particular amuse you ? Explain.

4. Between lines 125 and 155 Pope is clearly building up the mock suspense as the Baron prepares to snatch the lock. What devices does he use to achieve this end ?

5. The charm of mock-heroic often comes from the great gap between the matter and the manner. Is this effect particularly evident in this passage ? If so, where and how ?

6. Why does Ariel retire ? See note in the glossary on the Sylph and his duties.

Glossary p. 228

CANTO IV

And shall this prize, th' inestimable prize,
Expos'd thro' crystal to the gazing eyes,
And heighten'd by the diamond's circling rays,   115
On that rapacious hand for ever blaze ?
Sooner shall grass in Hyde-park Circus grow,
And wits take lodgings in the sound of Bow ;
Sooner let earth, air, sea, to Chaos fall,
Men, monkeys, lap-dogs, parrots, perish all !   120
   She said ; then raging to Sir Plume repairs,
And bids her Beau demand the precious hairs :
(Sir Plume of amber snuff-box justly vain,
And the nice conduct of a clouded cane)
With earnest eyes, and round unthinking face,   125
He first the snuff-box open'd, then the case,
And thus broke out—' My Lord, why, what the devil ?
' Z—ds ! damn the lock ! 'fore Gad, you must be civil !
' Plague on't ! 'tis past a jest—nay prithee, pox !
' Give her the hair'—he spoke, and rapp'd his box.   130
   It grieves me much (reply'd the Peer again)
Who speaks so well should ever speak in vain.
But by this Lock, this sacred Lock I swear,
(Which never more shall join its parted hair ;
Which never more its honours shall renew,   135
Clip'd from the lovely head where late it grew)
That while my nostrils draw the vital air,
This hand, which won it, shall for ever wear.
He spoke, and speaking, in proud triumph spread
The long-contended honours of her head.   140

Explorations

1. There is double irony in lines 131–132. Explain it fully.

2. What is the Baron's opinion of Sir Plume ? Is it shared by Pope ? What is your opinion ? Examine the evidence.

3. What sort of man is the Baron ? Seek further evidence in the preceding and following extracts.

4. What comic effects strike you particularly ? Have you encountered similar effects elsewhere in the extracts ?

5.   What satirical hints and insights into the attitudes and values of contemporary society do we get from this extract ? Where else in the poem do we get such intimations ? Is Pope, in general, angry or amused at the failings of his fellow-men? Explain in detail, not neglecting the question of tone.

Glossary p. 228

CANTO V

To arms, to arms ! the fierce Virago cries,
And swift as lightning to the combat flies.
All side in parties, and begin th' attack ;
Fans clap, silks russle, and tough whalebones crack ;   40
Heroes and Heroines shouts confus'dly rise,
And base, and treble voices strike the skies.
No common weapons in their hands are found,
Like Gods they fight, nor dread a mortal wound.
    So when bold Homer makes the Gods engage,   45
And heav'nly breasts with human passions rage ;
'Gainst Pallas, Mars ; Latona, Hermes arms ;
And all Olympus rings with loud alarms :
Jove's thunder roars, heav'n trembles all around,
Blue Neptune storms, the bellowing deeps resound :   50
Earth shakes her nodding towr's, the ground gives way,
And the pale ghosts start at the flash of day !
    Triumphant Umbriel on a sconce's height
Clap'd his glad wings, and sate to view the fight :
Prop'd on their bodkin spears, the Sprites survey   55
The growing combat, or assist the fray.
    While thro' the press enrag'd Thalestris flies,
And scatters death around from both her eyes,
A Beau and Witling perish'd in the throng,
One dy'd in metaphor, and one in song.   60
' O cruel nymph ! a living death I bear,'
Cry'd Dapperwit, and sunk beside his chair.
A mournful glance Sir Fopling upwards cast,
' Those eyes are made so killing '—was his last.
Thus on Mæander's flow'ry margin lies   65
Th' expiring Swan, and as he sings he dies.

When bold Sir Plume had drawn Clarissa down,
Chloe stepp'd in, and kill'd him with a frown ;
She smil'd to see the doughty hero slain,
But, at her smile, the Beau reviv'd again.   70
    Now Jove suspends his golden scales in air,
Weighs the Men's wits against the Lady's hair ;
The doubtful beam long nods from side to side ;
At length the wits mount up, the hairs subside.
    See fierce Belinda on the Baron flies,   75
With more than usual lightning in her eyes :
Nor fear'd the Chief th' unequal fight to try,
Who sought no more than on his foe to die.
But this bold Lord with manly strength endu'd,
She with one finger and a thumb subdu'd :   80
Just where the breath of life his nostrils drew,
A charge of Snuff the wily virgin threw ;
The Gnomes direct, to ev'ry atom just,
The pungent grains of titillating dust.
Sudden, with starting tears each eye o'erflows,   85
And the high dome re-echoes to his nose.

Explorations

1. In line 44 we are told that the combatants fight ' like Gods '. In
what sense is their fight like one waged by gods ? Is it Pope's purpose to
stress the resemblances or the differences ? Explain.

2. What is the purpose of the epic simile ? Does it succeed ?

3. What sort of battle is actually going on ? What sort of blows are
being struck ? Take your cue from line 60.

4. What sort of comment on society is involved in the balancing of
the ' Men's wits against the Lady's hair ' ? Where else in the poem
is such comment to be found ? Does Pope's sympathy lie with the men
or the women ? Explain.

5. Would you agree that anti-climax is a frequent device in the
passage ? Where is it found, and to what effect ?

Glossary p. 229

General Questions

1. It has often been suggested that while the poem is a satire on manners and morals in Pope's London, it is also a tribute to the grace and glamour of that society. Discuss, sifting the evidence carefully, attending to the recurrent images of light and brilliance and to the various glimpses of Belinda.

2. The heroic couplet is used with very remarkable flexibility in the poem. Incredibly, the poet manages to avoid all possibilities of monotony. Examine the verse, therefore, dwelling on those passages that you found most striking, and show how he uses antithesis, alliteration, assonance and other technical devices to vary the basic pattern.

3. What are the dominating images in the extracts ? What part do they play in the total effect ?

4. Where are the epics of Homer, Virgil and Milton deliberately invoked ? With what specific effects ?

5. This poem is supposed to be one of the great ironic masterpieces. Examine it with this in mind, showing the various shades of irony that the poet uses. Start, perhaps, with Canto III line 11, or Canto IV line 132.

6. Finally, what do you think was Pope's judgement on his society —contemptuous, admiring, affectionate, tolerant, amused, censorious . . . ? Was it a mixture of such feelings ? Support and illustrate your viewpoint.

Lines composed a few miles above

Tintern Abbey

Five years have past ; five summers, with the length
Of five long winters ! and again I hear
These waters, rolling from their mountain-springs
With a soft inland murmur.—Once again
Do I behold these steep and lofty cliffs,   5
That on a wild secluded scene impress
Thoughts of more deep seclusion ; and connect
The landscape with the quiet of the sky.
The day is come when I again repose
Here, under this dark sycamore, and view   10
These plots of cottage-ground, these orchard-tufts,
Which at this season, with their unripe fruits,
Are clad in one green hue, and lose themselves
'Mid groves and copses. Once again I see
These hedge-rows, hardly hedge-rows, little lines   15
Of sportive wood run wild : these pastoral farms,
Green to the very door ; and wreaths of smoke
Sent up, in silence, from among the trees !
With some uncertain notice, as might seem
Of vagrant dwellers in the houseless woods,   20
Or of some Hermit's cave, where by his fire
The Hermit sits alone.
                     These beauteous forms,
Through a long absence, have not been to me
As is a landscape to a blind man's eye :
But oft, in lonely rooms, and 'mid the din   25
Of towns and cities, I have owed to them,
In hours of weariness, sensations sweet,
Felt in the blood, and felt along the heart ;
And passing even into my purer mind,
With tranquil restoration :—feelings too   30
Of unremembered pleasure : such, perhaps,
As have no slight or trivial influence
On that best portion of a good man's life,
His little, nameless, unremembered, acts

Of kindness and of love. Nor less, I trust,   35
To them I may have owed another gift,
Of aspect more sublime ; that blessed mood,
In which the burthen of the mystery,
In which the heavy and the weary weight
Of all this unintelligible world,   40
Is lightened :—that serene and blessed mood,
In which the affections gently lead us on,—
Until, the breath of this corporeal frame
And even the motion of our human blood
Almost suspended, we are laid asleep   45
In body, and become a living soul :
While with an eye made quiet by the power
Of harmony, and the deep power of joy,
We see into the life of things.
                              If this
Be but a vain belief, yet oh ! how oft—   50
In darkness and amid the many shapes
Of joyless daylight ; when the fretful stir
Unprofitable, and the fever of the world,
Have hung upon the beatings of my heart—
How oft, in spirit, have I turned to thee,   55
O sylvan Wye ! thou wanderer thro' the woods,
How often has my spirit turned to thee !

    And now, with gleams of half-extinguished thought,
With many recognitions dim and faint,
And somewhat of a sad perplexity,   60
The picture of the mind revives again :
While here I stand, not only with the sense
Of present pleasure, but with pleasing thoughts
That in this moment there is life and food
For future years. And so I dare to hope,   65
Though changed, no doubt, from what I was when first
I came among these hills ; when like a roe
I bounded o'er the mountains, by the sides
Of the deep rivers, and the lonely streams,
Wherever nature led : more like a man   70
Flying from something that he dreads than one
Who sought the thing he loved. For nature then

(The coarser pleasures of my boyish days,
And their glad animal movements all gone by)
To me was all in all.—I cannot paint   75
What then I was. The sounding cataract
Haunted me like a passion : the tall rock,
The mountain, and the deep and gloomy wood,
Their colours and their forms, were then to me
An appetite ; a feeling and a love,   80
That had no need of a remoter charm,
By thought supplied, nor any interest
Unborrowed from the eye.—That time is past,
And all its aching joys are now no more,
And all its dizzy raptures. Not for this   85
Faint I, nor mourn nor murmur ; other gifts
Have followed ; for such loss, I would believe,
Abundant recompense. For I have learned
To look on nature, not as in the hour
Of thoughtless youth ; but hearing oftentimes   90
The still, sad music of humanity,
Nor harsh nor grating, though of ample power
To chasten and subdue. And I have felt
A presence that disturbs me with the joy
Of elevated thoughts ; a sense sublime   95
Of something far more deeply interfused,
Whose dwelling is the light of setting suns,
And the round ocean and the living air,
And the blue sky, and in the mind of man :
A motion and a spirit, that impels   100
All thinking things, all objects of all thought,
And rolls through all things. Therefore am I still
A lover of the meadows and the woods,
And mountains ; and of all that we behold
From this green earth ; of all the mighty world   105
Of eye, and ear,—both what they half create,
And what perceive ; well pleased to recognise
In nature and the language of the sense
The anchor of my purest thoughts, the nurse,
The guide, the guardian of my heart, and soul   110
Of all my moral being.

Nor perchance,
If I were not thus taught, should I the more
Suffer my genial spirits to decay :
For thou art with me here upon the banks
Of this fair river ; thou my dearest Friend,   115
My dear, dear Friend ; and in thy voice I catch
The language of my former heart, and read
My former pleasures in the shooting lights
Of thy wild eyes. Oh ! yet a little while
May I behold in thee what I was once,   120
My dear, dear Sister ! and this prayer I make,
Knowing that Nature never did betray
The heart that loved her ; 'tis her privilege,
Through all the years of this our life, to lead
From joy to joy : for she can so inform   125
The mind that is within us, so impress
With quietness and beauty, and so feed
With lofty thoughts, that neither evil tongues,
Rash judgments, nor the sneers of selfish men,
Nor greetings where no kindness is, nor all   130
The dreary intercourse of daily life,
Shall e'er prevail against us, or disturb
Our cheerful faith, that all which we behold
Is full of blessings. Therefore let the moon
Shine on thee in thy solitary walk ;   135
And let the misty mountain-winds be free
To blow against thee : and, in after years,
When these wild ecstasies shall be matured
Into a sober pleasure ; when thy mind
Shall be a mansion for all lovely forms,   140
Thy memory be as a dwelling-place
For all sweet sounds and harmonies ; oh ! then,
If solitude, or fear, or pain, or grief,
Should be thy portion, with what healing thoughts
Of tender joy wilt thou remember me,   145
And these my exhortations ! Nor, perchance—
If I should be where I no more can hear
Thy voice, nor catch from thy wild eyes these gleams
Of past existence—wilt thou then forget
That on the banks of this delightful stream   150

We stood together ; and that I, so long
A worshipper of Nature, hither came
Unwearied in that service : rather say
With warmer love—oh ! with far deeper zeal
Of holier love. Nor wilt thou then forget   155
That after many wanderings, many years
Of absence, these steep woods and lofty cliffs,
And this green pastoral landscape, were to me
More dear, both for themselves and for thy sake !

Explorations

1. It has been suggested that this is a poem not about nature but about memory ; memory stimulated by a return to the Wye valley. What part does memory play in the opening paragraph ? By what means does the poet impress upon us that he has been here before ?

2. What is the dominant mood of the landscape as he describes it in the first paragraph ? By what words and images is this mood conjured up ?

3. How are description and contemplation blended in the first paragraph ? Is the description objective or is the poet using the landscape to reflect his inner mood ? You might begin by looking at how often the word ' I ' recurs.

4. In the second paragraph Wordsworth attributes to this landscape —and his memory of it—three related benefits. What are they ? In what sense are they related ?

5. In the second paragraph Wordsworth moves skilfully from the obvious and external to the most profound and spiritual form of consolation. Trace the movement of the thought and show how the poet has shaped it in terms of metre and punctuation.

6. What is the tone of this second paragraph—quiet, intense, vehement, contemplative, reverent . . . ? Does it change in any way as the thought develops ? If so, what sort of words and phrases convey this change particularly ?

7. What might the poet mean by ' the power of harmony ' ? Does it imply, for instance, a relationship between man and nature ? Read the paragraph again.

8. What is the effect of the third paragraph—lines 49 to 57 ? How does the thought connect with that of the first, and of the second paragraphs ? What rôle does the landscape play in the poet's life ?

9. Is there any suggestion of doubt in the poet's mind about the claims he is making for nature in this paragraph ? Is there anything to suggest that the poet is trying to convince himself ? Explain.

10. In the next great paragraph of the ode—lines 58 to 111—Wordsworth describes his earlier, pre-reflective contact with nature and contrasts it with his later, more philosophic attitude. Identify roughly each attitude, then show how they differ from each other.

11. Wordsworth asserts that he does not mourn or murmur at the loss of these ' aching joys ' and ' dizzy raptures '. What reasons does he give ? Is he altogether convinced ? altogether convincing ? Glance again at questions 8 and 9 and read the opening lines of the fourth paragraph again.

12. When Wordsworth refers to ' The still, sad music of humanity ' what does he mean ? Glance back at lines 25/26 and 34/35 which may provide an answer. Is Wordsworth suggesting in any way that the harmony in nature described in lines 93 to 102 can heal the wounds in man's loneliness and sadness ? Read the third paragraph again.

13. Would you agree that this fourth paragraph is one of great power and energy ? If so, analyse how these qualities are achieved in **language, image and rhythm.**

14. In the final apostrophe to his sister Wordsworth asserts that she represents ' what I was once '. What lines and phrases in his description of her accord with his own youthful delight in nature ?

15. Why does Dorothy's presence preserve his ' genial spirits ' from decay and strengthen his ' cheerful faith ' that everything they see ' is full of blessings ' ? Is it because of his love for her, because she represents his former self, because they share a common faith in nature . . . ?

16. Wordsworth predicts that Dorothy's present ecstasy will mature, like his, into a ' sober pleasure '. In what ways, as he anticipates it, does it resemble his ' sense sublime ' as portrayed in the previous paragraph ?

17. Do you find his evocation of his sister's presence and personality vivid ? Do you feel that he ought to have introduced her to this landscape and meditation at all ? Why does he ? Explain and discuss.

18. What is the dominant tone of the ode—joy, regret, anxiety, triumph, nostalgia, hope . . . ? Do the casual statements of apprehension—take them separately and together—undermine the poem's affirmations, or do they merely modify them ? As critical opinion is by no means unanimous on this point, it provides a fruitful field for discussion and a valuable exercise in sensitive reading.

Glossary p. 229

Loud is the Vale

Loud is the Vale! the Voice is up
With which she speaks when storms are gone,
A mighty unison of streams !
Of all her Voices, One !

Loud is the Vale ;—this inland Depth   5
In peace is roaring like the Sea ;
Yon star upon the mountain-top
Is listening quietly.

Sad was I, even to pain deprest,
Importunate and heavy load !   10
The Comforter hath found me here,
Upon this lonely road ;

And many thousands now are sad—
Wait the fulfilment of their fear ;
For he must die who is their stay,   15
Their glory disappear.

A Power is passing from the earth
To breathless Nature's dark abyss ;
But when the great and good depart
What is it more than this—   20

That Man, who is from God sent forth,
Doth yet again to God return ?—
Such ebb and flow must ever be,
Then wherefore should we mourn ?

Explorations

1. The occasion of the poem is the illness and expected death of the great English statesman, Charles James Fox. Where does the poem refer to him ?

2. The poet is both disturbed and comforted. Where is each mood expressed ? What is the cause of each ? Does he suggest that nature shares each of these moods ? Explain and specify.

3. What sort of relationship between God, man and nature is suggested in the poem ?

4. Can you suggest why certain words are capitalised ?

5. What answer does Wordsworth expect to his final rhetorical question ? Has the poem earned such an answer ?

6. Analyse the metre and the rhyme scheme of the poem. Is it regular throughout ? Is it suitable for the development of the poet's thought ? Explain.

7. For comparison read Dylan Thomas's *A Refusal to Mourn.*

Glossary p. 230

Surprised by Joy

Surprised by joy—impatient as the Wind
I turned to share the transport—Oh ! with whom
But Thee, deep buried in the silent tomb,
That spot which no vicissitude can find ?
Love, faithful love, recalled thee to my mind—   5
But how could I forget thee ? Through what power,
Even for the least division of an hour,
Have I been so beguiled as to be blind
To my most grievous loss !—That thought's return
Was the worst pang that sorrow ever bore,   10
Save one, one only, when I stood forlorn,
Knowing my heart's best treasure was no more ;
That neither present time, nor years unborn
Could to my sight that heavenly face restore.

Explorations

1. Would you agree that there is great passion in this poem in memory of the poet's dead child ? If so, where in particular is the regret and the tenderness most evident ?

2. In line 10 the poet refers to his ' worst pang ' of sorrow ' save one '. What were the two pangs of sorrow ? Now trace the thought of the poem carefully from beginning to end.

3. What is the poet's mood—grief, resentment, resignation . . . ?

4. Normally a Petrarchan sonnet moves in clearly marked stages through its three formal divisions. Is this the case here ? Point out carefully the tension between the metrical units and the sentence units. What is the effect of this tension in terms of thought and emotion ? What is the effect of the exclamation and question marks ?

5. Read *Loud is the Vale* and contrast it with the present poem as an attempt to come to terms with the fact of death. Read also Dylan Thomas's poem *A Refusal to Mourn*.

Glossary p. 230

O Friend ! I know not

O Friend ! I know not which way I must look
For comfort, being, as I am, opprest,
To think that now our life is only drest
For show ; mean handy-work of craftsman, cook,
Or groom !—We must run glittering like a brook   5
In the open sunshine, or we are unblest :
The wealthiest man among us is the best :
No grandeur now in nature or in book
Delights us. Rapine, avarice, expense,
This is idolatry ; and these we adore :   10
Plain living and high thinking are no more :
The homely beauty of the good old cause
Is gone ; our peace, our fearful innocence,
And pure religion breathing household laws.

Explorations

1.   The poem expresses nostalgia for England's past, disgust at her present. Point out where each mood is expressed.

2.   What qualities in contemporary English life produced each of these feelings ? Is it of any help to recall that the Industrial Revolution was making rapid strides at this time, that people were leaving the land and flocking into the cities, and that commerce was booming ?

3.   The poet contrasts ' pure religion ' with ' idolatry '. What does he mean by each ? What does he wish to convey by the contrast ? What other words or images carry a religious connotation ?

4.   Would it be too much to claim that the poet manages to evoke two distinct ways of life by the suggestiveness of his language and images in this short poem ? Do you honestly think that this is a successful poem ?

5.   Compare the poem with *Surprised by Joy* with regard to the relationship between the formal scheme of the sonnet and the movement of the thought within it. Are the transitions in the present sonnet as successful as in the other ? Are the rhymes, for instance, as spontaneous ? Read both poems aloud as you think they ought to be read.

Ode to the West Wind

O wild West Wind, thou breath of Autumn's being,
Thou, from whose unseen presence the leaves dead
Are driven, like ghosts from an enchanter fleeing,
Yellow, and black, and pale, and hectic red,
Pestilence-stricken multitudes : O thou,   5
Who chariotest to their dark wintry bed
The wingèd seeds, where they lie cold and low,
Each like a corpse within its grave, until
Thine azure sister of the Spring shall blow
Her clarion o'er the dreaming earth, and fill   10
(Driving sweet buds like flocks to feed in air)
With living hues and odours plain and hill :
Wild Spirit, which art moving everywhere ;
Destroyer and preserver ; hear, oh, hear !

Thou on whose stream, mid the steep sky's commotion, 15
Loose clouds like earth's decaying leaves are shed,
Shook from the tangled boughs of Heaven and Ocean,
Angels of rain and lightning : there are spread
On the blue surface of thine aëry surge,
Like the bright hair uplifted from the head   20
Of some fierce Maenad, even from the dim verge
Of the horizon to the zenith's height,
The locks of the approaching storm. Thou dirge
Of the dying year, to which this closing night
Will be the dome of a vast sepulchre,   25
Vaulted with all thy congregated might
Of vapours, from whose solid atmosphere
Black rain, and fire, and hail will burst : oh, hear !

Thou who didst waken from his summer dreams
The blue Mediterranean, where he lay,   30
Lulled by the coil of his crystalline streams,
Beside a pumice isle in Baiae's bay,
And saw in sleep old palaces and towers

Quivering within the wave's intenser day,
All overgrown with azure moss and flowers   35
So sweet, the sense faints picturing them ! Thou
For whose path the Atlantic's level powers
Cleave themselves into chasms, while far below
The sea-blooms and the oozy woods which wear
The sapless foliage of the ocean, know   40
Thy voice, and suddenly grow gray with fear,
And tremble and despoil themselves : oh, hear !

If I were a dead leaf thou mightest bear ;
If I were a swift cloud to fly with thee ;
A wave to pant beneath thy power, and share   45
The impulse of thy strength, only less free
Than thou, O uncontrollable ! If even
I were as in my boyhood, and could be
The comrade of thy wanderings over Heaven,
As then, when to outstrip thy skiey speed   50
Scarce seemed a vision ; I would ne'er have striven
As thus with thee in prayer in my sore need.
Oh, lift me as a wave, a leaf, a cloud !
I fall upon the thorns of life ! I bleed !
A heavy weight of hours has chained and bowed   55
One too like thee : tameless, and swift, and proud.

Make me thy lyre, even as the forest is :
What if my leaves are falling like its own !
The tumult of thy mighty harmonies
Will take from both a deep, autumnal tone,   60
Sweet though in sadness. Be thou, Spirit fierce,
My spirit ! Be thou me, impetuous one !
Drive my dead thoughts over the universe
Like withered leaves to quicken a new birth !
And, by the incantation of this verse,   65
Scatter, as from an unextinguished hearth
Ashes and sparks, my words among mankind !
Be through my lips to unawakened earth
The trumpet of a prophecy ! O, Wind,
If Winter comes, can Spring be far behind ?   70

Explorations

1. The wind, in the first movement, is hailed as ' Destroyer and preserver '. Show how the poet introduces us to this dual notion both in the thought and in the imagery of the movement. How successfully do you think he reconciles the opposing notions of life and death ?

2. From what does the movement derive its terrific energy ? Read it aloud. What words strike you as particularly vigorous ? What contribution does the rhythm make ? How is it combined with the sentence structure ? Examine it carefully.

3. The might of the wind is finely rendered in the second movement. How are these effects of power and destructive energy achieved in terms of image, language, and sound ? Explain the simile of the Maenad. What aspects of the wind is the poet trying to portray in this image ?

4. Which aspect of the wind—destroyer or preserver—is celebrated in the second movement ? Examine carefully the images of death and explain their meaning.

5. In the third movement the wind is imagined over the Mediterranean and the Atlantic Ocean. What differences of tone and atmosphere are evident in the two treatments ? Would it be true to say that each represents a different aspect of the West Wind ? Give reasons for your views.

6. Looking back over the earlier passages of the poem from this vantage-point, describe the sort of character the poet gives the West Wind—its powers, effects, potentialities.

7. In what senses does the poem change with the beginning of the fourth movement ? What does Shelley wish for in this stanza ? What qualities in the wind does he envy ? Trace the thought carefully.

8. What is the tone of this fourth stanza—angry, baffled, self-pitying, defiant, bitter, despairing . . . ? Do you sympathise with the poet in the final lines ? Explain your reaction.

9. What does the poet demand of the West Wind in the final stanza ? Trace the thought carefully.

10. In what sense does the last movement recall the first ? Look carefully at the imagery and comment on its appropriateness.

11. Would you agree that this is a poem of great eloquence and power ? If so, try to explain the source of that power and how it is bodied forth in the language.

12.   Read the poem aloud as you think it should be read, and try to suggest how sound, image, colour and sense combine to produce the total effect.

13.   Examine the formal structure of each stanza considering rhythm and rhyme, in particular.   Does the movement of the verse strike you as a successful way of conveying the gusts of energy and eloquence that make up the poem's totality ?

Glossary p. 230

Stanzas written in Dejection near Naples

The sun is warm, the sky is clear,
   The waves are dancing fast and bright,
Blue isles and snowy mountains wear
   The purple noon's transparent might,
   The breath of the moist earth is light,   5
Around its unexpanded buds ;
   Like many a voice of one delight,
The winds, the birds, the ocean floods,
The City's voice itself, is soft like Solitude's.

I see the Deep's untrampled floor   10
   With green and purple seaweeds strown ;
I see the waves upon the shore,
   Like light dissolved in star-showers, thrown :
   I sit upon the sands alone,—
The lightning of the noontide ocean   15
   Is flashing round me, and a tone
Arises from its measured motion,
How sweet ! did any heart now share in my emotion.

Alas ! I have nor hope nor health,
   Nor peace within nor calm around,   20
Nor that content surpassing wealth
   The sage in meditation found,
   And walked with inward glory crowned—
Nor fame, nor power, nor love, nor leisure.
   Others I see whom these surround—   25
Smiling they live, and call life pleasure ;—
To me that cup has been dealt in another measure.

Yet now despair itself is mild,
   Even as the winds and waters are ;
I could lie down like a tired child,   30
   And weep away the life of care
   Which I have borne and yet must bear,
Till death like sleep might steal on me,
   And I might feel in the warm air
My cheek grow cold, and hear the sea   35
Breathe o'er my dying brain its last monotony.

Some might lament that I were cold,
  As I, when this sweet day is gone,
Which my lost heart, too soon grown old,
  Insults with this untimely moan ;   40
  They might lament—for I am one
Whom men love not,—and yet regret,
  Unlike this day, which, when the sun
Shall on its stainless glory set,
Will linger, though enjoyed, like joy in memory yet.   45

Explorations

1. What is the tone of the first stanza ? What sort of atmosphere is conjured up ? What sort of language and imagery is used to create the mood ?

2. Does the mood persist through the second stanza ? If not, where are there hints of a change ? What sort of change ? Why does the poet delay his entry into the poem until this point ?

3. What are the poet's complaints in the third stanza ? Are they particular or general ? Do we learn anything more specific about them as the poem proceeds ?

4. Do you find the death-wish in the last two stanzas sinister, chilling, pleasant, caressing ? How is this effect achieved ? Consider language, rhythm and imagery.

5. What is the poet's despair caused by—loneliness, weariness, self-contempt . . . ? Is it entirely unrelieved ? Examine the thought of the last three stanzas carefully.

6. By what sort of images and sounds are the lapsing, dream-like mood and atmosphere created ? Examine the language minutely, reading aloud to get the texture of it.

7. Read Keats's *Ode to a Nightingale* and compare the two poems in terms of the death-wish that is expressed in each, showing the differences as well as the resemblances.

Glossary p. 231

Ozymandias

I met a traveller from an antique land
Who said : Two vast and trunkless legs of stone
Stand in the desert . . . Near them, on the sand,
Half sunk, a shattered visage lies, whose frown,
And wrinkled lip, and sneer of cold command,   5
Tell that its sculptor well those passions read
Which yet survive, stamped on these lifeless things,
The hand that mocked them, and the heart that fed :
And on the pedestal these words appear :
" My name is Ozymandias, king of kings :   10
Look on my works, ye Mighty, and despair ! "
Nothing beside remains. Round the decay
Of that colossal wreck, boundless and bare
The lone and level sands stretch far away.

Explorations

1. Would you agree that this is an extremely ironic poem ? Where-
in does its irony lie ? Is the irony driven home in the last lines ?
Explain.

2. Would you say that this is a poem with a message ? If so, say
briefly what you think the message is.

3. What is the effect of the word ' antique ' in the first line ? What
does it mean ? What images does it conjure up ? What other words in
the sonnet do you find striking, evocative or unusual ? Show their
relevance to the total mood and meaning.

4. Are there any marked changes of pace or tone in the poem ?
Read it aloud so as to bring out their significance. Do you feel that the
poem has the completeness that a good sonnet should have ? What is
the effect of the quiet monosyllables in the final lines ?

5. Describe the rhyme scheme of the sonnet and examine the
relationship of the sentence structure to the metrical form.

Glossary p. 231

Ode to a Nightingale

My heart aches, and a drowsy numbness pains
  My sense, as though of hemlock I had drunk,
Or emptied some dull opiate to the drains
  One minute past, and Lethe-wards had sunk :
'Tis not through envy of thy happy lot,   5
  But being too happy in thine happiness,—
    That thou, light-winged Dryad of the trees,
      In some melodious plot
  Of beechen green, and shadows numberless,
    Singest of summer in full-throated ease.   10

O, for a draught of vintage ! that hath been
  Cool'd a long age in the deep-delved earth,
Tasting of Flora and the country green,
  Dance, and Provencal song, and sunburnt mirth !
O for a beaker full of the warm South,   15
  Full of the true, the blushful Hippocrene,
    With beaded bubbles winking at the brim,
      And purple-stained mouth ;
  That I might drink, and leave the world unseen,
    And with thee fade away into the forest dim :   20

Fade far away, dissolve, and quite forget
  What thou among the leaves hast never known,
The weariness, the fever, and the fret
  Here, where men sit and hear each other groan ;
Where palsy shakes a few, sad, last gray hairs,   25
  Where youth grows pale, and spectre-thin, and dies ;
    Where but to think is to be full of sorrow
      And leaden-eyed despairs,
  Where Beauty cannot keep her lustrous eyes,
    Or new Love pine at them beyond to-morrow.   30

Away ! away ! for I will fly to thee,
  Not charioted by Bacchus and his pards,
But on the viewless wings of Poesy,
  Though the dull brain perplexes and retards :

Already with thee ! tender is the night,   35
  And haply the Queen-Moon is on her throne,
    Cluster'd around by all her starry Fays ;
      But here there is no light,
  Save what from heaven is with the breezes blown
    Through verdurous glooms and winding mossy ways.   40

I cannot see what flowers are at my feet,
  Nor what soft incense hangs upon the boughs,
But, in embalmed darkness, guess each sweet
  Wherewith the seasonable month endows
The grass, the thicket, and the fruit-tree wild ;   45
  White hawthorn, and the pastoral eglantine ;
    Fast fading violets cover'd up in leaves ;
      And mid-May's eldest child,
  The coming musk-rose, full of dewy wine,
    The murmurous haunt of flies on summer eves.   50

Darkling I listen ; and, for many a time
  I have been half in love with easeful Death,
Call'd him soft names in many a mused rhyme,
  To take into the air my quiet breath ;
Now more than ever seems it rich to die,   55
  To cease upon the midnight with no pain,
    While thou art pouring forth thy soul abroad
      In such an ecstasy !
  Still wouldst thou sing, and I have ears in vain—
    To thy high requiem become a sod.   60

Thou wast not born for death, immortal Bird !
  No hungry generations tread thee down ;
The voice I hear this passing night was heard
  In ancient days by emperor and clown :
Perhaps the self-same song that found a path   65
  Through the sad heart of Ruth, when, sick for home,
    She stood in tears amid the alien corn ;
      The same that oft-times hath
  Charm'd magic casements, opening on the foam
    Of perilous seas, in faery lands forlorn.   70

Forlorn ! the very word is like a bell
　To toll me back from thee to my sole self !
Adieu ! the fancy cannot cheat so well
　As she is fam'd to do, deceiving elf.
Adieu ! adieu ! thy plaintive anthem fades　　　　　　　75
　　Past the near mountains, over the still stream,
　　　Up the hill-side ; and now 'tis buried deep
　　　　In the next valley-glades :
　Was it a vision, or a waking dream ?
　　Fled is that music :—Do I wake or sleep ?　　　　　80

Explorations

This poem is basically a meditation on human life which is transient and imperfect, and on art—represented by the song of the nightingale—which is not only perfect but immortal.

1.　What words, phrases or images serve to create the mood of ' drowsy numbness ' with which the poem opens ? In what respects does the nightingale contrast with the poet's mood ?

2.　In the second stanza the poet longs for ' a draught of vintage ' so that he may ' fade away into the forest ' with the nightingale. What sort of world does the bird symbolise ? What effect, for instance, is created by such words as ' earth ', ' Flora ', ' sunburnt ', ' Hippocrene ' ? Do such words echo any idea in the first stanza ? Consult the glossary before answering. In what way does the ' draught of vintage ' contrast with the hemlock in the opening lines ?

3.　What sort of change takes place in the third stanza ? What words or images establish this change most vividly ? What is the connection between the thought of this stanza and that of the previous two ? Consider the theme of life and death. What has the nightingale to do with this ?

4.　In the fourth stanza the poet dismisses wine as a means of escape. What does he put in its place ? Looking back over the poem so far, point out how often the poet has mentioned or implied flight or escape. What sort of escape do you think he has in mind ?

5.　In the fifth stanza the poet again writes about the world in which he is situated. In what way does the view taken here by the poet differ from that in the third stanza ?

6. The theme of escape recurs in the sixth stanza. What form does it now take ? What is the poet hoping he might achieve through death—immortality, beauty, a perfect state of being ? Is this a development of his previous thoughts on death ?

7. In the seventh stanza—one of the most celebrated in the language—the poet summarises much of his feeling about the nightingale. What attributes of the bird does the poet envy, admire, aspire after ? He suggests that the bird had been heard in medieval and biblical times. In what sense does he mean this ? The last two lines have fascinated readers and critics by their mystery. What do these lines suggest to you ? Does this stanza help you to answer question 6 ?

8. The last stanza brings the poet back from the world of the nightingale to his ' sole self '. What is the difference between the two worlds ? Why does he seem disappointed with ' the fancy ' or imagination in line 73 ? Why does the poem end with a question ? What, in fact, has the poem been about ?

9. Trace the development of the thought through the whole poem, paying attention to the sustained contrast between imagination and everyday reality, to the themes of flight, escape and death, to the theme of immortality.

10. Trace the references to the song of the nightingale through the poem. What do they contribute to the shape of the poem ?

11. Keats is noted for the sensuousness of his poetry. To how many senses does he appeal in the fifth stanza ? Read Marvell's *Thoughts in a Garden* for comparison.

12. Read *Ode on a Grecian Urn* and compare it with this ode as an exploration of similar themes. Read also Yeats's *Sailing to Byzantium* for comparison.

Glossary p. 231

Ode on a Grecian Urn

Thou still unravish'd bride of quietness,
  Thou foster-child of silence and slow time,
Sylvan historian, who canst thus express
  A flowery tale more sweetly than our rhyme :
What leaf-fring'd legend haunts about thy shape   5
  Of deities or mortals, or of both,
    In Tempe or the dales of Arcady ?
What men or gods are these ? What maidens loth ?
  What mad pursuit ? What struggle to escape ?
    What pipes and timbrels ? What wild ecstasy ?   10

Heard melodies are sweet, but those unheard
  Are sweeter ; therefore, ye soft pipes, play on ;
Not to the sensual ear, but, more endear'd,
  Pipe to the spirit ditties of no tone :
Fair youth, beneath the trees, thou canst not leave   15
  Thy song, nor ever can those trees be bare ;
    Bold Lover, never, never canst thou kiss,
Though winning near the goal—yet, do not grieve ;
  She cannot fade, though thou hast not thy bliss,
    For ever wilt thou love, and she be fair !   20

Ah, happy, happy boughs ! that cannot shed
  Your leaves, nor ever bid the Spring adieu ;
And, happy melodist, unwearied,
  For ever piping songs for ever new ;
More happy love ! more happy, happy love !   25
  For ever warm and still to be enjoy'd,
    For ever panting, and for ever young ;
All breathing human passion far above,
  That leaves a heart high-sorrowful and cloy'd,
    A burning forehead, and a parching tongue.   30

Who are these coming to the sacrifice ?
  To what green altar, O mysterious priest,
Lead'st thou that heifer lowing at the skies,
  And all her silken flanks with garlands drest ?

What little town by river or sea shore,   35
   Or mountain-built with peaceful citadel,
      Is emptied of this folk, this pious morn ?
And, little town, thy streets for evermore
   Will silent be ; and not a soul to tell
      Why thou art desolate, can e'er return.   40

O Attic shape ! Fair attitude ! with brede
   Of marble men and maidens overwrought,
With forest branches and the trodden weed :
   Thou, silent form, dost tease us out of thought
As doth eternity : Cold Pastoral !   45
   When old age shall this generation waste,
      Thou shalt remain, in midst of other woe
Than ours, a friend to man, to whom thou say'st,
   Beauty is truth, truth beauty,—that is all
      Ye know on earth, and all ye need to know.   50

Explorations

1. In the first stanza the poet moves from a contemplation of the urn itself to a consideration of the scenes depicted on it. Explain the three images in which he describes it—' bride of quietness ', ' foster-child of silence and slow time ', ' Sylvan historian '.

2. The scene depicted is of a pagan festival, probably in honour of the god Bacchus, celebrated with a sacrifice, wine and love-making. Are there any paradoxes involved in the way the poet describes this scene as against the way in which he first describes the urn ? Consider the first and last lines of the first stanza.

3. In the second stanza the poet suggests that the world of art is finer than the world of reality—the ' unheard ' melodies are sweeter than real music. In what sense can this be so ? Does he go on to make a similar distinction about love ? Trace the theme through to the end of stanza three.

4. In the fourth stanza we get a description of the participants in the sacrifice and the little town they have left empty. Why is it done with questions ? Is the word ' mysterious ' in any way important ? Is there a deliberate ambiguity here ?

5. In the first stanza the urn was addressed as a ' Sylvan historian '. Is the term in any sense justified by this fourth stanza ? What sort of

history does this ' historian ' write ? How does it differ from ordinary history ? In what sense might it be superior to it ?

6.   In the final stanza the poet calls the urn ' Cold Pastoral '. What are the possible meanings of this description ? Consider your answer to question 5. In what sense does the beauty of the design ' tease us out of thought ' ? See the glossary.

7.   In how far does the entire poem lead towards the final statement in the last two lines ? Is the statement justified ? Glance back at question 5.

8.   For similar poems about the relation between immortality, life and art, read *Ode to a Nightingale* and *Sailing to Byzantium*.

Glossary p. 232

La Belle Dame sans Merci

O what can ail thee, knight-at-arms,
  Alone and palely loitering?
The sedge has wither'd from the lake,
  And no birds sing.

O what can ail thee, knight-at-arms!   5
  So haggard and so woe-begone?
The squirrel's granary is full,
  And the harvest's done.

I see a lilly on thy brow,
  With anguish moist and fever dew,   10
And on thy cheeks a fading rose
  Fast withereth too.

I met a lady in the meads,
  Full beautiful—a faery's child,
Her hair was long, her foot was light,   15
  And her eyes were wild.

I made a garland for her head,
  And bracelets too, and fragrant zone;
She look'd at me as she did love,
  And made sweet moan.   20

I set her on my pacing steed,
  And nothing else saw all day long,
For sidelong would she bend, and sing
  A faery's song.

She found me roots of relish sweet,   25
  And honey wild, and manna dew,
And sure in language strange she said—
  " I love thee true ".

She took me to her elfin grot,
  And there she wept, and sigh'd full sore,   30
And there I shut her wild wild eyes
  With kisses four.

And there she lulled me asleep,
    And there I dream'd—Ah ! woe betide !
The latest dream I ever dream'd   35
    On the cold hill side.

I saw pale kings and princes too,
    Pale warriors, death-pale were they all ;
They cried—" La Belle Dame sans Merci
    Hath thee in thrall ! "   40

I saw their starved lips in the gloam,
    With horrid warning gaped wide,
And I awoke and found me here,
    On the cold hill's side.

And this is why I sojourn here,   45
    Alone and palely loitering,
Though the sedge has wither'd from the lake,
    And no birds sing.

Explorations

1. The poem opens dramatically in typical ballad style with a question to the knight who had been found wandering by the lake. What do the first three stanzas tell us of his condition ? How is the notion of desolation suggested ?

2. Now read the ballad through to the end. From the fourth stanza on, who is telling the story ?

3. This is a story of enchantment. How is this atmosphere built up ? Is there a quality of nightmare in it ? Explain. Is the title " La Belle Dame sans Merci " apt ? Give reasons for your answer.

4. Is this in any sense a moral tale ? What notion of love is contained in the poem ?

5. There is a chill about the entire experience. How is this feeling created in the words and phrases in which the story is told ?

6. There is a notable absence of detail. Why ?

7. How appropriate is the ballad form to the purpose of the tale ? What part do rhythm and archaic diction play ?

8. What is the final effect of the ballad on you—chilling, frightening, touching ? How is this effect brought about ?

Glossary p. 233

Terror of Death

When I have fears that I may cease to be
  Before my pen has glean'd my teeming brain,
Before high-piled books, in charact'ry,
  Hold like rich garners the full-ripen'd grain ;
When I behold, upon the night's starr'd face,   5
  Huge cloudy symbols of a high romance,
And think that I may never live to trace
  Their shadows, with the magic hand of chance ;
And when I feel, fair creature of an hour !
  That I shall never look upon thee more,   10
Never have relish in the faery power
  Of unreflecting love !—then on the shore
Of the wide world I stand alone, and think
Till love and fame to nothingness do sink.

Explorations

1. The first eight lines concern the poet's dread that death may come before he has completed what he wants to write. Consider the metaphors in each of the first two quatrains through which he expresses this fear. Do you find them vivid, accurate, satisfying ? What might the poet mean by ' the magic hand of chance ' ?

2. In what way does the thought change in the sestet ? Is it a natural extension of the thought and imagery of the octet ? Explain, giving reasons for your answer.

3. Would you agree that the poem gives us the picture of a man trying to understand the mystery of life and its transience ? If so, where, and how well, is this expressed ?

4. Why, for the poet, is the awareness of the passage of time so acute and depressing ? What aspects of the poet's life are mentioned in this connection ? Reconsider the poem in this light, paying special attention to the last two lines.

5. Keats was very much concerned with the mystery of the world and of the human being's place in it. Is this concern expressed in the poem ? If so, in what phrases and images ? What is his feeling in the face of this mystery—hope, despair, fear . . . ?

6. Note how Keats has shaped his thought. Pay particular attention to the use of the words ' when ' and ' then ' in the poem.

Glossary p. 233

Bright Star ! Would I were

Bright star ! would I were steadfast as thou art—
  Not in lone splendour hung aloft the night
And watching, with eternal lids apart,
  Like nature's patient, sleepless Eremite,
The moving waters at their priestlike task   5
  Of pure ablution round earth's human shores,
Or gazing on the new soft fallen mask
  Of snow upon the mountains and the moors—
No—yet still steadfast, still unchangeable,
  Pillow'd upon my fair love's ripening breast,   10
To feel for ever its soft fall and swell,
  Awake for ever in a sweet unrest,
Still, still to hear her tender-taken breath,
And so live ever—or else swoon to death.

Explorations

1. The poet wishes, in the first lines, for the steadfastness of the star but not for its loneliness. Trace how he renders this distinction through the sonnet. What, therefore, is his ideal of happiness ?

2. Is the reference to death in the last line prepared for in the body of the sonnet, or does it come as a surprise ?

3. Keats wishes to ' so live ever—or else swoon to death '. How are these apparently contradictory wishes reconcilable ?

4. How is the coldness of the inanimate world conveyed ? How is its beauty expressed ? Examine the imagery carefully and contrast it with the imagery in which human happiness is conveyed.

5. Do you consider the images in the poem vivid and apt ? Give reasons for your answer.

6. Do you find it an altogether satisfying poem ? Read *Ode to a Nightingale* for another statement of the poet's attitude to life and death.

7. Examine the structure of the sonnet. Does the thought move in a single unit or can certain stages in its development be marked ? Show how the single sentence makes its way through the lines and quatrains. Read it aloud.

Glossary p. 233

On the Sea

It keeps eternal whisperings around
   Desolate shores, and with its mighty swell
   Gluts twice ten thousand caverns, till the spell
Of Hecate leaves them their old shadowy sound.
Often 'tis in such gentle temper found,   5
   That scarcely will the very smallest shell
   Be moved for days from where it sometime fell,
When last the winds of heaven were unbound.
Oh ye ! who have your eye-balls vexed and tired,
   Feast them upon the wideness of the Sea ;   10
      Oh ye ! whose ears are dinn'd with uproar rude,
      Or fed too much with cloying melody,—
      Sit ye near some old cavern's mouth, and brood
Until ye start, as if the sea-nymphs quired !

Explorations

1. In the first quatrain a certain aspect of the sea is rendered. What aspect ? What word or image strikes you as especially vivid ?

2. What aspect of the sea is dealt with in the second quatrain ? Where do you find the poet's use of significant detail in these first eight lines especially effective ?

3. Would you agree that the poet combines the matter-of-fact with the mysterious in these first eight lines ? If so, is it a successful combination ? Explain.

4. Do you find that the sestet completes the thought satisfactorily ? Trace the argument of the sonnet. Is the sestet something of an anti-climax ?

5. Read the poem aloud and see whether you find it satisfying, in terms of sound and sense. Give specific reasons for your opinions.

Glossary p. 233

Choric Song of the Lotos-Eaters

There is sweet music here that softer falls
Than petals from blown roses on the grass,
Or night-dews on still waters between walls
Of shadowy granite, in a gleaming pass ;
Music that gentlier on the spirit lies,   5
Than tired eyelids upon tired eyes ;
Music that brings sweet sleep down from the blissful
    skies.
Here are cool mosses deep,
And thro' the moss the ivies creep,
And in the stream the long-leaved flowers weep,   10
And from the craggy ledge the poppy hangs in sleep.

Why are we weigh'd upon with heaviness,
And utterly consumed with sharp distress,
While all things else have rest from weariness ?
All things have rest : why should we toil alone,   15
We only toil, who are the first of things,
And make perpetual moan,
Still from one sorrow to another thrown :
Nor ever fold our wings,
And cease from wanderings ;   20
Nor steep our brows in slumber's holy balm ;
Nor harken what the inner spirit sings,
" There is no joy but calm ! "
Why should we only toil, the roof and crown of things ?

Lo ! in the middle of the wood,   25
The folded leaf is woo'd from out the bud
With winds upon the branch, and there
Grows green and broad, and takes no care,
Sun-steep'd at noon, and in the moon
Nightly dew-fed ; and turning yellow   30
Falls, and floats adown the air.

Lo ! sweeten'd with the summer light,
The full-juiced apple, waxing over-mellow,
Drops in a silent autumn night.
All its allotted length of days,   35
The flower ripens in its place,
Ripens and fades, and falls, and hath no toil,
Fast-rooted in the fruitful soil.

Hateful is the dark-blue sky,
Vaulted o'er the dark-blue sea.   40
Death is the end of life ; ah ! why
Should life all labour be ?
Let us alone. Time driveth onward fast,
And in a little while our lips are dumb.
Let us alone. What is it that will last ?   45
All things are taken from us, and become
Portions and parcels of the dreadful Past.
Let us alone. What pleasure can we have
To war with evil ? Is there any peace
In ever climbing up the climbing wave ?   50
All things have rest, and ripen toward the grave
In silence, ripen, fall and cease.
Give us long rest or death, dark death, or dreamful ease !

How sweet it were, hearing the downward stream,
With half-shut eyes ever to seem   55
Falling asleep in a half-dream !
To dream and dream, like yonder amber light,
Which will not leave the myrrh-bush on the height ;
To hear each other's whisper'd speech ;
Eating the Lotos, day by day,   60
To watch the crisping ripples on the beach,
And tender curving lines of creamy spray :
To lend our hearts and spirits wholly
To the influence of mild-minded melancholy ;
To muse and brood and live again in memory,   65
With those old faces of our infancy
Heap'd over with a mound of grass,
Two handfuls of white dust, shut in an urn of brass !

Dear is the memory of our wedded lives,
And dear the last embraces of our wives   70
And their warm tears : but all hath suffer'd change ;
For surely now our household hearths are cold :
Our sons inherit us : our looks are strange :
And we should come like ghosts to trouble joy.
Or else the island princes over-bold   75
Have eat our substance, and the minstrel sings
Before them of the ten-years' war in Troy,
And our great deeds, as half-forgotten things.
Is there confusion in the little isle ?
Let what is broken so remain.   80
The Gods are hard to reconcile :
'Tis hard to settle order once again.
There *is* confusion worse than death,
Trouble on trouble, pain on pain,
Long labour unto aged breath,   85
Sore task to hearts worn out with many wars
And eyes grown dim with gazing on the pilot-stars.

But, propt on beds of amaranth and moly,
How sweet (while warm airs lull us, blowing lowly,)
With half-dropt eyelids still,   90
Beneath a heaven dark and holy,
To watch the long bright river drawing slowly
His waters from the purple hill—
To hear the dewy echoes calling
From cave to cave thro' the thick-twined vine—   95
To hear the emerald-colour'd water falling
Thro' many a wov'n acanthus-wreath divine !
Only to hear and see the far-off sparkling brine,
Only to hear were sweet, stretch'd out beneath the pine.

The Lotos blooms below the flowery peak :   100
The Lotos blows by every winding creek :
All day the wind breathes low with mellower tone :
Thro' every hollow cave and alley lone
Round and round the spicy downs the yellow Lotos-dust
      is blown.

We have had enough of action, and of motion we,   105
Roll'd to starboard, roll'd to larboard, when the surge was
    seething free,
Where the wallowing monster spouted his foam-fountains
    in the sea.
Let us swear an oath, and keep it with an equal mind,
In the hollow Lotos-land to live and lie reclined
On the hills like Gods together, careless of mankind.   110
For they lie beside their nectar, and the bolts are hurl'd
Far below them in the valleys, and the clouds are lightly
    curl'd
Round their golden houses, girdled with the gleaming
    world :
Where they smile in secret, looking over wasted lands,
Blight and famine, plague and earthquake, roaring deeps
    and fiery sands,   115
Clanging fights, and flaming towns, and sinking ships,
    and praying hands.
But they smile, they find a music centred in a doleful
    song,
Steaming up, a lamentation and an ancient tale of
    wrong,
Like a tale of little meaning though the words are strong;
Chanted from an ill-used race of men that cleave the soil, 120
Sow the seed, and reap the harvest with enduring toil,
Storing yearly little dues of wheat, and wine and oil ;
Till they perish and they suffer—some, 'tis whisper'd—
    down in hell
Suffer endless anguish, others in Elysian valleys dwell,
Resting weary limbs at last on beds of asphodel.   125
Surely, surely, slumber is more sweet than toil, the shore
Than labour in the deep mid-ocean, wind and wave
    and oar ;
Oh rest ye, brother mariners, we will not wander more.

Note

This choric song is part of a poem based on an episode in Homer's
Odyssey. It describes how Odysseus and his mariners come ashore
on a strange island inhabited by the mild-eyed, melancholy lotos-
eaters. Those who ate the lotos no longer felt any desire to return to
their home and former life.

In Tennyson's poem the lotos-eaters gather on the beach and intone
this song. Now read this poem through at least once to get the feel of
its mood and atmosphere.

Explorations

1. What atmosphere is created in the first stanza? What sort of
mood does the passage evoke in you? Is the mood sustained, strength-
ened or varied as the poem proceeds? Is there a point at which it
changes altogether? If so, indicate what sort of change, by quotation
and comment.

2. What part does sound play in creating the mood and atmos-
phere? Examine the vowel and consonant combinations, the use of
repetitions, the varying length of the lines. Glance, for instance, at the
passage beginning with line 54. Read it aloud and feel the texture of
the sounds.

3. The feeling of a twilight world, of 'Falling asleep in a half-
dream' dominates the first part of the poem. Examine the imagery,
the word-painting, the use of tone and colour, the recurring references
to light and shade.

4. What part does memory play in the thought of the poem?
You might begin with the passage which opens at line 65. How vivid
is the evocation of the sailors' past? How is the effect created?

5. What are the sailors' arguments in favour of remaining in Lotos-
land? Do you find them persuasive? Which ones in particular?
What elements in the poem help to persuade us to accept the sailors'
opinions of the world?

6. What view of the gods is put forward in the final passage of the
poem? In what sense can the lotos-eaters claim to be 'like Gods
together'? In what tone is the description of the ordinary human's
life stated—'Storing yearly little dues of wheat, and wine and oil'?

7. In how far does this poem manage to build up a lavish impression
of Mediterranean life in Homeric times? Examine the extraordinary
range of detail which the poet deploys in creating this world—natural,
civil, religious . . .

8. Consider the sensuousness with which the poet depicts the land of the lotos-eaters and their way of life. Examine the poet's appeal to the various senses.

9. Would you agree that a sense of energy enters the poem with line 105 ? What emotion causes this upsurge of energy ? How is it conveyed ? Read the passage aloud and then look at the movement of the lines, the verbs, the adjectives, the swing of the metre.

10. Read aloud any passage at what you consider its proper pace. How is this sense of pace created and sustained ? Examine such contributory factors as the line lengths, the organisation of the sentences, the use of adjectives. At what point or points does this change ? In all cases does the pace reflect the mood ?

Glossary p. 233

Because I could not stop for Death

Because I could not stop for Death—
He kindly stopped for me—
The Carriage held but just Ourselves—
And Immortality.

We slowly drove—He knew no haste   5
And I had put away
My labor and my leisure too,
For His Civility—

We passed the School, where Children strove
At Recess—in the Ring—   10
We passed the Fields of Gazing Grain—
We passed the Setting Sun—

Or rather—He passed Us—
The Dews drew quivering and chill—
For only Gossamer, my Gown—   15
My Tippet—only Tulle—

We paused before a House that seemed
A Swelling of the Ground—
The Roof was scarcely visible—
The Cornice—in the Ground—   20

Since then—'tis Centuries—and yet
Feels shorter than the Day
I first surmised the Horses Heads
Were toward Eternity—

Explorations

1. Having read the poem, now read all Emily Dickinson's poems
in this book. Don't feel that you have to make sense ' of them, don't
bully them in the hope that they will yield up their message in a
manner that can be summarised and paraphrased. If you find that
you like them, only one thing is required. It can be best expressed by

the advice that the great Olympic athlete, Jesse Owens, gave to those who wish to be great long-jumpers. His three rules were that you sprint, then sprint, and finally sprint. For the word ' sprint ' we might here substitute ' read ' with equal emphasis and repetition.

2. Because the poet ' could not stop for Death ', so Death, personified, intervened to show her something of his nature. What sights does he show her ?

3. What is the significance of each of the images he presents to her in stanzas three, four and five ? Examine each of them carefully. Are they threatening, sinister, natural, inevitable, attractive . . . ? Can you find any progression from one to another ?

4. Do you find a dream quality in the poem ? Or would it be truer to say that it has a suggestion of nightmare ? The objects of the poem's landscape are spare and unadorned. What is the effect of this starkness ?

5. The last stanza suggests that Death leads to Eternity. How does this eternity strike you—as pleasant, empty, terrifying . . . ? What view of life is implied in this vision of death ? How does the poem leave you—depressed, contented, happy ? Point out the images or phrases that tend to create this feeling.

6. Trace the forward movement of the poem, paying particular attention to the verbs and repetitions. Is a sense of the inexorable created ? If so, how ?

Glossary p. 234

I felt a Funeral, in my Brain

I felt a Funeral, in my Brain,
And Mourners to and fro
Kept treading—treading—till it seemed
That Sense was breaking through—

And when they all were seated,   5
A Service, like a Drum—
Kept beating—beating—till I thought
My Mind was going numb—

And then I heard them lift a Box
And creak across my Soul   10
With those same Boots of Lead, again,
Then Space—began to toll,

As all the Heavens were a Bell,
And Being, but an Ear,
And I, and Silence, some strange Race   15
Wrecked, solitary, here—

And then a Plank in Reason, broke,
And I dropped down, and down—
And hit a World, at every plunge,
And Finished knowing—then—   20

Explorations

1. See Exploration 1 on *Because I could not stop for Death.*

2. The poem is clearly about death. What concrete images or details are especially suggestive of death or funerals? Examine each stanza carefully for the images it contains.

3. The poetess feels a funeral in the brain. In what sense does she mean this—is it a dream, a reality, a memory, or merely a metaphor? Trace the images from stanza to stanza and the progress of thought.

4. The poem dramatises the growth or dawning within the mind of an insight into the reality of death. Trace this from stanza to stanza with particular reference to those words which suggest mind, soul, consciousness.

5. What is the tone of the meditation—apprehensive, resigned or coldly factual? What words or phrases are especially typical of the tone?

6. Consider the part played by repetitions and other sound effects in the poem. What do they contribute to the movement and meaning? Consider the long sequences of conjunctions with this question in mind.

7. What is the effect of the final plunge downwards? Is this plunge prepared for in previous stanzas? Explain. Read the poem, paying particular attention to the effect of suspense created.

8. Examine the grammar and punctuation of the poem. How does it combine with the stanza division?

9. Read *Because I could not stop for Death* for comparison.

The Soul selects her own Society

The Soul selects her own Society—
Then—shuts the Door—
To her divine Majority—
Present no more—

Unmoved—she notes the Chariots—pausing—   5
At her low Gate—
Unmoved—an Emperor be kneeling
Upon her Mat—

I've known her—from an ample nation—
Choose One—   10
Then—close the Valves of her attention—
Like Stone—

Explorations

1. See Exploration 1 on *Because I could not stop for Death.*

2. Would you agree that this poem presents a human soul as alone, majestic, self-sufficient, proud ? If so, how is the impression conveyed ? In what images is the notion of seclusion and exclusiveness given ?

3. Is the poem an open-ended meditation inviting the reader to complete it or is it a complete statement ? What, for instance, is the effect of the curious punctuation ?

4. Examine the images to see what they contribute either singly or in groups to the meaning of the poem. Say honestly what picture each image conveys to your mind. In what way does one image work upon another ?

5. Read the poem aloud, at its proper pace, and let it reverberate in your mind.

Glossary p. 234

Of all the Souls that stand create

Of all the Souls that stand create—
I have elected—One—
When Sense from Spirit—files away—
And Subterfuge—is done—
When that which is—and that which was—   5
Apart—intrinsic—stand—
And this brief Tragedy of Flesh—
Is shifted—like a Sand—
When Figures show their royal Front—
And Mists—are carved away,   10
Behold the Atom—I preferred—
To all the lists of Clay !

Explorations

1. See Exploration 1 on *Because I could not stop for Death.*

2. This is a richly suggestive poem which is open to more than one interpretation, but it is clearly the poet's meditation on the immortality of the spirit. What do you take ' the Atom ' in line 11 to mean ? Is it God or is it the poet's own perfected soul ? Is it the same as ' One ' referred to in the second line ?

3. The poem begins and ends with the notion of a soul in isolation. Trace the progress of the thought by which the sense, the flesh, the material, is shorn away from the spirit. Look at the possible meanings of ' files ', ' shifted ', ' carved '.

4. What can the poet mean by ' Tragedy of Flesh ' ? What words or phrases in the poem suggest permanence on the one hand and impermanence on the other ?

5. Is it a poem that describes and defines, or rather does it suggest possibilities ? Read it aloud with the pace and tone that you would think appropriate, giving it the pauses and inflections that its unusual scheme of punctuation seems to suggest.

Glossary p. 234

At Half past Three

At Half past Three, a single Bird
Unto a silent Sky
Propounded but a single term
Of cautious melody.

At Half past Four, Experiment   5
Had subjugated test
And lo, Her silver Principle
Supplanted all the rest.

At Half past Seven, Element
Nor Implement, be seen—   10
And Place was where the Presence was
Circumference between.

Explorations

1. See Exploration 1 on *Because I could not stop for Death*.

2. Like most of Emily Dickinson's poems this one is very compressed in thought. It begins with a concrete fact—the bird's song. It proceeds to suggest that this song, in itself important, can be seen as an expression of something more significant. Can you discern a progress not only in time but also in thought? Trace the progression of the thought in terms of the following words :—' melody ', ' Experiment ', ' test ', ' Principle ', ' Element ', ' Implement ', ' Place ', ' Presence '. What has each of these to do with the bird?

3. Reading the poem we discern a progress in time. Is there a progress in tone? Take the words ' propounded ' and ' cautious ' in the first stanza, ' subjugated ' and ' supplanted ' in the second, and ' was ' in the third. What progress is implied in this sequence of statements?

4. Would you agree that the entire movement is towards ' Circumference ' in the last line? It may be useful to know that the poet defined ' Circumference ' as ' comprehension of essentials '.

5. Instead of seeing the poem as a progression of thought you may prefer to see it as an exercise in thoughtful observation. In the first stanza the poet hears the bird experiment with song. In the second, she hears the ' silver Principle ' of song triumphantly achieved. In the third, the bird and the song have departed leaving the essence, the ' Circumference ' behind. Reflect on all of these possibilities and suggest your own reading of the piece.

Glossary p. 234

That Nature is a Heraclitean Fire

Cloud-puffball, torn tufts, tossed pillows flaunt forth, then
    chevy on an air-
built thoroughfare : heaven-roysterers, in gay-gangs they
    throng ; they glitter in marches.
Down roughcast, down dazzling whitewash, wherever an elm
    arches,
Shivelights and shadowtackle in long lashes lace, lance, and
    pair.
Delightfully the bright wind boisterous ropes, wrestles, beats
    earth bare   5
Of yestertempest's creases ; in pool and rut peel parches
Squandering ooze to squeezed dough, crust, dust ; stanches,
    starches
Squadroned masks and manmarks treadmire toil there
Footfretted in it. Million-fuelèd, nature's bonfire burns on.
But quench her bonniest, dearest to her, her clearest-selvèd
    spark   10
Man, how fast his firedint, his mark on mind, is gone !
Both are in an unfathomable, all is in an enormous dark
Drowned. O pity and indignation ! Manshape, that shone
Sheer off, disseveral, a star, death blots black out ; nor mark
            Is any of him at all so stark   15
But vastness blurs and time beats level. Enough ! the
    Resurrection,
A heart's-clarion ! Away grief's gasping, joyless days,
    dejection.
            Across my foundering deck shone
A beacon, an eternal beam. Flesh fade, and mortal trash
Fall to the residuary worm ; world's wildfire, leave but ash : 20
            In a flash, at a trumpet crash,
I am all at once what Christ is, since he was what I am, and
This Jack, joke, poor potsherd, patch, matchwood, immortal
    diamond,
            Is immortal diamond.

Explorations

1. The full title of this poem is *That Nature is a Heraclitean Fire and of the Comfort of the Resurrection*. Read the gloss on ' Heraclitean '. The theme is that man seems obliterated and lost in a constantly changing world, but the poet finds comfort in the thought of the Resurrection. In the opening lines does the poet view the changing world with joy, wonder or despair ? Try reading the first nine lines in a way that brings out the mood and spirit. Point out such words and phrases as seem particularly expressive.

2. The poem begins in the clouds and plunges splendidly downwards through images of light. Trace this movement. It comes to rest for a moment in ' nature's bonfire burns on '. Does it continue through to the end of the poem ? What transition in thought and feeling begins with line 9 ? What significant change in the imagery occurs here ?

3. What is the cause of the ' pity and indignation ', the ' grief's gasping ', the ' dejection ' that supervene at this point ? Is the sense of dismay vividly conveyed ?

4. The poem soars upwards again in the final lines. Where is the turning point ? What makes this upsurge of joy possible ? How is it assisted by the light/darkness imagery ? Do you find the image of the ship especially powerful ? Why ? How is it supported by the image of light ?

5. Now re-read the poem. Examine the relevance of the idea of Heraclitean fire to the theme. Trace the fire imagery. How is the metaphor of the diamond connected with the images of fire and of light/darkness ?

6. Where and how is the prodigality and richness of Nature conveyed ? What phrase sums up this aspect of Nature ? Is there a paradox here ?

7. Do you sense a remarkable energy in the language ? If so, what does it derive from—the rhythm, the brilliant word-combinations, the verbs, the images of light and shade ? Or is it from the blending of all these ? Read the poem again, you will find few better examples of words strenuously about their proper business.

8. Can you explain how the sense of dismay and dejection is conveyed, beginning with line 10 ? Look at the movement of the phrases, the exclamations, the adjectives, the verbs.

9. Read the poem aloud until you can really feel its miraculous energy.

Glossary p. 234

The Windhover :

To Christ our Lord

I caught this morning morning's minion, king-
   dom of daylight's dauphin, dapple-dawn-drawn Falcon, in
      his riding
Of the rolling level underneath him steady air, and striding
High there, how he rung upon the rein of a wimpling wing
In his ecstasy ! then off, off forth on swing,   5
   As a skate's heel sweeps smooth on a bow-bend : the hurl
      and gliding
Rebuffed the big wind. My heart in hiding
Stirred for a bird,—the achieve of, the mastery of the thing !

Brute beauty and valour and act, oh, air, pride, plume, here
   Buckle ! AND the fire that breaks from thee then, a billion   10
Times told lovelier, more dangerous, O my chevalier !

No wonder of it : shéer plód makes plough down sillion
Shine, and blue-bleak embers, ah my dear,
   Fall, gall themselves, and gash gold-vermilion.

Explorations

1. Hopkins said that this poem was ' the best thing I ever wrote '.
Let us first get the feel of the poem by reading it more than once
silently and then aloud. Now let us consider the first eight lines merely
as a description of a bird in flight. Would you agree that it is superbly
done ? What phrases or images strike you as especially vivid ? Show—
if only by reading it aloud—how the movement of the lines mimes or
reflects the energy and grace of the windhover's flight—' the achieve
of, the mastery of the thing ! '

2. The bird is compared consistently to a knight on horseback.
Trace this image through the poem. Where and how is the sense of
nobility and daring registered ?

3. The poem is addressed to ' Christ our Lord ', whom Hopkins
sees as the great Chevalier, battling heroically against evil. Read the
poem again with the idea that the falcon/knight is a symbol of Christ
himself. Where is the struggle against evil suggested in the description
of flight ?

4. We now come to the word ' Buckle ! ' It is on the meaning of this word that readers of the poem have disagreed in the most interesting way. Some readers hold that the word means ' Challenge ! ', ' Tackle ! ' or ' Come to grips with ! ' adversity ; others believe that it means ' Collapse ' or ' Crumple ' before the assault of evil. See the glossary for a third possible meaning. Read the poem again before moving to question 5.

5. The last three lines give us two images which stand for triumph arising out of defeat. The soil that has been ploughed and trodden upon gives off a splendid ' shine ' or radiance ; the embers when they part and fall produce a victorious ' gold-vermilion ' brightness. Look back at ' Buckle ! ' and say which of the two meanings you favour. Do you think that the ambiguity is, in fact, deliberate and enriching, that one meaning need not exclude the other ?

6. Think of the victory which Christ brought out of defeat. Read the poem again ; consider its full symbolic resonance and grapple with its meaning. Isn't it a remarkable celebration of the Christian mystery ?

7. Look back over the poem and note the use of detail that goes to make the poem's eloquence, the effects achieved by alliteration and vowel quality, by exclamation, by the tension between line and sentence, form and sense, by the use of colour and a heraldic image, by the passionate rise and fall of the meditation, by the expert daring of it all.

8. Read *That Nature is a Heraclitean Fire* for its contemplation of the beauty of the world when seen in Christian vision. Contrast *The Windhover* with *Thou art indeed just, Lord.*

Glossary p. 235

Felix Randal

Felix Randal the farrier, O he is dead then ? my duty all
    ended,
Who have watched his mould of man, big-boned and hardy-
    handsome
Pining, pining, till time when reason rambled in it and some
Fatal four disorders, fleshed there, all contended ?

Sickness broke him. Impatient he cursed at first, but mended 5
Being anointed and all ; though a heavenlier heart began some
Months earlier, since I had our sweet reprieve and ransom
Tendered to him. Ah well, God rest him all road ever he
    offended !

This seeing the sick endears them to us, us too it endears.
My tongue had taught thee comfort, touch had quenched thy
    tears,   10
Thy tears that touched my heart, child, Felix, poor Felix
    Randal ;

How far from then forethought of, all thy more boisterous
    years,
When thou at the random grim forge, powerful amidst peers,
Didst fettle for the great grey drayhorse his bright and battering
    sandal !

Explorations

1. The first three stanzas describe the farrier's sickness. What is
the poet's feeling for Felix Randal—pity, tenderness, dismay, incom-
prehension ? Give reasons for your answer.

2. Is it as priest, friend or fellow-human being that Hopkins thinks
of the dead man ? Point out any words or phrases that give especial
support to your view.

3. Is it a vivid evocation of sickness ? Is it in any sense frightening ?
Trace the movement of the thought and feeling from line 2 where Felix
is described as ' big-boned and hardy-handsome ' to the end of the
third stanza—' child, Felix, poor Felix Randal '.

4. Would you agree that the poet's feelings involve both pity and admiration ? In what respect was the farrier magnificent ? Does the powerful up-beat of the final stanza affirm his strength and simplicity ? If so, what phrases and images register these qualities ? Read the poem aloud from its seemingly casual opening, ' O he is dead then ' to that final statement, so as to bring out the force and meaning.

5. The poem deals with the perplexing mystery of strength and sickness, life and death. Where is this mystery expressed in the poem ? Is the mystery sustained in the final stanza ?

6. Analyse in detail how much the poem tells us about Felix Randal, his life, his death, his sickness. Consider the vividness and economy of the picture of Felix at work. What is the effect of ' random grim forge ' ? Show how the language rises in the final stanza towards that magnificent last line.

Glossary p. 235

No Worst, there is None

No worst, there is none. Pitched past pitch of grief,
More pangs will, schooled at forepangs, wilder wring.
Comforter, where, where is your comforting ?
Mary, mother of us, where is your relief ?
My cries heave, herds-long ; huddle in a main, a chief   5
Woe, world-sorrow ; on an age-old anvil wince and sing—
Then lull, then leave off. Fury had shrieked " No ling-
ering ! Let me be fell : force I must be brief."

O the mind, mind has mountains ; cliffs of fall
Frightful, sheer, no-man-fathomed. Hold them cheap   10
May who ne'er hung there. Nor does long our small
Durance deal with that steep or deep. Here ! creep,
Wretch, under a comfort serves in a whirlwind : all
Life death does end and each day dies with sleep.

Explorations

1. St. Ignatius Loyola, whose *Spiritual Exercises* Hopkins had studied intimately, described a state of mind called ' desolation ' as a ' darkening of the soul, trouble of mind, movement to base and earthly things . . . moving to distrust, loss of hope, loss of love ; when the soul feels herself thoroughly apathetic, sad, and as it were, separated from her Creator and Lord '. Now read the poem again with this in mind. Is this the sort of feeling that the poem expresses ? Is there any hope of relief ? Look again at the opening and closing lines.

2. The poet seeks to express a great intensity of suffering. How do the first four lines convey this intensity ? Do they give us a clue to the cause and nature of the suffering ?

3. Explain the images in the second quatrain. By what common theme are the metaphors related ? What is the effect of the strained, labouring syntax ? Where is the sense of strain and labour most intense ? Examine the predominant vowel and consonant combinations.

4. How does the thought and imagery change in the sestet ? Do you find a sense of mental terror, almost of nightmare here ? If so, how is it conjured up ? Explain the inversions. What do they contribute to the mood and sense ?

5. There are several complex images in this poem which merit attention. Choose two and pursue the ideas they suggest in the context of the poem.

6. Pope laid it down that in poetry the sound should be ' an echo to the sense '. Is this the case here ? Read the poem aloud carefully before commenting.

7. Read *Thou art indeed just, Lord* and *I wake and feel* with the themes of grief and desolation in mind.

Glossary p. 236

I wake and feel the Fell of Dark

I wake and feel the fell of dark, not day.
What hours, O what black hoürs we have spent
This night ! what sights you, heart, saw ; ways you went !
And more must, in yet longer light's delay.
    With witness I speak this. But where I say   5
Hours I mean years, mean life. And my lament
Is cries countless, cries like dead letters sent
To dearest him that lives alas ! away.

    I am gall, I am heartburn. God's most deep decree
Bitter would have me taste : my taste was me ;   10
Bones built in me, flesh filled, blood brimmed the curse.
    Selfyeast of spirit a dull dough sours. I see
The lost are like this, and their scourge to be
As I am mine, their sweating selves ; but worse.

Explorations

1.   The poet wakes in darkness—read the gloss on ' fell '. What does the darkness symbolise ? The poet speaks to his heart. What aspect of himself does the heart stand for—the part that thinks, suffers, dreads ? In what context is the word ' heart ' repeated later ?

2.   The poet sees no end to his pain. How do the words convey desperation, loneliness of soul, the endless, unanswering immensity of existence ? To whom is he directing his cries ? Read the second quatrain with the sort of tone and emphasis you think it demands.

3.   Trace the images of gall, bitterness, scourge, blood, bones, flesh, sweat, in the sestet. There are obvious echoes of Christ's passion here. What do these images tell us of the poet's inner torment ?

4.   In line 9 the poet first wrote ' God's most deep decree ', changed it to ' God's most just decree ' and finally changed it back to its original form. In the light of the pain and desperation can you understand why ? What possible meanings has the word ' deep ' ?

5.   How does the imagery change ? Is the sense of physical sourness more or less terrible than the spiritual isolation of the octet ?

6.   Read question 1, *No Worst, there is None*. Do you find that the present sonnet reflects a kind of ' desolation ' ? In what way does the sestet extend the feeling of spiritual loneliness of the first eight lines ?

7.   How would you describe the poet's predicament ? Read *No Worst, there is None* and *Thou art indeed just, Lord*. Can you understand why these are called ' the terrible sonnets ' ?

Glossary p. 236

Thou art indeed just, Lord

Justus quidem tu es, Domine, si disputem tecum : verumtamen justa loquar
ad te : Quare via impriorum prosperatur ? &c.

Thou art indeed just, Lord, if I contend
With thee ; but, sir, so what I plead is just.
Why do sinners' ways prosper ? and why must
Disappointment all I endeavour end ?
    Wert thou my enemy, O thou my friend,   5
How wouldst thou worse, I wonder, than thou dost
Defeat, thwart me ? Oh, the sots and thralls of lust
Do in spare hours more thrive than I that spend,
Sir, life upon thy cause. See, banks and brakes
Now, leavèd how thick ! lacèd they are again   10
With fretty chervil, look, and fresh wind shakes
Them ; birds build—but not I build ; no, but strain,
Time's eunuch, and not breed one work that wakes.
Mine, O thou lord of life, send my roots rain.

Explorations

1. The poem is a questioning of God. In what spirit are the questions put—anger, rebelliousness, reverence, resentment, trust, despair . . . ? What are the questions ?

2. Would you agree that there is a sense of pain in the poem ? Does it intensify ? If so, where is it especially present ? Has the jerky and abrupt movement of the verse any function in the poem's feeling ?

3. The sestet is largely non-metaphorical. What sort of change takes place in line 9 ? How does the imagery of nature support the central theme ? Trace the images of fertility to the final line.

4. What image of God emerges from the poem ? What sort of relationship is suggested between the poet and his Maker ? Examine the several titles which the poet gives to God.

5. Examine the relation between the sentence units and the regularity of the metrical organisation. What form of sonnet is it ?

6. What sort of ' work ' has Hopkins in mind in line 13 ? Is he speaking as priest or poet ?

7. Compare Hopkins's relationship with God in this sonnet with that of Herbert in *The Collar* or of Donne in *A Hymn to God the Father*.

Glossary p. 236

During Wind and Rain

They sing their dearest songs—
He, she, all of them—yea,
Treble and tenor and bass,
    And one to play ;
With the candles mooning each face. . . .   5
    Ah, no ; the years O !
How the sick leaves reel down in throngs !

They clear the creeping moss—
Elders and juniors—aye,
Making the pathways neat   10
    And the garden gay ;
And they build a shady seat. . . .
    Ah, no ; the years, the years ;
See, the white storm-birds wing across !

They are blithely breakfasting all—   15
Men and maidens—yea,
Under the summer tree,
    With a glimpse of the bay,
While pet fowl come to the knee. . . .
    Ah, no ; the years O !   20
And the rotten rose is ript from the wall.

They change to a high new house,
He, she, all of them—aye,
Clocks and carpets and chairs
    On the lawn all day,   25
And brightest things that are theirs. . . .
    Ah, no ; the years, the years ;
Down their carved names the rain-drop ploughs.

Explorations

1. Read the poem through and then read it aloud at the tone and pace that you think suits its mood and thought. How would you describe its mood—wistful, sad, cheerful, regretful, gloomy? The mood emerges from two sets of images, one gay, the other sorrowful. Point out how these two sets of images are played off against each other in each stanza throughout the poem. Having done this do you feel you should revise your idea of what the poem's dominant mood is?

2. Several images tend to build up a feeling of family tenderness and joy. Where are they? Which of them succeed best? Explain.

3. There are also images of decay and transience. Where are these? Are they so powerful as to eclipse the images referred to in question 2? Which of them strike you as most vivid? Why?

4. Do you consider the title appropriate to the poem's mood, atmosphere and feeling? Examine and explain.

5. Note the poet's repeated invocation of ' the years '. What is it meant to convey? Does the evocation take on a greater poignancy as the familial images accumulate?

6. How has the poet structured his thought? Consider the individual stanzas, the manner in which the thought develops from one to the other. Does each stanza in some way re-state and extend the theme of the preceding ones? What is the poem's central theme?

Glossary p. 236

When I set out for Lyonnesse

When I set out for Lyonnesse,
  A hundred miles away,
  The rime was on the spray,
And starlight lit my lonesomeness
When I set out for Lyonnesse   5
  A hundred miles away.

What would bechance at Lyonnesse
  While I should sojourn there
  No prophet durst declare,
Nor did the wisest wizard guess   10
What would bechance at Lyonnesse
  While I should sojourn there.

When I came back from Lyonnesse
  With magic in my eyes,
  All marked with mute surmise   15
My radiance rare and fathomless,
When I came back from Lyonnesse
  With magic in my eyes !

Explorations

1. The poet comes home from Lyonnesse with magic in his eyes. How is the sense of the magical and wonderful built up through the poem ? Point out the words and phrases in which it is especially evident. Read the glossary note on Lyonnesse.

2. Stanzas one and three deal with the going and returning. What happened to the poet in between ? In how far is it defined in stanza two ? Or is it deliberately left in mystery ? Purely from the evidence of the poem, what sort of change was it ?

3. The poet uses a form reminiscent of the ballad. In what way is this particularly appropriate to the linked themes of romance, legend, magic and love ?

4. Read the poem aloud in such a way as to bring out its mood and melody. Would you agree that there is a particularly happy marriage of sound and sense in the poem ? In what lines or phrases is it especially prominent ?

Glossary p. 237

Afterwards

When the Present has latched its postern behind my
    tremulous stay,
  And the May month flaps its glad green leaves like
    wings,
Delicate-filmed as new-spun silk, will the neighbours
    say,
  " He was a man who used to notice such things " ?

If it be in the dusk when, like an eyelid's soundless
    blink,   5
  The dewfall-hawk comes crossing the shades to alight
Upon the wind-warped upland thorn, a gazer may think,
  " To him this must have been a familiar sight."

If I pass during some nocturnal blackness, mothy and
    warm,
  When the hedgehog travels furtively over the lawn,   10
One may say, " He strove that such innocent creatures
    should come to no harm,
  But he could do little for them ; and now he is gone."

If, when hearing that I have been stilled at last, they
    stand at the door,
  Watching the full-starred heavens that winter sees,
Will this thought rise on those who will meet my face no
    more,   15
  " He was one who had an eye for such mysteries " ?

And will any say when my bell of quittance is heard in
    the gloom,
  And a crossing breeze cuts a pause in its outrollings,
Till they rise again, as they were a new bell's boom,
  " He hears it not now, but used to notice such
    things " ?   20

Explorations

1.   Read the poem more than once ; read it aloud to get the rise and fall of its rhythms.   At first glance what is its central theme ?

2.   The poet reflects that his neighbours, after his death, will think of him as a man to whom certain things were important.   What kind of things ?   Take these details one by one and see what they all have in common.   What picture of Hardy the man emerges ?

3.   This is a poem about death, yet how many of the images dealt with in question 2 suggest life ?   How do these images assist the development of the thought ?   Would you agree that the death images increase towards the end of the poem ?

4.   Is this a meditation on death or on life ?   Is it concerned with the value of life in any way ?   Is the poet hopeful or despondent, cheerful or gloomy ?   Support your view by references to key words, phrases or images.

5.   Does the poet believe in *any sort* of immortality ?   If so, precisely what kind of immortality is involved ?

6.   Read a passage aloud.   How appropriate to the thought and mood are the slow lapsing rhythms and the long lines ?

7.   In how far is the poem an exploration of ' mysteries ' ?   Explain.

Glossary p. 237

In Time of " The Breaking of Nations "

Only a man harrowing clods
    In a slow silent walk
With an old horse that stumbles and nods
    Half asleep as they stalk.

Only thin smoke without flame   5
    From the heaps of couch-grass ;
Yet this will go onward the same
    Though Dynasties pass.

Yonder a maid and her wight
    Come whispering by :   10
War's annals will cloud into night
    Ere their story die.

Explorations

1. What is the poem's central theme ? What does the man harrow-
ing with his horse stand for ?

2. What is meant by the ' Dynasties ' in the second stanza ? What
contrast is intended between them and the figures in the first and last
stanzas ? What have the ' maid and her wight ' in common with the
man in the first stanza ? In what way is ' War's annals ' related to
' Dynasties ' ?

3. What is the function of the image in lines 5 and 6 ? Gather this
image into the poem's general meaning.

4. This poem was written in 1915. Does this fact alter or confirm
your opinion of the poem ? Why ?

Glossary p. 237

The Love Song of J. Alfred Prufrock

S'io credesse che mia risposta fosse
A persona che mai tornasse al mondo,
Questa fiamma staria senza piu scosse.
Ma perciocche glammai di questo fondo
Non torno vivo alcun, s'i'odo il vero,
Senza tema d'infamia ti rispondo.

Let us go then, you and I,
When the evening is spread out against the sky
Like a patient etherised upon a table ;
Let us go, through certain half-deserted streets,
The muttering retreats   5
Of restless nights in one-night cheap hotels
And sawdust restaurants with oyster-shells :
Streets that follow like a tedious argument
Of insidious intent
To lead you to an overwhelming question . . .   10
Oh, do not ask, " What is it ? "
Let us go and make our visit.

In the room the women come and go
Talking of Michelangelo.

The yellow fog that rubs its back upon the window-panes,   15
The yellow smoke that rubs its muzzle on the window-panes
Licked its tongue into the corners of the evening,
Lingered upon the pools that stand in drains,
Let fall upon its back the soot that falls from chimneys,
Slipped by the terrace, made a sudden leap,   20
And seeing that it was a soft October night,
Curled once about the house, and fell asleep.

And indeed there will be time
For the yellow smoke that slides along the street
Rubbing its back upon the window-panes ;   25
There will be time, there will be time
To prepare a face to meet the faces that you meet ;
There will be time to murder and create,
And time for all the works and days of hands
That lift and drop a question on your plate ;   30

Time for you and time for me,
And time yet for a hundred indecisions,
And for a hundred visions and revisions,
Before the taking of a toast and tea.

In the room the women come and go   35
Talking of Michelangelo.

And indeed there will be time
To wonder, " Do I dare ? " and, " Do I dare ? "
Time to turn back and descend the stair,
With a bald spot in the middle of my hair—   40
[They will say : " How his hair is growing thin ! "]
My morning coat, my collar mounting firmly to the chin,
My necktie rich and modest, but asserted by a simple pin—
[They will say : " But how his arms and legs are thin ! "]
Do I dare   45
Disturb the universe ?
In a minute there is time
For decisions and revisions which a minute will reverse.

For I have known them all already, known them all—
Have known the evenings, mornings, afternoons,   50
I have measured out my life with coffee spoons ;
I know the voices dying with a dying fall
Beneath the music from a farther room.
   So how should I presume ?

And I have known the eyes already, known them all—   55
The eyes that fix you in a formulated phrase,
And when I am formulated, sprawling on a pin,
When I am pinned and wriggling on the wall,
Then how should I begin
To spit out all the butt-ends of my days and ways ?   60
   And how should I presume ?

And I have known the arms already, known them all—
Arms that are braceleted and white and bare
[But in the lamplight, downed with light brown hair !]
Is it perfume from a dress   65
That makes me so digress ?

Arms that lie along a table, or wrap about a shawl.
   And should I then presume ?
   And how should I begin ?

     .   .   .   .   .

Shall I say, I have gone at dusk through narrow streets   70
And watched the smoke that rises from the pipes
Of lonely men in shirt-sleeves, leaning out of windows ? . . .

I should have been a pair of ragged claws
Scuttling across the floors of silent seas.

     .   .   .   .   .

And the afternoon, the evening, sleeps so peacefully !   75
Smoothed by long fingers,
Asleep . . . tired . . . or it malingers,
Stretched on the floor, here beside you and me.
Should I, after tea and cakes and ices,
Have the strength to force the moment to its crisis ?   80
But though I have wept and fasted, wept and prayed,
Though I have seen my head [grown slightly bald]
    brought in upon a platter,
I am no prophet—and here's no great matter ;
I have seen the moment of my greatness flicker,
And I have seen the eternal Footman hold my coat, and
    snicker,   85
And in short, I was afraid.

And would it have been worth it, after all,
After the cups, the marmalade, the tea,
Among the porcelain, among some talk of you and me,
Would it have been worth while,   90
To have bitten off the matter with a smile,
To have squeezed the universe into a ball
To roll it toward some overwhelming question,
To say : " I am Lazarus, come from the dead,
Come back to tell you all, I shall tell you all "—   95
If one, settling a pillow by her head,
    Should say : " That is not what I meant at all.
    That is not it, at all."

And would it have been worth it, after all,
Would it have been worth while,   100

After the sunsets and the dooryards and the sprinkled streets,
After the novels, after the teacups, after the skirts that trail
    along the floor—
And this, and so much more ?—
It is impossible to say just what I mean !
But as if a magic lantern threw the nerves in patterns on a
    screen :   105
Would it have been worth while
If one, settling a pillow or throwing off a shawl,
And turning toward the window, should say :
  " That is not it at all,
    That is not what I meant, at all."   110

    .   .   .   .   .   .

No ! I am not Prince Hamlet, nor was meant to be ;
Am an attendant lord, one that will do
To swell a progress, start a scene or two,
Advise the prince ; no doubt, an easy tool,
Deferential, glad to be of use,   115
Politic, cautious, and meticulous ;
Full of high sentence, but a bit obtuse ;
At times, indeed, almost ridiculous—
Almost, at times, the Fool.

I grow old . . . I grow old . . .   120
I shall wear the bottoms of my trousers rolled.

Shall I part my hair behind ? Do I dare to eat a peach ?
I shall wear white flannel trousers, and walk upon the beach.
I have heard the mermaids singing, each to each.

I do not think that they will sing to me.   125

I have seen them riding seaward on the waves
Combing the white hair of the waves blown back
When the wind blows the water white and black.

We have lingered in the chambers of the sea
By sea-girls wreathed with seaweed red and brown   130
Till human voices wake us, and we drown.

Explorations

This poem is regarded by many as one of the very first great modern poems. It is modern in theme because it expresses the confusion and indecision arising from the self-doubt of modern man facing a world in which the traditional religious and social certainties were losing force. It is modern in method, making its impact by means of images and symbols which are not held together by any strict or obvious logic, but by free association of ideas. In other words, the confusion and incoherence of Prufrock's mind and of his world are to some extent reflected in the *apparent* incoherence of the poem. Close study of the poem will reveal that it has a coherence and logic of its own.

1.   As there are some initial obstacles to an understanding of this poem it is advisable to read it through more than once. Then read it through with the help of the glossaries. Pay special attention to the function of the pronouns, ' us ', ' you ', ' I ', ' we ', in the poem.

2.   In the first fourteen lines Prufrock sets out towards his destination, a room in which the women come and go ' Talking of Michelangelo '. What route does he take ? Is it the expected one ? What sort of scenes and images does he encounter on his way ?

3.   The second and third lines give us an image of the world Prufrock inhabits. What sort of world is it ?

4.   The women talk of Michelangelo. Do you get the impression that their conversation about the great painter is profound or trivial ? Can you suggest why the poet makes them talk of Michelangelo ? Be alert for the contrast between Prufrock—especially in his public life— and the other heroic presences in the poem, John the Baptist, Lazarus, Hamlet.

5.   Lines 15 to 22 compare the fog to a cat. Trace the image to its conclusion.   What does the cat symbolise—indolence, sleepiness, sensuality . . . ? What does the passage tell you about Prufrock's world in terms of mood and atmosphere ?

6.   What dominant aspect of Prufrock is suggested in lines 23 to 34 ? Why does time play so important a part in his life ? How is his manner of life suggested ? What is wrong with his life ? Why can't he mend it ? In what sense can he ' murder ' or ' create ' ? Explain the irony involved in ' visions and revisions '. Is one really the opposite of the other ? What have they to do with ' indecisions ' ?

7.   Lines 37 to 48 give us a vivid image of Prufrock's social self. What sort of man is he ? What is the governing trait of his personality ?

Does he ' dare ' do what—make his declaration of love ? Reveal his inner self ? Or does the one necessarily involve the other ? In what sense can he possibly ' Disturb the universe ' ?

8. Trace the references to time in this paragraph. How do they continue and intensify the impression created in lines 23 to 34 ?

9. In lines 49 to 54 the speaker conveys the quality of his daily life. What sort of life is it ? What particular image here focuses it best ? Refer also to lines 23 to 34. Is this life responsible in any way for the inadequacy expressed in line 54 ? Explain.

10. How is this sense of inadequacy and self-consciousness further underlined in the passage that follows ? What is Prufrock comparing himself to in line 57 ? Why does he use an image from entomology ? What is the feeling expressed in line 60—tedium, annoyance, self-disgust ?

11. In lines 62 to 74 Prufrock builds up towards his declaration, his ' overwhelming question ', fails to ask it and relapses into self-contempt. Work out the movement of the thought and the imagery. Can you suggest a reason why he should consider prefacing his question with a reference to ' lonely men in shirt-sleeves, leaning out of windows ' ? Glance back at the opening passage of the poem. Would you agree that Prufrock's self-disgust reaches its nadir in lines 73 and 74 ?

12. Prufrock has apparently failed to put his question. Now from line 75 onwards he seeks to justify his failure to himself. There is a succession of brilliant, bitter ironies in the next eleven lines. Comment on them. Explain in particular the ironic discrepancy between John the Baptist and Prufrock, as well as their points of similarity. Interpret the image of the footman.

13. Perhaps you do not agree with the interpretation advanced in questions 11 and 12, especially in locating the point of crisis. If so, suggest an alternative reading, giving your reasons.

14. Between lines 87 and 110 Prufrock contemplates the possible consequences of his declaration, had he made it. What does he seem most afraid of—the woman's scorn, insensitivity, indifference, incomprehension . . . ? Ponder this one deeply, it is crucial to the poem's meaning.

15. Between lines 111 and 119 Prufrock settles for a lesser version of himself. Show how the passage plunges downwards from ' Prince Hamlet ' to ' Fool '. Read it aloud in the tone you think suits the mood.

16. What is the effect of the deliberate triviality in lines 120 to 124 ? What sort of finality is implied in ' I do not think that they will sing to me ' ? Glance back at the sea imagery in lines 73 and 74 and elsewhere. What do the mermaids represent ? Why won't they sing to Prufrock ? Has he himself destroyed the possibility that they might ? If so, how ?

17. Prufrock—his private and his public self—has ' lingered in the chambers of the sea '. What does he mean by this ? What does the sea represent—his unfulfilled potential, the poetic side of his nature, his heroic possibilities, his dream world . . . ? What, therefore, is meant by his being finally drowned to the sound of ' human voices ' ? Why does Prufrock speak as ' we ' and not ' I ' in the last three lines ?

18. Consider the structure of the poem, taking into account not only its stanza pattern but the four movements into which it is formally divided.

19. This poem is one of the finest poetic statements about the human condition in the modern world. Read it again and again until you absorb its meaning, mood and movement.

Glossary p. 237

A Song for Simeon

Lord, the Roman hyacinths are blooming in bowls and
The winter sun creeps by the snow hills ;
The stubborn season has made stand.
My life is light, waiting for the death wind,
Like a feather on the back of my hand.   5
Dust in sunlight and memory in corners
Wait for the wind that chills towards the dead land.

Grant us thy peace.
I have walked many years in this city,
Kept faith and fast, provided for the poor,   10
Have given and taken honour and ease.
There went never any rejected from my door.
Who shall remember my house, where shall live my children's
    children
When the time of sorrow is come ?
They will take to the goat's path, and the fox's home,   15
Fleeing from the foreign faces and the foreign swords.

Before the time of cords and scourges and lamentation
Grant us thy peace.
Before the stations of the mountain of desolation,
Before the certain hour of maternal sorrow,   20
Now at this birth season of decease,
Let the Infant, the still unspeaking and unspoken Word,
Grant Israel's consolation
To one who has eighty years and no to-morrow.

According to thy word.   25
They shall praise Thee and suffer in every generation
With glory and derision,
Light upon light, mounting the saints' stair.
Not for me the martyrdom, the ecstasy of thought and prayer,
Not for me the ultimate vision.   30
Grant me thy peace.
(And a sword shall pierce thy heart,
Thine also).

I am tired with my own life and the lives of those after me,
I am dying in my own death and the deaths of those after me.   35
Let thy servant depart,
Having seen thy salvation.

Explorations

1.   Read the poem and the gloss on Simeon. How does Eliot suggest
in the first movement of the poem that Simeon stands at a sort of cross-
roads in history ? Examine, for instance, the ideas at work in the
imagery, with special reference to the contrasts.

2.   In the second and third movements Simeon foresees the suffering
of Christ and of his people. What images of suffering are employed ?
Are these images original ? Are they effective ?

3.   What does the poet mean by ' this birth season of decease ' ?
Work it out for yourself before going to the gloss. Consider it in con-
junction with the contrasts of the first movement and the thought of
the last.

4.   Does Simeon regret that he cannot share ' the martyrdom, the
ecstasy of thought and prayer ' ? Explain. What is meant by ' the
ultimate vision ' and why does he say that this also is not for him ?

5.   What kind of ' peace ' does Simeon want ? Explain. How
would you describe the tone of his meditation—ecstatic, regretful,
bitter, weary, resigned . . . ?

6.   Does your awareness that Simeon had the gift of prophecy give
a new and deeper poignancy to his song ? In the poem trace the refer-
ences to past, present and future.

7.   Say, without looking, whether the poem is rhymed. Now
examine it and explain its stanzaic and metrical pattern. Examine the
repetitions. Does this form suit the meditation of a man such as
Simeon ? Show how the thought moves within the poem's structure.

Glossary p. 239

Fern Hill

Now as I was young and easy under the apple boughs
About the lilting house and happy as the grass was green,
    The night above the dingle starry,
      Time let me hail and climb
    Golden in the heydays of his eyes,   5
And honoured among the wagons I was prince of the apple
      towns
And once below a time I lordly had the trees and leaves
    Trail with daisies and barley
    Down the rivers of the windfall light.

And as I was green and carefree, famous among the barns   10
About the happy yard and singing as the farm was home,
    In the sun that is young once only,
      Time let me play and be
    Golden in the mercy of his means,
And green and golden I was huntsman and herdsman, the
      calves   15
Sang to my horn, the foxes on the hills barked clear and cold,
    And the sabbath rang slowly
    In the pebbles of the holy streams.

All the sun long it was running, it was lovely, the hay
Fields high as the house, the tunes from the chimneys, it was
      air   20
    And playing, lovely and watery
      And fire green as grass,
    And nightly under the simple stars
As I rode to sleep the owls were bearing the farm away,
All the moon long I heard, blessed among stables, the nightjars 25
    Flying with the ricks, and the horses
    Flashing into the dark.

And then to awake, and the farm, like a wanderer white
With the dew, come back, the cock on his shoulder : it was all
    Shining, it was Adam and maiden,   30
      The sky gathered again
    And the sun grew round that very day.

So it must have been after the birth of the simple light
In the first, spinning place, the spellbound horses walking warm
    Out of the whinnying green stable   35
        On to the fields of praise.

And honoured among foxes and pheasants by the gay house
Under the new made clouds and happy as the heart was long,
    In the sun born over and over,
        I ran my heedless ways,   40
    My wishes raced through the house high hay
And nothing I cared, at my sky blue trades, that time allows
In all his tuneful turning so few and such morning songs
    Before the children green and golden
        Follow him out of grace,   45

Nothing I cared, in the lamb white days, that time would take
        me
Up to the swallow thronged loft by the shadow of my hand,
    In the moon that is always rising,
        Nor that riding to sleep
I should hear him fly with the high fields   50
And wake to the farm forever fled from the childless land.
Oh as I was young and easy in the mercy of his means,
        Time held me green and dying
        Though I sang in my chains like the sea.

Explorations

1. A good way to begin an exploration of this poem would be to apportion each stanza to a pupil and, after five minutes silent preparation, have it read aloud, giving full value to its sound and resonance.

2. The poem is a celebration of childhood joy, pride and innocence. Identify some of the images which Thomas uses to register each of these qualities throughout the poem.

3. Trace the references to weather in the poem. What impression do these convey? What words denoting light, shade and colour help to give this impression? Is it a convincing backward look at childhood?

4. Would you agree that nature is altogether benign in the poem? If so, how is this feeling achieved? Consider the imagery at the end of

stanza two. In what way is the imagery sacramental ? What other religious or biblical imagery or language can you find in the poem ? What does it contribute in general and in particular ?

5. Would you agree that there is a remarkable blending of sound and sense ? Choose a single stanza and read it aloud so as to bring out this quality. Are the senses of sight and sound confused in certain passages ? What about the last three lines of the second stanza ? Is this confusion deliberate ? successful ?

6. In the poem there are numerous references to the sun, the moon and night. Take the sun first and trace the references to it one by one. In what ways do they work together with the total meaning and mood of the poem ? Study the other references similarly.

7. The poem deals with childhood innocence. Is there any suggestion that this is the innocence of Eden ? How are Genesis and the Creation suggested ? What part does innocence play in the poem's thought and atmosphere ? Follow the thought through the last three stanzas in particular. Is the poem in any sense a prayer ?

8. Would you agree that the poem gives a sense of delighted energy ? How is this achieved—through the forward rush of the adjectives, the activeness of the verbs, the sparkle of the imagery, the fluid punctuation, or is it a combination of these ? Take a stanza in which you sense this energy and analyse how it is achieved. It will help to read aloud.

9. What new thought and feeling enter the poem in the last two stanzas ? Show how it is expressed and developed. How does it affect the vision of innocence and joy of the previous stanzas ? Does it darken or intensify it ?

10. Read Hopkins's *That Nature is a Heraclitean Fire* for the sake of contrast and comparison with this poem in respect of theme, language and imagery.

Glossary p. 239

A Refusal to Mourn

Never until the mankind making
Bird beast and flower
Fathering and all humbling darkness
Tells with silence the last light breaking
And the still hour   5
Is come of the sea tumbling in harness

And I must enter again the round
Zion of the water bead
And the synagogue of the ear of corn
Shall I let pray the shadow of a sound   10
Or sow my salt seed
In the least valley of sackcloth to mourn

The majesty and burning of the child's death.
I shall not murder
The mankind of her going with a grave truth   15
Nor blaspheme down the stations of the breath
With any further
Elegy of innocence and youth.

Deep with the first dead lies London's daughter,
Robed in the long friends,   20
The grains beyond age, the dark veins of her mother,
Secret by the unmourning water
Of the riding Thames.
After the first death, there is no other.

Explorations

1. The poem is a single rush of thought and image to the end of
line 13. The construction of the main clause is ' Never . . . Shall
I let pray . . .' See can you work out the subclauses. If necessary,
consult the glossary for help. Now read it again, responding to the
images as well.

2. Thomas believed that the world and everything in it was perpetually dying and at the same time perpetually being reborn : where is this notion to be found in these opening lines ? Is it vividly or effectively realised ?   Explain.

3. In the second section of the poem Thomas suggests his reasons for not mourning : what, as far as you can judge, are these reasons ? One is suggested in stanza three, the other more directly expressed in the final lines.

4. In what sense can the child's death have ' majesty ' or the speaking of a ' grave truth ' be blasphemy ? In what precise sense is the Thames ' unmourning ', or the dead girl ' Robed in the long friends ' ?

5. Would you agree that while the poem is difficult to unravel in terms of thought and syntax, it delivers its impact vividly on the level of sound and image ? Read it aloud and draw attention to any effects that strike you as especially powerful or expressive in bringing out the central theme.

6. The poem uses biblical and religious language, images and allusions. What sort of tone and atmosphere do these give the poem ? Where do you find them particularly effective ? Do you find any of them mysterious ? If so, would you say the mystery works for or against the poem's purpose ? Be specific.

7. Can you suggest a reason why the first movement of the poem is unpunctuated while the second is punctuated ? Can you connect this with the theme, pace or tone ? Explain.

8. Read the passage in *Lycidas* which begins ' Weep no more, woful Shepherds, weep no more ' and compare it in theme and imagery with this poem.

Glossary p. 240

No Second Troy

Why should I blame her that she filled my days
With misery, or that she would of late
Have taught to ignorant men most violent ways,
Or hurled the little streets upon the great,
Had they but courage equal to desire ?   5
What could have made her peaceful with a mind
That nobleness made simple as a fire,
With beauty like a tightened bow, a kind
That is not natural in an age like this,
Being high and solitary and most stern ?   10
Why, what could she have done, being what she is ?
Was there another Troy for her to burn ?

Explorations

1. The poem, clearly, is about the poet's relation with his beloved,
Maud Gonne. Is it a poem of reproach, admiration, jealousy or
forgiveness ? Does it, perhaps, show traces of all four ? Read it aloud
so as to exhibit its tone and mood.

2. Why has the poet suffered misery ? Who or what has been his
rival in Maud Gonne's affections ? Explain the image in line 4.

3. The poet asserts that his beloved had to act as she did ' being
what she is '. What does he mean by this ? What qualities does he
ascribe to her ? Do you find his similes here especially apt or vivid ?
Explain.

4. In what way does Yeats present Maud Gonne as a woman
singled out by fate ? Trace this idea through the poem. How is this
notion related to the question in line 1 ?

5. What does his reference to Troy tell us about his beloved ?
What does it tell us about the political situation described in the
opening quatrain ?

6. The poem is organised in terms of four rhetorical questions.
What sort of answer is implied in each of these questions ? Examine
how these questions are related to the movement of the quatrains
and the lines.

7. For an example of the same heroic sentiment in Yeats read
his poem *September 1913*.

Glossary p. 240

September 1913

What need you, being come to sense,
But fumble in a greasy till
And add the halfpence to the pence
And prayer to shivering prayer, until
You have dried the marrow from the bone ? 5
For men were born to pray and save :
Romantic Ireland's dead and gone,
It's with O'Leary in the grave.

Yet they were of a different kind,
The names that stilled your childish play, 10
They have gone about the world like wind,
But little time had they to pray
For whom the hangman's rope was spun,
And what, God help us, could they save ?
Romantic Ireland's dead and gone, 15
It's with O'Leary in the grave.

Was it for this the wild geese spread
The grey wing upon every tide ;
For this that all that blood was shed,
For this Edward Fitzgerald died, 20
And Robert Emmet and Wolfe Tone,
All that delirium of the brave ?
Romantic Ireland's dead and gone,
It's with O'Leary in the grave.

Yet could we turn the years again, 25
And call those exiles as they were
In all their loneliness and pain,
You'd cry, " Some woman's yellow hair
Has maddened every mother's son " :
They weighed so lightly what they gave, 30
But let them be, they're dead and gone,
They're with O'Leary in the grave.

Explorations

1. You may find it helpful to read the note on this poem in the glossary.

2. Describe the tone of the opening stanza. Is it angry, contemptuous, bitter . . . ? Where is the tone most vividly in evidence ? Explain the ambiguity and then the irony in line 6.

3. The second stanza calls up a vision of different men with different attitudes to life. Explain the contrast. What has this vision to do with Romantic Ireland ' and O'Leary ? Explain the meaning of ' save ' in line 14. Glance back again at line 6.

4. Would you agree that the feeling in the poem reaches its climax in stanza three ? What is the effect of the historical allusions, the proper names ? Is there a feeling of generous admiration in the lift of the lines ? Discuss this aspect of the poem and how it relates to the feeling in the first stanza. What do you make of the phrase 'All that delirium of the brave ' ?

5. In the final stanza Yeats asserts that his opponents, even if confronted with the patriots, would not be able to understand their generosity. Work out the thought and mood of the stanza. How would you interpret lines 28 and 29 ? (See glossary.)

6. In the contrast between meanness and generosity, which is more vividly realised ? Point out specific phrases or images.

7. Read the poem through as a whole and explain what the poet means by ' Romantic Ireland '. Can you find any echo of the theme in *No Second Troy* ? Explain. Read *The Fisherman* with similar considerations in mind.

8. Comment on the structure of the poem, bearing in mind the repetitions, rhyme scheme and rhythm. Does the poem gain or lose by the refrain ?

Glossary p. 241

The Fisherman

Although I can see him still,
The freckled man who goes
To a grey place on a hill
In grey Connemara clothes
At dawn to cast his flies,   5
It's long since I began
To call up to the eyes
This wise and simple man.
All day I'd looked in the face
What I had hoped 'twould be   10
To write for my own race
And the reality ;
The living men that I hate,
The dead man that I loved,
The craven man in his seat,   15
The insolent unreproved,
And no knave brought to book
Who has won a drunken cheer,
The witty man and his joke
Aimed at the commonest ear,   20
The clever man who cries
The catch-cries of the clown,
The beating down of the wise
And great Art beaten down.

Maybe a twelvemonth since   25
Suddenly I began,
In scorn of this audience,
Imagining a man,
And his sun-freckled face,
And grey Connemara cloth,   30
Climbing up to a place
Where stone is dark under froth,
And the down-turn of his wrist
When the flies drop in the stream ;
A man who does not exist,   35
A man who is but a dream ;

And cried, " Before I am old
I shall have written him one
Poem maybe as cold
And passionate as the dawn."   40

Explorations

1.   The poem begins and ends with an ideal picture of a ' wise and
simple ' fisherman, living and working in a quiet world of nature.
How does this man differ from the people described in lines 15 to 24 ?
Examine the phrases and images in which this distinction is conveyed.

2.   In lines 10 to 13 the poet draws a distinction between what his
hopes as an Irish writer had been and ' the reality '. Is he distressed
by ' the reality ' ? What does he mean by the last two lines of the first
stanza ? See the glossary.

3.   Yeats is distressed that his efforts to give his country ' great Art '
—literature, drama, art galleries—are met with hostility and indiffer-
ence. (See biographical note on Yeats and the note on *September 1913*.)
He decides to take refuge in his imagination. Show how this decision
is expressed in the second stanza. What does his fisherman symbolise ?

4.   In what tone are the last four lines of the poem expressed—
bitter, resolute, ironic, hopeful . . . ? Can you explain why the poem
will be both ' cold ' and ' passionate ' ? Are these qualities present in
this poem ?

5.   In what respects does the tone of the poem vary ? Read it aloud.
Examine the poem's metre. Would you agree that the beat varies in
vehemence as the poet moves from reverie to satire and back again ?

6.   Another poem in which Yeats expresses the difference between
his ideal for Ireland and ' the reality ' is *September 1913*. Read it for the
sake of comparison. Also read *No Second Troy*.

7.   Yeats obviously prizes the seemingly contradictory qualities of
coldness and passion in poetry. Take any one of his poems and explore
the extent to which these qualities are combined in it.

Glossary p. 241

Sailing to Byzantium

That is no country for old men. The young
In one another's arms, birds in the trees
—Those dying generations—at their song,
The salmon-falls, the mackerel-crowded seas,
Fish, flesh, or fowl, commend all summer long   5
Whatever is begotten, born, and dies.
Caught in that sensual music all neglect
Monuments of unageing intellect.

An aged man is but a paltry thing,
A tattered coat upon a stick, unless   10
Soul clap its hands and sing, and louder sing
For every tatter in its mortal dress,
Nor is there singing school but studying
Monuments of its own magnificence ;
And therefore I have sailed the seas and come   15
To the holy city of Byzantium.

O sages standing in God's holy fire
As in the gold mosaic of a wall,
Come from the holy fire, perne in a gyre,
And be the singing-masters of my soul.   20
Consume my heart away ; sick with desire
And fastened to a dying animal
It knows not what it is ; and gather me
Into the artifice of eternity.

Once out of nature I shall never take   25
My bodily form from any natural thing,
But such a form as Grecian goldsmiths make
Of hammered gold and gold enamelling
To keep a drowsy Emperor awake ;
Or set upon a golden bough to sing   30
To lords and ladies of Byzantium
Of what is past, or passing, or to come.

Explorations

1. In this poem Yeats explores—as Keats had done in *Ode on a Grecian Urn*—the changing life of the natural world and the immortality of art. You may find it helpful to read the glossary note on Byzantium and what it meant to Yeats. Now, having read the poem through, examine how in the first stanza he portrays the changing world of nature. What ambiguity is involved in ' dying generations ' ? What is the effect of the other images of fertility and death ? How are they contrasted with ' Monuments of unageing intellect ' ? Why is Ireland ' no country for old men ' ?

2. Work out the contrast between the soul and the body expressed in the second stanza. What has this contrast to do with ' Monuments of its own magnificence ' ? Is the voyage to Byzantium real or imagined ?

3. In stanza three the poet entreats the sages, represented in the mosaic, first to ' be the singing-masters ' of his soul, and also to ' gather ' him into the ' artifice of eternity '. Explain both these ideas and relate them to the ideas of change and permanence enunciated in the previous stanzas. Glance back at question 2 and at the glossaries on stanza three.

4. What does the poet mean by ' out of nature ' in the final stanza ? Why does the poet wish for the ' form ' of a golden bird ? Because of its beauty, rareness, immortality, perfection . . . ? Why, when having taken such shape, does he wish to sing of ' what is past, or passing, or to come ' ? Review the whole poem with this in mind.

5. Trace how the poet has structured his thought from the opening line to the end, noting how he has balanced the notion of flux in life and death against the ideal of permanence through art.

6. Analyse the rhyme and metre structure of one stanza and show how this design has been carried through the poem.

7. Read Keats's *Ode on a Grecian Urn* and compare the two poems in terms of theme and structure. In doing so consider how each of them has achieved an eternal artifact in words.

Glossary p. 242

Among School Children

I walk through the long schoolroom questioning ;
A kind old nun in a white hood replies ;
The children learn to cipher and to sing,
To study reading-books and histories,
To cut and sew, be neat in everything   5
In the best modern way—the children's eyes
In momentary wonder stare upon
A sixty-year-old smiling public man.

I dream of a Ledaean body, bent
Above a sinking fire, a tale that she   10
Told of a harsh reproof, or trivial event
That changed some childish day to tragedy—
Told, and it seemed that our two natures blent
Into a sphere from youthful sympathy,
Or else, to alter Plato's parable,   15
Into the yolk and white of the one shell.

And thinking of that fit of grief or rage
I look upon one child or t'other there
And wonder if she stood so at that age—
For even daughters of the swan can share   20
Something of every paddler's heritage—
And had that colour upon cheek or hair,
And thereupon my heart is driven wild :
She stands before me as a living child.

Her present image floats into the mind—   25
Did Quattrocento finger fashion it
Hollow of cheek as though it drank the wind
And took a mess of shadows for its meat ?
And I though never of Ledaean kind
Had pretty plumage once—enough of that,   30
Better to smile on all that smile, and show
There is a comfortable kind of old scarecrow.

What youthful mother, a shape upon her lap
Honey of generation had betrayed,
And that must sleep, shriek, struggle to escape   35
As recollection or the drug decide,
Would think her son, did she but see that shape
With sixty or more winters on its head,
A compensation for the pang of his birth,
Or the uncertainty of his setting forth ?   40

Plato thought nature but a spume that plays
Upon a ghostly paradigm of things ;
Solider Aristotle played the taws
Upon the bottom of a king of kings ;
World-famous golden-thighed Pythagoras   45
Fingered upon a fiddle-stick or strings
What a star sang and careless Muses heard :
Old clothes upon old sticks to scare a bird.

Both nuns and mothers worship images,
But those the candles light are not as those   50
That animate a mother's reveries,
But keep a marble or a bronze repose.
And yet they too break hearts—O Presences
That passion, piety or affection knows,
And that all heavenly glory symbolise--   55
O self-born mockers of man's enterprise ;

Labour is blossoming or dancing where
The body is not bruised to pleasure soul,
Nor beauty born out of its own despair,
Nor blear-eyed wisdom out of midnight oil.   60
O chestnut-tree, great-rooted blossomer,
Are you the leaf, the blossom or the bole ?
O body swayed to music, O brightening glance,
How can we know the dancer from the dance ?

Explorations

1. This is regarded by many as Yeats's greatest poem ; it is certainly one of his most complex. It is an intense meditation on a theme that he explored constantly in his later poems. Looking at the children he reflects that both he and his beloved, Maud Gonne, had once been young like them and he goes on to contemplate the relation between the ageing body and the immortal soul. He thinks of how human beings, despite human decay, manage to preserve ideal ' images ', the mother of her child, the lover of his beloved. Like the images before which nuns pray, these ' Presences ' are both perfect and indestructible ; they symbolise ' heavenly glory '. In the final stanza the poet calls up two images in which there is complete unity and harmony of being, the dancer and the chestnut-tree. Read the poem through several times, with the help of the glossary, and feel your way into its mood and thought. For the moment it is perhaps better not to worry too much about the knottier difficulties.

2. The meditation of the first four stanzas has the classroom for its setting. Trace the theme of childhood and old age as it proceeds through them. What sets the meditation in motion ? How does the ' momentary wonder ' of the children call up the image of Maud Gonne, first as child, then as old woman ?

3. Why is the poet's heart ' driven wild ' ? What is his reaction to the present image of Maud Gonne ? How does the poet accommodate his inner grief to his outward appearance ?

4. Would you agree that there is a remarkable blend of recollection, thought, passion and humour in these four stanzas ? If so, show where each appears and how the blend is achieved. Discuss how the scene in the classroom frames the experience.

5. There are some superb lines and images in these four stanzas. Point out those that strike you especially. Say why you respond to them and how they contribute to the unfolding of the poem's thought up to this point. In what sense is this first half of the poem dramatic ?

6. Stanza five moves the poem into a new phase. What is its central thought ? How does this thought extend the meditation of the first four stanzas ? In answering these questions read the glossary and question 1 again.

7. Is there a change of tone in stanza five ? If so, can you account for it ?

8. Explain, perhaps with the help of the glossary, the thought in stanza six. How does it develop or extend the thought of the previous

five stanzas ? What is the significance of the scarecrow image ? Where else in the poem does this occur ? Is there a connection between these images ? What does the poet intend by the repetition ?

9. In stanza seven the poet refers to images. What sort of images ' animate a mother's reveries ' ? What sort of images do nuns ' worship ' ?

10. The poet writes first of those images worshipped by nuns and mothers. He then refers to the images as ' Presences ' which seem to have eternal existence and reality. Is there a change of tone as his thought moves towards the supernatural ? Does he speak of the Presences with wonder, pleasure, bitterness, exaltation . . . ? In what sense are they ' self-born ' ? How do they mock ' man's enterprise ' ?

11. Is the poet's reference to the ' self-born mockers of man's enterprise ' directly connected with the philosophers in stanza six, or the mother in stanza five, the lovers and the ' kind old nun ' in the first four stanzas ? Explain.

12. In the first four lines of the last stanza the poet names three attitudes to life that undermine its fullness and its harmony : the life of mortification, despair at the passing of beauty, exhausting scholarship. Can you connect each of these with some person or attitude already mentioned in the poem ? In what sense are the dancer and the tree images for the opposite ideals of harmony and fullness ?

13. Read *Sailing to Byzantium* for another approach to and treatment of the themes of youth, old age and immortality.

Glossary p. 242

The Circus Animals' Desertion

I sought a theme and sought for it in vain,
I sought it daily for six weeks or so.
Maybe at last, being but a broken man,
I must be satisfied with my heart, although
Winter and summer till old age began   5
My circus animals were all on show,
Those stilted boys, that burnished chariot,
Lion and woman and the Lord knows what.

What can I but enumerate old themes ?
First that sea-rider Oisin led by the nose   10
Through three enchanted islands, allegorical dreams,
Vain gaiety, vain battle, vain repose,
Themes of the embittered heart, or so it seems,
That might adorn old songs or courtly shows ;
But what cared I that set him on to ride,   15
I, starved for the bosom of his faery bride ?

And then a counter-truth filled out its play,
The Countess Cathleen was the name I gave it ;
She, pity-crazed, had given her soul away,
But masterful Heaven had intervened to save it.   20
I thought my dear must her own soul destroy,
So did fanaticism and hate enslave it,
And this brought forth a dream and soon enough
This dream itself had all my thought and love.

And when the Fool and Blind Man stole the bread   25
Cuchulain fought the ungovernable sea ;
Heart-mysteries there, and yet when all is said
It was the dream itself enchanted me :
Character isolated by a deed
To engross the present and dominate memory.   30
Players and painted stage took all my love,
And not those things that they were emblems of.

Those masterful images because complete
Grew in pure mind, but out of what began?
A mound of refuse or the sweepings of a street,   35
Old kettles, old bottles, and a broken can,
Old iron, old bones, old rags, that raving slut
Who keeps the till. Now that my ladder's gone,
I must lie down where all the ladders start,
In the foul rag-and-bone shop of the heart.   40

Explorations

1. This poem can be read both as Yeats's testimony as an artist and
as a man looking back over his life's work. Read it through, with the
help of the glossaries, and be especially alert to the idea that Yeats has
neglected the needs of his own heart in creating his works of literature.

2. Show how the predicament of the poet is announced in the first
stanza. What attitude to his creations is involved in the phrase ' My
circus animals ' ? Are there other such phrases ?

3. In what sense is the second stanza an extension of the meditation
in the first ? Why does Yeats call the gaiety, battle and repose of
Oisin's wanderings ' vain ' ? Because Oisin's wanderings were ulti-
mately fruitless ? Because these creations were of the mind, not of the
heart ? Because they were imagined not lived ? Because they were
written out of pride and not love . . . ? Does line 16 help you to an
answer ?

4. The ' Countess Cathleen ' is a ' counter-truth ' in that her pity
for the poor comes from the heart, whereas Yeats's literary enterprises
come from the mind and are vain. What contrast is made with Maud
Gonne's attitudes ? Is there any similarity between her dedication to
politics and the poet's to art ? Ponder this a little.

5. When Yeats writes that ' this brought forth a dream ', what has
he in mind ? Is it the inspiration for a new poetic work ? Or is the
poet in fact worried because he has been constantly turning the real
stuff of life into the ' dream ' of art ? Or can you suggest another
explanation ? When answering, glance back at questions 2 and 3.

6. What does Yeats mean in stanza four by ' It was the dream
itself enchanted me ' ? In what way is the dream distinguished from
the ' Heart-mysteries ' ? Is the poem's central idea to some extent
summarised in lines 31 and 32 ? Explain. Glance back at question 1.

7. In the final stanza the poet asserts that the images which he perfected in his work ' Grew in pure mind ', but he suggests that they had their real beginnings elsewhere. Read the glossary for this stanza. Explain the imagery in lines 35 to 37. What do you understand by his suggestion that all the ladders begin ' In the foul rag-and-bone shop of the heart ' ?

8. The poet imagines himself at the end as lying down among rags and bones. Glancing back over the poem does it strike you that the poet is pleased or disappointed with his life ? Is there pleasure, zest or weariness in the way he describes his work in the theatre ? In what sense is his claim to be ' a broken man ' borne out in the entirety of the poem ? How would you describe the tone of the poem ? Is it consistent throughout ?

9. Read and study *Sailing to Byzantium* and discuss in how far it is a contradiction or a confirmation of the poet's outlook here.

Glossary p. 243

The Lost Heifer

When the black herds of the rain were grazing
In the gap of the pure cold wind
And the watery hazes of the hazel
Brought her into my mind,
I thought of the last honey by the water   5
That no hive can find.

Brightness was drenching through the branches
When she wandered again,
Turning the silver out of dark grasses
Where the skylark had lain,   10
And her voice coming softly over the meadow
Was the mist becoming rain.

Explorations

1. What is there in this poem that evokes the Irish landscape and weather ? Show how the details of image and phrase work together to build the picture.

2. Read the poem aloud. How would you describe its mood ? Is it consistent throughout the poem ?

3. How much of the picture is built up of colour, light and shade ? In what ways do these contribute to the mood ?

4. Consider the metaphors used by the poet. Do they effectively convey the mood of the poet's recollection ? Which metaphor appeals to you most and why ?

5. What do you make of the implied metaphor in lines 5 and 6 ? Does the poet merely mean the rare wild honey which the hand of man will never touch ? Can you think of another meaning ?

6. Is it possible that the lost heifer is a symbol for something or someone else ? Consider the tone in which she is evoked. Is it affectionate, tender, admiring . . . ?

7. Examine the structure of the thought. Is there a sense of completeness in the poem ? Consider the first and last lines. Is a progression in time suggested ?

8. The poem has a very elaborate and ingenious sound pattern. Read it aloud and then show how the poet uses rhyme, line-length

and sound correspondence in the shaping of his lyric. Begin, perhaps, by tracing the ' ay ' sound through the poem. Read also Exploration 7 on *The Blackbird of Derrycairn*.

9. Read *The Blackbird of Derrycairn* and compare it with the present poem in terms of both theme and technique.

The Blackbird of Derrycairn

Stop, stop and listen for the bough top
Is whistling and the sun is brighter
Than God's own shadow in the cup now !
Forget the hour-bell. Mournful matins
Will sound as well, Patric, at nightfall.   5

Faintly through mist of broken water
Fionn heard my melody in Norway,
He found the forest track, he brought back
This beak to gild the branch and tell, there,
Why men must welcome in the daylight.   10

He loved the breeze that warns the black grouse,
The shout of gillies in the morning
When packs are counted and the swans cloud
Loch Erne, but more than all those voices,
My throat rejoicing from the hawthorn.   15

In little cells behind a cashel,
Patric, no handbell has a glad sound.
But knowledge is found among the branches.
Listen ! The song that shakes my feathers
Will thong the leather of your satchels.   20

Stop, stop and listen for the bough top
Is whistling . . .

Explorations

1. This is a translation from the Irish of a poem in a sequence known as the ' Colloquy of the Old Men '. The Fenian poet Oisin debates with St. Patrick the merits of paganism and christianity. What details in the poem establish time and place ?

2. There seems to be a contrast between the blackbird's song and Patric's religious way of life. Read the poem carefully and show how this contrast is made. What things in life does the bird stand for ? In what way are they associated with Fionn ? What precisely does Patric stand for ? Do you think that his values are presented fairly ?

3. Explain how in the first stanza ' God's own shadow ' can be bright. Is the paradox deliberate ? What ' cup ' has the poet in mind ? In what way does this complex image establish the theme of the poem ?

4. In what sense does the bird ' gild the branch ' ? What is the significance of the message it brought ? How does it contrast with the message of christianity as represented in the poem—for instance in lines 4 and 5 ?

5. How do the nature images in stanza three contribute to the general theme ? Which of the images strikes you as especially vivid ?

6. What kind of ' knowledge ' is found among the branches in the fourth stanza ? How does it differ from that of the cells and the satchels ? Consider the repetition in the final lines.

7. Read the poem aloud carefully so as to catch its sound patterns. Now look and see how these sound effects are achieved. Note, for instance, how in the first stanza the poet uses : (*a*) cross-rhyme— ' bough top '/' cup now ' ; (*b*) assonance—' brighter '/' nightfall ', and the more unexpected internal echoes like ' whistling '/' listen ' ; (*c*) alliteration—' Mournful matins ' and so on. Now examine the other stanzas with such hints in mind.

8. Read *The Lost Heifer* for the sake of comparison. Consider, for instance, the poet's attitude to nature, the sound patterns used, the theme and technique.

Glossary p. 244

The Planter's Daughter

When night stirred at sea
And the fire brought a crowd in,
They say that her beauty
Was music in mouth
And few in the candlelight   5
Thought her too proud,
For the house of the planter
Is known by the trees.

Men that had seen her
Drank deep and were silent,   10
The women were speaking
Wherever she went—
As a bell that is rung
Or a wonder told shyly
And O she was the Sunday   15
In every week.

Explorations

1.   In this simple lyric the beauty of the planter's daughter is
registered indirectly. Show the different ways in which this is done.

2.   Identify the metaphors and similes used to imply her beauty.
Examine these singly and say what each conveys to you.   What are
the implications of lines 7 and 8 ?

3.   Different kinds of response are described in stanza two. What
do these imply about the people who admired the planter's daughter ?

4.   What sort of community does the poem evoke ? What details
suggest the setting ? What is the effect of the poet's indirect treat-
ment of his subject ?

5.   Read question 7 on *The Blackbird of Derrycairn* and then describe
the sound pattern of the present poem. You may find it helpful to
read it aloud.

Glossary p. 244

Stony Grey Soil

O stony grey soil of Monaghan
The laugh from my love you thieved ;
You took the gay child of my passion
And gave me your clod-conceived.

You clogged the feet of my boyhood   5
And I believed that my stumble
Had the poise and stride of Apollo
And his voice my thick-tongued mumble.

You told me the plough was immortal !
O green-life-conquering plough !   10
Your mandril strained, your coulter blunted
In the smooth lea-field of my brow.

You sang on steaming dunghills
A song of cowards' brood,
You perfumed my clothes with weasel itch,   15
You fed me on swinish food.

You flung a ditch on my vision
Of beauty, love and truth.
O stony grey soil of Monaghan
You burgled my bank of youth !   20

Lost the long hours of pleasure
All the women that love young men.
O can I still stroke the monster's back
Or write with unpoisoned pen

His name in these lonely verses   25
Or mention the dark fields where
The first gay flight of my lyric
Got caught in a peasant's prayer.

Mullahinsha, Drummeril, Black Shanco—
Wherever I turn I see   30
In the stony grey soil of Monaghan
Dead loves that were born for me.

Explorations

1. What attitude towards his ' stony grey soil ' is expressed in the first five stanzas ? How would you describe the tone of his address— bitter, angry, affectionate . . . ?

2. In what ways do the last three stanzas differ from the first five ? Is there a change of tone in the sixth stanza ? Explain. What does the poet mean by his reference to the ' monster's back ' ? Test all the possible implications of this and the following line.

3. What would you say are the answers to the rhetorical questions asked in lines 23 to 28 ? Think these out carefully.

4. What forms might a ' peasant's prayer ' take ? In what way might it hamper the flight of a poet's lyric ?

5. In what way does the last stanza suggest the answer to the poet's questionings ? Has his love for his native Monaghan been completely destroyed ? What do you make of the paradox in the final line ? Read the poem through again before answering.

6. Take the poem stanza by stanza and explain each of the poet's complaints against his native soil. Which of the complaints strikes you as the most bitter ?

7. This poem is addressed to Kavanagh's native county. What do we learn from it about the man himself? Is there an element of self-hatred in the poem ?

8. Explain the metaphors of the poem one by one.

9. Read *Inniskeen Road* for the sake of comparison and contrast.

Glossary p. 245

Advent

We have tested and tasted too much, lover—
Through a chink too wide there comes in no wonder.
But here in the Advent-darkened room
Where the dry black bread and the sugarless tea
Of penance will charm back the luxury   5
Of a child's soul, we'll return to Doom
The knowledge we stole but could not use.

And the newness that was in every stale thing
When we looked at it as children : the spirit-shocking
Wonder in a black slanting Ulster hill   10
Or the prophetic astonishment in the tedious talking
Of an old fool will awake for us and bring
You and me to the yard gate to watch the whins
And the bog-holes, cart-tracks, old stables where Time begins.

O after Christmas we'll have no need to go searching   15
For the difference that sets an old phrase burning—
We'll hear it in the whispered argument of a churning
Or in the streets where the village boys are lurching.
And we'll hear it among decent men too
Who barrow dung in gardens under trees,   20
Wherever life pours ordinary plenty.
Won't we be rich, my love and I, and please
God we shall not ask for reason's payment,
The why of heart-breaking strangeness in dreeping hedges
Nor analyse God's breath in common statement.   25
We have thrown into the dust-bin the clay-minted wages
Of pleasure, knowledge and the conscious hour—
And Christ comes with a January flower.

Explorations

1. The first stanza presents the poet's desire to return from the
world of adult experience to that of childhood innocence. What has
the Advent fasting to do with this wish ? What does he mean by the
statement in the second line ? Explain the ' penance '/' luxury '
paradox of the fifth line. In what sense can luxury be predicated
of a child's soul ?

2. The notion of ' wonder ' is taken up and developed in the second stanza. Trace the movement of the thought. What has this wonder to do with childhood and innocence ? Why is ' newness ' associated with ' every stale thing ', and ' astonishment ' with ' tedious talking ' ?

3. Explain the last two lines of the second stanza, relating them to the thought of the lines which have gone before. Examine in particular the final phrase of the second stanza and relate ' Time begins ' to childhood innocence on one hand and to Advent on the other.

4. The third movement of the poem presents the poet's vision of the rewards which follow the Advent penance. What are the rewards ? Have they been indicated already in the poem ? Where ?

5. What does the poet mean by ' reason's payment ', ' the clay-minted wages/Of pleasure ' ? In what way are both these contrasted with the ' heart-breaking strangeness ' of the common sights and objects of the countryside ?

6. What relation exists in the poet's mind between penance, innocence, wonder and happiness ?

7. A good deal of the poem's attractiveness comes from the vividness of its detail. Which phrases or images strike you especially ?

8. Kavanagh tended to see this world as a reflection of the Divine. Is this evident here ?

Glossary p. 245

Memory of my Father

Every old man I see
Reminds me of my father
When he had fallen in love with death
One time when sheaves were gathered.

That man I saw in Gardner Street   5
Stumble on the kerb was one,
He stared at me half-eyed,
I might have been his son.

And I remember the musician
Faltering over his fiddle   10
In Bayswater, London,
He too set me the riddle.

Every old man I see
In October-coloured weather
Seems to say to me :   15
" I was once your father."

Explorations

1. Why does every old man remind the poet of his father ? What is the significance of the gathered sheaves and the ' October-coloured weather ' ?

2. What is the theme of the poem—memory of his father or the realisation by the old of the inevitability of death ? Explain.

3. In what sense, do you think, had his father ' fallen in love with death ' ? In answering, you might consider line 4.

4. What is the riddle referred to in line 12 ? Do stanzas two and four suggest an answer ?

5. The poem expresses itself very simply. Is the result vivid or merely commonplace ? Explain with detailed reference to language, rhythm and imagery.

Glossary p. 245

Inniskeen Road : July Evening

The bicycles go by in twos and threes—
There's a dance in Billy Brennan's barn to-night,
And there's the half-talk code of mysteries
And the wink-and-elbow language of delight.
Half-past eight and there is not a spot   5
Upon a mile of road, no shadow thrown
That might turn out a man or woman, not
A footfall tapping secrecies of stone.

I have what every poet hates in spite
Of all the solemn talk of contemplation.   10
Oh, Alexander Selkirk knew the plight
Of being king and government and nation.
A road, a mile of kingdom, I am king
Of banks and stones and every blooming thing.

Explorations

1. Why isn't the poet one of the people going to the dance ? Is he
in some way cut off from the ' half-talk code of mysteries ' and ' the
wink-and-elbow language of delight ' ? If so, why ?

2. Kavanagh states at the beginning of the sestet that he has
' what every poet hates '. What is this ? Does the poem suggest why
poets hate it ?

3. What might the poet mean by ' secrecies of stone ' in line 8 ?
Does it mean the human secrecies referred to in Exploration 1, or the
mysteries of the countryside which the poet, alone in his solitude,
now contemplates, or both ? Or perhaps it means something else ?

4. What is the poem about—the poet's loneliness, the loneliness
of being a poet, the joy of being ruler of ' every blooming thing ' ?
In answering, consider how much joy there is in the poem, and how
much sorrow.

5. Show how the poem combines features of the Shakespearean
and Petrarchan sonnet. Does the movement and the shape of the
thought justify this blend of forms ? Explain. Do you consider that
the thought is successfully completed within the framework ?

6. Read *Stony Grey Soil* and Kavanagh's two canal-bank sonnets
for the sake of contrast and comparison.

Glossary p. 245

Canal Bank Walk

Leafy-with-love banks and the green waters of the canal
Pouring redemption for me, that I do
The will of God, wallow in the habitual, the banal,
Grow with nature again as before I grew.
The bright stick trapped, the breeze adding a third   5
Party to the couple kissing on an old seat,
And a bird gathering materials for the nest for the Word
Eloquently new and abandoned to its delirious beat.
O unworn world enrapture me, enrapture me in a web
Of fabulous grass and eternal voices by a beech,   10
Feed the gaping need of my senses, give me ad lib
To pray unselfconsciously with overflowing speech
For this soul needs to be honoured with a new dress woven
From green and blue things and arguments that cannot be
    proven.

Explorations

1.   The poet sees nature as 'Pouring redemption' for him. What does he mean? Does the poet see nature as a kind of sacrament? In what other phrases is nature seen as a healing agency?

2.   The poet sees it as his duty to 'wallow in the habitual, the banal'. What commonplace things does he present to us in a new light? In what sense do all these body out the poem's central message?

3.   What is the effect of such words as 'delirious', 'enrapture', 'fabulous', 'overflowing'? How do they contrast and interact with the very ordinary objects named and described in the poem? How does this contrast contribute to the poem's total impact?

4.   What does the poet mean by 'unworn world'? Where else in the poem is the notion to be found? How is this idea connected with love? What kind of love is the poet writing about in line 1? In what way is it connected with the 'couple' and the 'bird'?

5.   What do the 'green and blue things' in the final line stand for? Why arguments that 'cannot be proven'?

6.   Is it helpful to know that when the poet wrote this sonnet he had come out of hospital having been very close to death? Read the poem through—perhaps aloud—and see in how far it expresses a new sense of gratitude and wonder at the world.

7.   Read Kavanagh's *Advent* and Hopkins's *The Windhover* for other approaches to the same sort of theme.

Glossary p. 246

Lines written on a Seat on the Grand Canal, Dublin
" Erected to the Memory of Mrs. Dermot O'Brien "

O commemorate me where there is water,
Canal water preferably, so stilly
Greeny at the heart of summer. Brother
Commemorate me thus beautifully.
Where by a lock Niagariously roars   5
The falls for those who sit in the tremendous silence
Of mid-July. No one will speak in prose
Who finds his way to these Parnassian islands.
A swan goes by head low with many apologies,
Fantastic light looks through the eyes of bridges—   10
And look ! a barge comes bringing from Athy
And other far-flung towns mythologies.
O commemorate me with no hero-courageous
Tomb—just a canal-bank seat for the passer-by.

Explorations

1. The poet wishes to be commemorated by a seat on the canal bank that he has loved. Where is this sense of love suggested, implied, or otherwise communicated in the poem ?

2. He asks to be commemorated ' thus beautifully '. What images or phrases convey this sense of beauty ?

3. Do you find a sense of wonder in the poem ? Where is it especially evident ? Point out the words and phrases that convey it. What would you say it stems from ? Read the poet's *Canal Bank Walk* before answering.

4. Why, in fact, does the poet prefer a canal-bank seat to a ' hero-courageous Tomb ' as his memorial ?

5. Consider the structure of the poem and say how skilfully you think the poet has shaped his thought. Think about the sonnet form of the poem, then look, perhaps, at the lines with which the poem opens and closes.

6. Work out the rhyme scheme of the poem. What pattern does it conform to ? How would you describe the sort of rhyme used ? Are they successful rhymes in the poem's context ? Explain.

Glossary p. 246

Another September

Dreams fled away, this country bedroom, raw
With the touch of the dawn, wrapped in a minor peace,
Hears through an open window the garden draw
Long pitch black breaths, lay bare its apple trees,
Ripe pear trees, brambles, windfall-sweetened soil,   5
Exhale rough sweetness against the starry slates.
Nearer the river sleeps St. John's, all toil
Locked fast inside a dream with iron gates.

Domestic Autumn, like an animal
Long used to handling by those countrymen,   10
Rubs her kind hide against the bedroom wall
Sensing a fragrant child come back again
—Not this half-tolerated consciousness
That plants its grammar in her yielding weather
But that unspeaking daughter, growing less   15
Familiar where we fell asleep together.

Wakeful moth-wings blunder near a chair,
Toss their light shell at the glass, and go
To inhabit the living starlight. Stranded hair
Stirs on the still linen. It is as though   20
The black breathing that billows her sleep, her name,
Drugged under judgment, waned and—bearing daggers
And balances—down the lampless darkness they came,
Moving like women : Justice, Truth, such figures.

Explorations

1. Like Thomas Kinsella's other poem in the anthology, *Another September* is dramatic : the poet captures himself in a particular mood, at a particular time and place. He has returned with his wife to the house in which she grew up. The scene is set in the first stanza. Identify the details which build up the sense of time and space. Which strike you as especially vivid ? What is the mood or tone of this first stanza—detached, reflective, gloomy, sad, . . .? How many of the details suggest sleep ? Might any suggest death ?

2. Why, in the second stanza, does Autumn welcome her rather than him ? Because it knows her already ? Because, unlike the poet, she is unthinking and therefore more in harmony with nature ? Why is his consciousness ' half-tolerated '—because he is awake, or is thinking, or is a poet planting ' grammar ' ? What irony is involved in this latter phrase ? With whom is the ' unspeaking daughter ' growing less familiar—with him, or with Autumn ? Examine how the contrast between the man and woman is worked out through this stanza and into the next.

3. Read the third stanza. There is a moment in it when the poet turns from description to vision. Where does it occur ? How is the transition managed ? What is the nature of the vision—is it gloomy, cheerful, threatening, frightening . . . ? What do the figures of the moving women stand for—death, judgement, fate . . . ?

4. What images in this stanza suggest sleep ? Do any suggest death ? Explain. Are the death/sleep images prepared for in the earlier stanzas ?

5. What would you say is the central theme of the poem ? Is this theme conveyed by definition, description or suggestion—or by a combination of all three ? Is it vividly conveyed ? What feeling does the poem chiefly convey to you—dread, dismay, tenderness, protectiveness, uncertainty . . . ?

6. Show how the poet has structured his thought, referring to the manner in which the first and third stanzas ' frame ' the experience of the second. Examine the stanzaic pattern and show what effect its tightness and regularity have on the thought and the impact of the theme.

7. Read *Mirror in February* for the sake of comparison, in terms of tone, theme and dramatic structure.

Glossary p. 246

Mirror in February

The day dawns with scent of must and rain,
Of opened soil, dark trees, dry bedroom air.
Under the fading lamp, half dressed—my brain
Idling on some compulsive fantasy—
I towel my shaven jaw and stop, and stare,   5
Riveted by a dark exhausted eye,
A dry downturning mouth.

It seems again that it is time to learn,
In this untiring, crumbling place of growth
To which, for the time being, I return.   10
Now plainly in the mirror of my soul
I read that I have looked my last on youth
And little more ; for they are not made whole
That reach the age of Christ.

Below my window the awakening trees,   15
Hacked clean for better bearing, stand defaced
Suffering their brute necessities,
And how should the flesh not quail that span for span
Is mutilated more ? In slow distaste
I fold my towel with what grace I can,   20
Not young and not renewable, but man.

Explorations

1. The poem opens dramatically ; the poet places himself in a certain posture in a certain place and in a certain time and season. Identify all of these.

2. The occasion of his return to familiar surroundings and to the awakening orchard tempts the poet to think about age, growth and decay. Why ? What details in his surroundings first prompt these meditations ? What direction does his thought take ?

3. What contrasts does he make between himself and his surroundings ? What conclusions does he draw, first in stanza two, then in stanza three ?

4. The poet realises that he has looked his 'last on youth'. How does he face up to the realisation—with courage, bitterness, good humour, self-mockery, ruefulness . . . ?

5. Comment on the possible meanings of the word 'grace' in the second last line. On what note does the poem end—triumph, defeat, resignation? In what way are we prepared for this ending throughout the poem? Explain.

6. How is the notion of death and decay conveyed—almost simultaneously at times—through the language and imagery? Examine the poem in detail with this in mind.

7. Examine the rhyme scheme of each stanza in turn. Is it regular throughout? What is the effect of such irregularities as you can discern? How is the sense of summary and finality achieved in the last two lines?

8. Read *Another September* for a meditation in the same sort of setting.

NOTES AND GLOSSARIES

The Canterbury Tales

1 *shoures* — showers.
  sote — sweet.
2 *perced to the rote* — pierced to the root.
3 *veyne* — vine.
  swich licour — such liquor, sap.
4 *engendred* — begotten.
  flour — flower.
5 *Zephirus* — the west wind.
  eek — also.
6 *holt* — small wood, copse.
  heeth — heath.
7 *sonne* — sun.
8 *Ram* — the first sign of the Zodiac, March 21–April 21.
10 *yë* — eyes.
11 *priketh* — pricks, spurs.
  hem — them.
  hir corages — their hearts.
12 *longen* — want, long for.
13 *palmers* — pilgrims. Pilgrims from the Holy Land carried a palm branch in their hands.
  straunge strondes — strange lands.
14 *ferne halwes* — distant shrines.
  couthe in sondry londes — known in various countries.
16 *Caunterbury* — Canterbury, the scene of the martyrdom of St. Thomas à Becket.
18 *holpen* — helped.
  seke — sick.
19 *Bifel* — it happened.
20 *Tabard* — the Tabard Inn in Southwark where Chaucer stayed on the way to Canterbury.
25–26 *by aventure y-falle/In felawshipe* — ' by chance, fell into company.'
27 *wolden* — would.
28 *wyde* — wide, spacious.
29 *And wel . . . beste* — ' we were entertained with the best of everything.'
31 *everichon* — everyone.
33 *made forward* — suggested, planned.
34 *devyse* — wish, propose.
35 *natheles* — nonetheless.
36 *Er that I . . . pace* — ' before I progress any further with this story.'
45 *chivalrye* — chivalry.

47 *werre* — war.
48 *hadde* — had.
ferre — farther.
49 *hethenesse* — heathen lands.
51 *Alisaundre* — the siege of Alexandria in 1365.
52 *bord bigonne* — sat at the top of the table.
53 *Pruce* — Prussia.
54 *Lettow* — Lithuania.
reysed — campaigned.
Ruce — Russia.
56 *Gernade* — Granada.
sege — siege.
57 *Algezir* — Algeciras.
Belmarye — Benamarin, a Moorish kingdom in north Africa.
58 *Lyeys* — the modern town of Ayas in Armenia.
Satalye — Attalia, the modern Adalia on the coast of Turkey.
59 *Grete See* — Mediterranean.
60 *aryve* — landing, disembarkation of soldiers.
62 *Tramissene* — the Moorish kingdom.
64 *ilke* — very, same.
65 *Palatye* — Palatia, in Turkey.
67 *prys* — reputation, renown.
69 *mayde* — maid.
70 *no vileinye ne sayde* — he never spoke rudely.
71 *maner wight* — kind of man.
73 *his array* — his dress.
74 *hors* — horses.
nat gay — not gaudily dressed.
75 *fustian* — a coarse cotton cloth.
gipoun — a short doublet or tunic.
76 *bismotered* — stained, spotted.
habergeoun — coat of mail.
77 *viage* — travels.
80 *lovyere* — lover.
81 *lokkes crulle* — curly hair.
leyd in presse — as if they had been pressed.
83 *evene lengthe* — moderate height.
84 *deliver* — agile, nimble.
85 *chivachye* — an expedition by mounted soldiers.
86 *Flaundres* — Flanders.
Artoys — Artois.
Picardye — Picardy.
87 *as of so litel space* — considering his short service.
89 *Embrouded* — embroidered.
mede — meadow.

91 *floytinge* — fluting.
95 *endyte* — compose.
96 *Juste* — joust.
   purtreye — draw.
97 *by nightertale* — by dawn.
100 *carf biforn* — carved before.
101 *Yeman* — yeoman.
   namo — no other.
102 *him liste ryde so* — he preferred to travel so.
104 *pecok-arwes* — peacock-feathered arrows.
105 *bar* — bore.
106 *takel* — equipment, weapons, especially arrows.
109 *not-heed* — nut head, with closely cropped hair.
110 *wel coude he al the usage* — he understood thoroughly.
111 *bracer* — an arm-guard used in archery.
112 *bokeler* — buckler, a small shield.
114 *Harneised* — mounted.
115 *A Cristofre* — a medal of St. Christopher, the patron saint of
   foresters.
116 *bawdrik* — baldric, a sword belt.
117 *forster* — forester, similar to the modern gamekeeper.
   soothly — truly.
120 *ooth* — oath.
   sëynt Loy — Saint Loy ; St. Eloi lived in France in the seventh
   century, and after resigning his post as Master of the Mint
   in France he became a priest and ultimately a bishop in
   Flanders.
121 *cleped* — named.
123 *Entuned* — intoned.
124 *fetisly* — elegantly.
125 *After the scole of Stratford atte Bowe* — ' according to the school of
   Stratford-at-Bowe.' This was the name of a priory outside
   London, and French was probably taught at the school there.
127 *At mete wel y-taught was she* — ' at meals she was well taught ',
   i.e., she had good table manners.
128 *leet* — let.
129 *Ne wette hir fingres in hir sauce depe* — ' nor did she wet her fingers
   deeply in her sauce.'
130–131 *Wel coude . . . brest* — ' well could she handle a morsel and
   make sure that no drop ever fell on her breast.'
132 *In curteisye . . . lest* — ' courtesy was her particular interest.'
134 *ferthing* — trace.
136 *Ful semely . . . raughte* — ' she reached politely for her food.'
137 *sikerly* — certainly.
   greet disport — cheerful.

138   *amiable of port* — of amiable disposition.
139–140 *And peyned . . . manere* — ' she tried hard to copy the behaviour of court and be stately in manner.'
141   *holden digne* — worthy of respect.
146   *houndes* — religious were forbidden to keep household pets.
147   *wastel-breed* — fine bread.
149   *smoot it with a yerde smerte* — ' hit it smartly with a stick.'
151   *Ful semely . . . was* — ' her wimple was pleated very neatly.'
      wimpel — a garment covering the head and neck of a woman.
152   *tretys* — shapely.
154   *But sikerly . . . forheed* — ' she certainly had a good forehead.'
155   *a spanne brood* — a span in breadth, i.e., the width of a hand.
      I trowe — I believe.
156   *nat undergrowe* — not undersized.
157   *Ful fetis . . . war* — ' her cloak was very neat, as I was aware.'
159   *A peire of bedes . . . grene* — a pair of rosary beads, with large green stones. Religious were forbidden to wear jewellery.
      gauded — having larger or dividing beads. Obviously the larger beads of green were used for the Our Fathers.
160   *And ther-on . . . shene* — ' and on this there hung a brooch of shining gold.'

Sonnet No. 15

2   *Holds in* — take these words as a single verb, in the sense of ' contains ' or ' retains '.
3   *shows* — plays, shadows, representations.
4   *secret . . . comment* — in Shakespeare's day the stars were believed to influence men's actions ; in this case they are seen as spectators witnessing and commenting on the drama of human life which they secretly control.
6   *Cheered and check'd* — encouraged and retarded. The audience sometimes cheer the players and sometimes interrupt them, just as the changes from night to day, and from season to season, encourage and retard the growth of plants.
9   *conceit* — realisation.
      inconstant — transient.
14   *I engraft you new* — ' I give you a new life ', i.e., in his poetry.

Sonnet No. 23

1   *unperfect* — not well versed in his lines.
2   *is put besides his part* — is ill at ease in his part.

5 *for fear of trust* — 'fearing to trust myself'.
10 *presagers* — prophets, spokesmen.
12 *More . . . express'd* — 'more than the poems of another which express love for you.'

Sonnet No. 29

2 *beweep* — bemoan, lament.
3 *bootless* — useless.
7 *art* — talent.
  scope — skill.

Sonnet No. 30

6 *dateless* — endless.
8 *sight* — sigh. There was an old belief that excessive sighing affected the health. The line here means ' I lament the sighs that wasted me long ago.'
9 *foregone* — gone before.
10 *tell* — count.
11 *fore-bemoaned* — already lamented.

Sonnet No. 55

2 *rime* — rhyme, poetry.
3 *these contents* — in this poetry.
6 *broils* — quarrels.
9 *all-oblivious enmity* — ' everything that would cause you to be forgotten.'
13 *till . . . arise* — ' until the day of judgment when you will arise.'

Sonnet No. 60

2 *our minutes* — our lives.
4 *sequent* — following one another.
  contend — strive.
5 *the main of light* — the world of light. See the image of waves in line 1.

7 *Crooked* — malignant.
  eclipses — believed to bring ill-luck, especially at sea. See 'Lycidas', line 101.
8 *confound* — destroy.
9 *transfix* — destroy.
13 *times in hope* — times in my imagination.

Sonnet No. 64

1 *fell* — cruel, destructive.
1–2 The general sense of these two lines is clear enough, but their syntax has puzzled scholars. They may be crudely summarised like this : 'when I see the damage which time has inflicted on the ruins and burial monuments of ancient times.'
4 *brass* — a symbol of durability.
  mortal rage — the rage of death.
9 *state* — condition, state.
10 *state* — majesty, authority.
  confounded — doomed.

Sonnet No. 65

4 *action* — power to preserve itself.
6 *wrackful* — destructive.
10 *Time's best jewel* — the poet's beloved. The image of a jewel in its casket is a favourite one with Shakespeare.
  Time's chest — the coffin, death.
13 *unless . . . might* — 'unless I can live poetically and truthfully.'

Sonnet No. 73

4 *late* — lately.
8 *Death's second self* — black night.
9–12 He sees his life in terms of a fire smothered by its own ashes.
13 *thou* — his beloved.

Sonnet No. 86

3 *inhearse* — stifle, imprison.
5 *by spirits taught to write* — the rival to whom Shakespeare is referring in this sonnet may have been Chapman (1559–1634), who claimed to have been inspired by Homer's ghost.

7   *compeers* — equals, associates.
8   *astonished* — amazed, stunned.
9   *affable familiar ghost* — see note on line 5.
10   *gulls* — fools or tricks.
13   *when your countenance fill'd up his line* — 'when I saw that he had successfully created an image of you in his poetry.'
14   *Then lack'd I . . . enfeebled mine* — 'I felt that my inspiration had been taken away.'

Sonnet No. 87

2   *estimate* — value, worth.
3   *charter* — deed conferring certain rights or privileges, in this case liberty.
4   *bonds* — binding agreements.
     determinate — expired, out of date.
8   *patent* — literally, letter patent; here 'the grant of my right to your love is revoked'.
     swerving — returning (to you).
11   *misprision* — misapprehension.
14   *no such matter* — no such thing.

Sonnet No. 116

2   *impediments* — obstacles, something that might make a marriage invalid.
8   *Whose worth's . . . taken* — 'although the height and position of the star in the sky has been determined, its occult powers or intrinsic worth are still unknown.'
9   *Time's fool* — love is not the sport of time.

Sonnet No. 130

3   *dun* — brown.
5   *damask'd* — variegated.
8   *reeks* — emits or exhales. The word had not yet taken on its modern meaning of 'stinks'.
12   *treads* — walks. Shakespeare does not mean that his mistress walks heavily but that she is a real woman and not imaginary.
14   *As any . . . compare* — as any woman who has been ever praised by false comparison.
     she — used as a noun to mean 'woman'.

Sonnet No. 146

3   *dearth* — want, poverty.
8   *charge* — body, over which you have charge.
9   *live . . . loss* — ' live on the losses of the body which is your servant.'
10   *aggravate* — increase.
11   *dross* — worthless rubbish, literally, the clippings of coins.

A Hymne to God the Father

4   *rod* — punishment.
19–20   *That gav'st a Sonne . . . slave* — the redemption of man enslaved by sin through the incarnation and death of Christ.
27   *slight* — blaspheme.
28   *I'le come in* — I will repent.

An Ode. To himselfe

5   *Moath* — moth.
7   *Aonian springs* — the springs of Hippocrene and Agaippe, sacred to the Muses, situated on Mount Helicon, in Greece.
8   *Thespia* — from Thespis, a Greek poet of the sixth century B.C., who is credited with the invention of tragedy in dramatic art.
9   *Clarius* — Apollo, from the temple and oracle of Apollo at Claros.
12   *Pies* — magpies.
19   *Frie* — fry, young fish.
20   *Baytes* — baits.
21   *Balladrie* — balladry. A keen rivalry existed between poets and the more common ballad-makers.
27   *Japhets lyne* — in Greek mythology, a Titan, whose son Prometheus stole fire from heaven to give to mankind. Prometheus is often seen as a prototype of the artist.
     aspire — inspire.
28   *Sols Chariot* — the sun's chariot. See note on line 27 above.
30   *issue of Joves braine* — Minerva (known as Pallas Athene in Greek mythology), like Prometheus a patron of the arts, sprang fully armed from the head of Jove.
34   *strumpet* — prostitute.
     that strumpet the Stage — Jonson does not wish to prostitute his art.

The Good-Morrow

4 *snorted* — snored.
    the Seven Sleepers' den — Donne refers to a story about seven young men who, to escape the persecution of Decius, took refuge in a cave. They were walled in by their pursuers and, instead of starving to death, they slept for 187 years.
11 *an everywhere* —the universe.
13 *maps* — this could refer to maps of the heavens showing newly discovered stars and planets.
17 *two better hemispheres* — the reflection of each other in their eyes.
19 *Whatever dies . . . equally* — this is a reference to a chemical process.

The Anniversary

11 *Two graves* — they would be buried in separate graves as they are not married.
    corse — corpse.
18 *inmates* — temporary lodgers.
    prove — experience, feel.
21 *throughly blest* — in heaven they will enjoy the rewards of the blessed.
22 *now* — the ' now ' here is the present graphic for ' then '.
    But now . . . rest — the poet feels that this love, experienced on earth and unique, is to be preferred to the bliss which will be enjoyed in heaven but which will have to be shared with everyone else there.
27 *refrain* — keep from.
30 *second of our reign* — the second year of their love.

A Hymn to God the Father

1 *sin . . . begun* — original sin.

Batter my Heart

5 *due* — owing loyalty to.
9 *fain* — readily, gladly.

O, My Black Soul

4 *durst not* — did not dare.
7 *haled* — dragged forcibly.

The Collar

2 *abroad* — at liberty.
4 *rode* — road.
6 *in suit* — in service to another.
8 *To let me bloud* — to bleed me.
9 *cordiall* — healing.
14 *bayes* — bay leaves, used in victory garlands.
20 *double pleasures* — the double pleasure of throwing off restraint
    and at the same time embracing unaccustomed enjoyments.
    dispute — debate.
31 *To suit and serve his need* — to follow and look after his own needs.

Life

2 *remnant* — remainder (of life).
9 *admonition* — reproof, reminder.
12 *surging* — sweetening.
15 *And . . . cures* — the dead rose was used in certain medicines.
17 *sent* — scent.

Vertue

2 *bridall* — marriage.
10 *sweets* — perfumes.
11 *closes* — closing cadences.
14 *gives* — gives way, yields.
15 *coal* — ashes. The poet is thinking of the world being finally
    destroyed by fire.

The Retreate

4 The poet believes in an existence prior to our life on earth,
    an existence in which we are closer to heaven.
24 *traine* — companions.
27 *stay* — delay.

The Showre

1 *drowsie* — heavy with sleep.
2 *faint* — sickly.

Man

9   *staidness* — steadiness, constancy.
10 *appointments* — ordinances, arrangements.
15 *toyes* — amusements, pleasures.
23 *some stones* — lodestones, which are naturally magnetised.
26 *shuttle* — moving bobbin on a weaver's loom.

Peace

3   *Centrie* — sentry.
8   *files* — ranks.
17 *ranges* — wanderings.

Thoughts in a Garden

6   *upbraid* — reproach.
29 *Apollo hunted Daphne* — Daphne, the nymph in Greek mythology, was pursued by Apollo and on appealing to the gods was changed into a bay tree.
31 *Pan . . . Syrinx* — Pan, the Greek god of flocks and shepherds, invented a musical pipe of seven reeds which he called Syrinx after the nymph of the same name whom he loved but who was changed into a reed to escape him.
37 *nectarine* — a kind of peach.
44 *resemblance* — image.
51 *body's vest* — the mantle of the soul.
54 *whets* — preens.
57 *Garden-state* — i.e., the Garden of Eden.
66 *dial new* — sun-clock, here, a floral sun-clock.
68 *fragrant zodiac* — the yearly cycle of the flowers in bloom.

Lycidas

2   *Myrtles, Ivy* — evergreens, symbols of the fame won by poets, or the fame conferred by them on those whom they choose as the subjects of their poetry.
    never-sear — unripe, unwithered.
3   *crude* — unripe.
4   *rude* — fumbling, inexperienced.
6   *dear* — grievous.
8   *Lycidas* — traditional name of a goat-herd in Greek classical poetry, here referring to Milton's friend Edward King.
11 *lofty* — noble.

12 *watry bear* — watery bier. Edward King was drowned at sea.
14 *meed* — reward.
15 *Sisters . . . well* — the Muses, patronesses of the Arts.
16 *seat of Jove* — the altar of Jupiter.
20 *destin'd Urn* — the grave or coffin destined for the poet.
22 *sable shrowd* — black shroud or winding cloth.
24 *Fed the same flock* — followed the same literary pursuits.
28 *the Gray-fly* — grey-fly, probably the dor-beetle which makes a loud noise when flying.
29 *Batt'ning* — fattening.
33 *th'Oaten Flute* — pipe made from an oaten straw.
34 *Satyrs* — Greek woodland demi-gods, with the horns, ears and legs of a goat.
   Fauns — rural demi-gods, protectors of shepherds.
36 *Damœtas* — a name used in the classical pastoral poetry of Theocritus (*c.* 270 B.C.).
44 *layes* — lays, short lyrics.
46 *Taint-worm* — a parasite.
   weanling — newly weaned.
47 *wardrop* — wardrobe.
52 *steep* — mountain near the coast of Wales.
54 *Mona* — island of Anglesey.
55 *Deva* — the Latin name of the river Dee in Cheshire.
   wisard — the river Dee was reputed to have magical properties.
56 *fondly* — foolishly.
58 *Orpheus* — legendary Greek lyre player, whose mother was Calliope, the Muse of Epic Poetry.
60–63 Orpheus was torn to pieces by the Thracian Maenads and his head, still singing, floated down the river Hebrus until it reached the island of Lesbos where it was buried.
61 *rout* — disorderly band.
64 *What boots it* — ' what profits it '.
68 *Amaryllis* — from the Greek, meaning a country girl. It is also the name of an autumn-flowering plant. Sporting with Amaryllis and Neæra is meant to stand for the lighter forms of poetry.
69 *Neæra* — a water nymph. See note on Amaryllis above.
73 *Guerdon* — a reward, a prize.
75 *Fury* — one of the three Furies: Atropos, the eldest, who was represented with shears to cut the thread of life at the moment of death ; ' blind ' to emphasise her irresponsibility.
79 *glistering foil* — the bright setting of a gem.
83 *pronounces lastly* — gives the final judgment.
85 *Arethuse* — the Greek nymph Arethusa was changed into a fountain by Artemis.

86 *Mincius* — a river in northern Italy near Mantua, the birth-place of Virgil, hence ' honour'd '.

88 *Oate* — flute.

89 *Herald of the Sea* — Triton, the son of Neptune. He summoned the sea gods by blowing on a shell. Here he defends Neptune against the charge of being responsible for the death of Lycidas.

91 *Fellon* — felon, wicked.

96 *Hippotades* — Aeolus, the Greek god of winds.

99 *Panope* — a sea nymph.

103 *Camus* — a river god, symbolising the river Cam, which flows through Cambridge where Milton and King were students.

104 *sedge* — a coarse grass which grows near water.

106 *sanguine flower* — the hyacinth, emblem of death in ancient Greece.

107 *reft . . . pledge* — ' taken away my dearest child '.

109 *Pilot . . . lake* — St. Peter.

114 *Anow* — enough.

115 *Creep . . . fold* — secretively and unworthily enter the Church.

116 *care* — duty.

121 *Herdmans* — shepherds, here clergymen.

122 *recks* — means.
     sped — provided for.

123 *list* — desire.
     flashy — worthless.

124 *scrannel* — thin, reedy.

128 *grim Woolf* — the Catholic Church, a traditional term of abuse.
     privy — treacherous.

130 *two-handed engine* — The general meaning is that retribution will fall on the wicked. The precise meaning of the ' two-handed engine ' has been disputed among scholars.

132 *Alpheus* — a river in Greece. This river was associated in legend with the fountain of Arethusa which in turn inspired the Sicilian pastoral poets.

133 *Sicilian Muse* — see note line 132.

138 *the swart Star* — Sirius, the dog star. The heat of the dog days which scorched vegetation was attributed to this star.

141 *vernal* — springtime.

142 *rathe* — early flowering.
     forsaken — in the shade, out of the sunshine.

143 *Crow-toe* — crow-foot or buttercup.
     Gessamine — jasmine.

144 *jeat* — jet, black.

149 *Amaranthus* — a legendary flower which never fades.

151 *Laureat Herse* — bier decorated with laurels.

158 *monstrous* — inhabited by monsters.
159 *moist vows* — weeping prayers.
160 *Bellerus* — legendary giant after whom Land's End was named in Roman times.
161 *guarded Mount* — St. Michael's Mount in Cornwall.
162 *Namancos and Bayona* — two Spanish towns.
163 *ruth* — compassion, tenderness.
168 *day-star* — the sun.
170 *Ore* — gold.
175 *oozy* — wet from the sea.
176 *unexpressive* — inexpressible.
    nuptiall Song — marriage song ; refers to the union of the soul with its Maker in heaven.
183 *Genius* — guardian spirit.
188 *stops* — holes in wind instruments.
189 *Dorick* — i.e., doric, a pastoral.
192 *blew* — blue.

How soon hath Time

1 *suttle* — subtle.
3 *full career* — full speed.
4 *But my late . . . shew'th* — Milton may be referring here to his failure to achieve great spirituality or, on the other hand, it may mean that he has not yet written a great work.
5 *semblance* — appearance. Milton looked younger than his years.
7 *inward ripenes* — mental maturity.
8 *indu'th* — endows, invests with.
10 *in strictest measure eev'n* — in complete conformity.
13 *All is* — i.e., all depends on whether.

When I Consider

1 *light* — sight.
    spent — lost, gone forever.
3 *Talent* — gift, faculty.
4 *bent* — determined.
7 *Doth God . . . deny'd* — ' does God expect the same work from me, a blind man.'
8 *fondly* — foolishly.
11 *yoak* — yoke, burden.

Avenge O Lord

1 *slaughter'd Saints* — this poem was inspired by the news of the massacre in 1655, by Italian troops, of Piedmontese Protestants known as the Waldensians.

3 *them* — the Waldensians traced their origins back to the apostles.

12 *The triple Tyrant* — the Pope, as wearer of the tiara.

14 *Babylonian wo* — Protestant writers sometimes identified the papacy with Babylon.

Paradise Lost, Book I

2 *mortal taste* — mortal because the eating of the fruit brought death.

6 *Heavenly Muse* — though following classical convention, Milton does not invoke one of the nine Muses of mythology, but the sacred Muse who inspired Moses and David.

7 *Oreb* — another name for Mount Sinai.

8 *That shepherd* — Moses.

10-11 *Sion hill . . . Siloa's brook* — Mount Sion and the river Siloam in Jerusalem.

12 *the oracle of God* — the temple in Jerusalem.

14 *middle flight* — Milton's intention is to attempt a more difficult task than has ever been tried before, to justify the ways of God to man.

15 *Aonian mount* — Mount Helicon in Greece, the home of the Muses.

21 *vast Abyss* — chaos, the nothingness before creation.

22 *pregnant* — fruitful.

29 *our grand parents* — our first parents.

32 *For one restraint* — the one condition imposed on Adam and Eve to try obedience.

33 *seduced* — tempted.

36 *The Mother of Mankind* — Eve.

45 *ethereal* — airy, heavenly.

48 *adamantine chains* — unbreakable chains ; adamant, a stone of impenetrable hardness.

49 *durst* — darest.

53 *Confounded* — overthrown, vanquished.

56 *baleful* — full of evil, also, full of woe.

58 *obdúrate* — stubborn.

69 *ever-burning sulphur unconsumed* — though the sulphur burns continually, it is never exhausted.

72 *portion* — destiny.

74 *the centre . . . pole* — refers to the distance between the centre of the universe, the earth, and the outermost point.
81 *Beëlzebub* — the prince of devils, ranking second to Satan.
82 *Satan* — the Hebrew word satan means enemy.
87 *mutual league* — alliance in which both parties are in complete agreement.
94 *The force . . . arms* — the fearful power of God.
96 *else* — in addition.
104 *In dubious battle* — to Satan the outcome appeared doubtful. To him the rebel angels were not utterly vanquished.
109 *And what . . . overcome* — ' and what can this mean but that we cannot be conquered.'
110 *That glory* — homage.
116–117 *since . . . fail* — Satan speaks of himself and his fellow angels as gods, and therefore of heavenly substance.
127 *compeer* — equal, associate.
128 *Powers* — Satan's forces.
132 *put to proof* — tested.
138 *essences* — spirits.
144 *Of force* — of necessity.
148 *suffice* — satisfy.
149 *thralls* — slaves, servants.
153 *What . . . avail* — of what use is it?
157 *Cherub* — cherubim.
weak — cowardly.
158 *Doing or suffering* — doing God's bidding or enduring punishment.
162–164 *If then . . . end* — ' if it is God's plan to bring good out of our evil-doing, it must be our task to thwart his aim.'
172 *o'erblown* — blown over.
178 *slip the occasion* — allow the opportunity to pass.
178–179 *whether scorn . . . foe* — ' whether our enemy allows it through contempt or satisfied wrath '.
183 *tend* — move, go.
188 *our own . . . repair* — how to restore our own loss, heaven.
198 *Titanian* — Titans, in Greek mythology the children of Uranus and Ge. They were of immense size.
Earth-born — the Giants of Greek mythology.
199 *Briareos* — a giant with a hundred arms, in Greek mythology.
Typhon — a monster with a hundred heads, in Greek mythology.
200 *Tarsus* — the capital city of Cilicia, where Typhon was reputed to live.
201 *Leviathan* — a sea monster, a whale. In ancient Egypt Leviathan referred to a crocodile.
204 *night-foundered* — caught out by night.

207   *under the lee* — on the sheltered side.

213   *at large* — free.

226   *incumbent* — resting on, supported by.

231   *subterranean wind* — earthquakes were attributed to winds within the earth.

232   *Pelorus* — a cave in Sicily near Mount Etna.

233   *Ætna* — Mount Etna, the volcano in Sicily.

239   *Stygian flood* — the river Styx, a principal river of Hades or Hell.

241   *supernal* — supernatural.

246   *sovran* — sovereign.

248   *Whom . . . equalled* — ' whom our reason had equalled.'

256–258   *What matter . . . greater* — ' surely it does not matter as long as I am still the same, only less than God.'

266   *astonished* — stunned.

      oblivious pool — the lake of fire inducing forgetfulness.

281   *erewhile* — previously, formerly.

282   *pernicious* — fatal.

285   *massy* — massive, large.

286   *cast* — slung.

288   *Tuscan artist* — Galileo, whom Milton visited in Italy.

289   *Fesolè* — Fiesole, near Florence.

290   *Valdarno* — i.e., Vald'arno, the valley of the river Arno.

294   *ammiral* — admiral, here flagship.

296   *marle* — marl, clay.

299   *Nathless* — nevertheless.

303   *Vallombrosa* — a beauty spot near Florence.

      Etrurian — Tuscan.

304   *sedge* — usually refers to a kind of flag or coarse grass growing near rivers, here refers to seaweed. The Red Sea was called ' the sea of sedge '.

305   *Orion* — the rising and setting of the constellation of this name was associated with bad weather.

307   *Busiris* — in Greek mythology, king of Egypt. To avert drought in his country, he slew strangers and offered them as sacrifices to Zeus. He was killed by Heracles.

      Memphian chivalry — Egyptian cavalry.

309   *Goshen* — the land given to the Israelites by Pharaoh.

317   *astonishment* — shock.

320   *virtue* — bravery.

338–343   This is a reference to the plague of locusts which Moses brought on Egypt. Moses was the son of Amram.

351–355   A reference to the barbarian invasions from northern Europe.

353   *Rhene* — Rhine.

      Danaw — Danube.

360 *erst* — formerly.

366 *Through . . . sufferance* — through God's tolerance.

378 *next in worth* — in order of rank.

380 *promiscuous* — confused.

383 *seats* — places of worship.

385 *abide* — face.

386 *Jehovah* — name given to God in the Old Testament.

392 *Moloch* — an idol to which the Ammonites and Phoenicians offered human sacrifice, particularly children.

394 *timbrels* — tambourines.

397 *Rabba* — capital of the Ammonites called the ' city of waters '.

398 *Argob, Basan* — towns which Milton believed were in the territory of the Ammonites.

399 *Arnon* — the territory east of the Jordan.

400 *Audacious* — daring, because so near to the Holy Land.

401–405 Solomon, in his old age, built a temple to false gods on the Mount of Olives (Mount of Offence) opposite the temple of Jerusalem. The nearby valley of Hinnom or Tophet, also desecrated, came to be called Gehenna or Hell.

406 *Chemos* — a Moabite god, related to Moloch.

407–411 The places mentioned in these lines lie to the east of the Jordan.

411 *Asphaltic pool* — the Dead Sea.

412 *Peor* — see line 406 above.

413 *Sittim* — a town east of the Jordan.

414 *cost them woe* — this refers to the plagues sent by God to punish the Israelites for their idolatry.

416 *hill of scandal* — i.e., Mount of Olives (Mount of Offence). See lines 401–405 above.

417 *lust hard by hate* — lust, represented by Chemos, side by side with hate, represented by Moloch.

418 *Josiah* — King of Judah who carried out a religious reform and dedicated the Temple of Jerusalem wholly to Yahweh (God).

419–421 *from . . . ground* — the Euphrates to the east and the river Essor to the west defined the area of Canaan or the Promised Land.

422 *Baalim and Ashtaroth* — these gods adopted many different forms and could assume either sex. Ashtaroth was the moon goddess, the counterpart of Baal.

425 *uncompounded* — ethereal.

433 *living Strength* — the living God.

435 *bestial gods* — animals adored as gods, such as the golden calf.

438 *Astoreth* — also known as Astarte, the moon goddess, also the goddess of fertility.

441 *Sidonian* — Phoenician.

443   *offensive mountain* — see lines 401–405 above.

444   *uxorious king* — a reference to Solomon who, in old age, was led astray by his wives. See 1 *Kings* 2 ; 1–4.

446   *Thammuz* — lover of Astarte, was the son of a Syrian king. Phoenician women held a ceremony of mourning for him each year.

450   *smooth Adonis* — the river Adonis was reputed to run red at certain times of the year. The Greek counterparts of Thammuz and Astoreth were Adonis and Aphrodite.

453   *Sion's daughters* — Israelite women.
      heat — passion.

455   *Ezekiel* — a prophet of the Old Testament who saw the idolatry of the Israelites in a vision.

457–463   ' Next came Dagon, half-man half-fish, who was worshipped by the Philistines. When the Philistines captured the Ark of the Covenant, they placed it in the temple of Dagon where, the following morning, the idol was found smashed on the ground.'

460   *grunsel-edge* — threshold.

464   *Azotus* — Ashtod, the site of the temple of Dagon.

464–466   The chief cities of the Philistines.

467   *Rimmon* — god of Damascus.

471   *A leper . . . gained a king* — see 2 *Kings* 5.

472   *Ahaz* — king of Judah and a follower of Rimmon, who erected an altar to idols in front of the Temple in Jerusalem.
      sottish — foolish.

475–476   *the gods . . . vanquished* — Ahaz had persuaded the king of Assyria to capture Damascus, the city of Rimmon.

478   *Osiris* — chief god of the Egyptians.
      Isis — sister and wife of Osiris.
      Orus — son of Isis and Osiris.

479   *monstrous shapes* — Osiris was represented by a bull, Isis by a cow, and Orus by a hawk.
      abused — deceived.

481   *wandering gods* — in Roman legend when the giants declared war on the gods some of the latter fled to Egypt and assumed the disguise of animals.

483–484   *borrowed gold . . . Oreb* — the Israelites made an idol in the form of a calf from gold borrowed from the Egyptians.

484   *Oreb* — Mount Horeb, Mount Sinai.

484–485   *rebel king . . . Dan* — Jeroboam, a rebel in the time of Rehoboam, who made two calves of gold for worship and located them in the cities of Bethel and Dan.

488   *equalled with one stroke* — made equal in death.

490   *Belial* — the Evil One ; not the name of any specific god. In Hebrew the word means ' the worthless one '.

504   *Gibeah* — a city of the Old Testament. (See *Judges* 20.)

508   *The Ionian gods* — the Ionians, a branch of the Greeks, were said to be descended from Javan, a descendant of Noah.

510   *Titan* — see note on line 198.

512   *Saturn* — the Titans were led by Saturn in their revolt against Uranus, their father ; here Milton makes it appear that Saturn revolted against Titan the eldest son of Uranus and Ge.

      Jove — son of Saturn and Rhea, who deposed his father and drove him out of Greece to Italy.

515   *Ida* — the mountain in Crete where Jove was born.

516   *the middle air* — the region between heaven and earth in which the aforementioned gods ruled.

517   *Delphian cliff* — the temple of Apollo at Delphi was situated on a rocky cleft of Mount Parnassus.

518   *Dodona* — refers to the shrine of the oracle of Zeus in Epirus.

519   *Doric* — Greek. The Dorians, one of the Greek races, lived in Doris.

      Saturn — see note on line 512 above.

520   *Adria* — the Adriatic Sea.

      Hesperian — western : Hesperia was the poetic name for Italy or Spain.

534   *Azazel* — an Old Testament name, here given by Milton to one of the fallen angels.

547   *helms* — helmets.

550   *Dorian mood* — i.e., Dorian mode. Greek music was composed in one of three modes—Dorian, Phrygian or Lydian. The Dorian mode was simple and solemn.

556   *swage* — assuage, soothe.

573–576   These lines mean that Satan's army, now drawn up in hell, is the most powerful force assembled since the creation of man.

575–576   *small infantry . . . cranes* — a reference to the Homeric tale that the pygmies, a race of dwarfs, were attacked by flocks of cranes.

577   *Phlegra* — the site of the battle between the Titans and the gods.

578   *Thebes . . . Ilium* — the cities of Thebes and Ilium (Troy) were the scenes of battles in Greek legend.

580   *Uther's son* — King Arthur.

581   *Armoric* — from Amorica, the ancient name for Brittany and closely linked with Arthurian legend.

583   *Aspramont* — probably refers to a range of mountains in Calabria where Charlemagne fought the Saracens.

      Montalban — in southern France, site of battle fought by Charlemagne.

584   *Trebisond* — a town in Asia Minor.

585   *Biserta* — a town on the coast of north Africa from which the Saracens were reputed to have set sail when attacking Europe.

587   *Fontarabbia* — a fortress on the frontier between France and Spain, it was the site of many conflicts.

597–599   *In dim eclipse . . . monarchs* — eclipses were believed to herald calamity, hence ' disastrous '.

603   *considerate* — deliberate.

609   *amerc'd* — punished, deprived.

619   *assayed* — attempted.

632   *puissant* — powerful.

651   *a fame* — a rumour.

656   *eruption* — expedition.

670   *grisly* — horrible.

672   *scurf* — scales, crust.

676   *pioneers* — engineers or sappers, who prepare or fortify ground for an army.

678   *Mammon* — the god of riches.

690   *admire* — wonder.

692   *bane* — a curse or poison ; ' precious bane ' is usually understood to be an oxymoron.

694   *Memphian* — Egyptian.

703   *founded* — smelted, cast.

704   *Severing* — separating.

    bullion dross — impurities floating on the top of the liquid metal.

709   *sound-board* — that part of an organ which distributes the air to various pipes.

710   *fabric* — edifice.

713   *pilasters* — rectangular columns.

714   *Doric pillars* — fluted, circular pillars.

715   *architrave* — the main beam which rests on pillars.

716   *Cornice* — the top portion of the entablature in classical architecture.

    frieze — the middle section of the entablature, coming above the architrave and below the cornice.

718   *Alcairo* — Cairo.

720   *Belus* — Baal.

    Sérapis — a god worshipped by Greeks and Egyptians.

728   *cressets* — metal bowls which held oil for lamps.

729   *naphtha* — an inflammable oil produced from coal.

    asphaltus — pitch, tar.

739   *Ausonian* — Italian.

740   *Mulciber* — name for Vulcan, meaning ' smelter of metals '.

750 *engines* — inventions, contrivances.
764 *Soldan's* — Sultan's.
765 *Panim* — pagan.
769 *Taurus* — the second sign of the Zodiac, April and May.
772 *smoothèd plank* — the landing-board of a beehive.
780–781 A race of pygmies was reputed to have lived in India, perhaps near the Himalayas.
783 *belated* — out late at night.
785 *arbitress* — presiding.
797 *Frequent* — numerous.

Mac Flecknoe

3 *Fleckno* — Flecknoe, probably an Irish priest who was known as the writer of a considerable amount of indifferent poetry.
 Augustus — Caesar Augustus.
5 *own'd* — considered.
8 *issue . . . increase* — offspring (here followers) who will in turn produce more followers.
15 *Sh* — Shadwell (1642–1692), who was constantly feuding with Dryden. They wrote many satires against each other, Dryden writing both *The Medal* and *Mac Flecknoe*, and Shadwell replying with *The Medal of John Bayes* and a translation of the *Tenth Satire of Juvenal*. Shadwell wrote popular comedies, some of which excelled those of Dryden. At the time of the 1689 revolution Shadwell replaced Dryden as Poet Laureate.
23 *ray* — of light (intelligence).
25 *Fabrick* — body.
28 *supinely* — listlessly, lethargically.
29 *Heywood and Shirley* — Heywood (1575–1641) a dramatist and Shirley (1595–1666) also a dramatist.
30 *Tautology* — repetition.
33 *Drugget* — a coarse woollen fabric used for covering floors.
35 *whilom* — formerly.
36 *King John of Portugal* — reference to a poem by Flecknoe addressed to King John of Portugal.
38–40 See note on line 15 above.

Absalom and Achitophel

Absalom — the favourite son of King David who, under the influence of Achitophel, revolted against his father. Dryden uses the name here to refer to James, Duke of Monmouth, illegitimate son of Charles II.

Achitophel — tutor of Absalom. Here the name refers to Lord Shaftesbury whose party wanted as heir to the throne the protestant Duke of Monmouth, thus excluding the catholic Duke of York from the succession.

3 *close Designs* — secret plots.
6 *unpleased* — dissatisfied.
9 *Tenement of Clay* — the body.
19 *Bankrupt of Life* — growing old.
   Prodigal of Ease — recklessly wasteful of his remaining years of leisure.
22 *Got* — begotten.
   huddled Notions trie — consider secret plans.
26 *To Compass* — to achieve.
   Triple Bond — the triple alliance formed by England, Holland and Sweden against Louis XIV.
28 *Israel* — here, England.
31 *Factious* — troublesome.
44 *Gown* — the robes of a judge.
45 *rankness* — foulness.
47 *David* — Charles II of England.

The Rape of the Lock

Canto I

121 *the Toilet* — the dressing table with its array of toilet requisites.
123 *Nymph* — Belinda.
127 *inferior Priestess* — the maid, Betty.
128 *sacred rites* — solemn ceremonies.
131 *nicely* — precisely.
   culls — selects, chooses.
139 *awful* — awe-inspiring.
144 *keener lightnings* — Belinda used belladonna to brighten her eyes.
145 *Sylphs* — any spirits that have the care of young unmarried girls. Here they have the task of protecting Belinda.
148 *Betty* — the maid.

Canto II

47 *secure* — safe.
51 *Zephyrs* — west winds.

53   *Sylph* — Ariel, who is commander of the sylphs assigned to protect Belinda.

55   *Denizens* — inhabitants.

56   *lucid* — light.

57   *shrouds* — ropes.

58   *train* — company.

67   *transient* — fleeting.

Canto III

1   *meads* — meadows.

3   *structure of majestic frame* — Hampton Court built by Cardinal Wolsey and presented by him to Henry VIII in 1526.

5   *foredoom* — plot.

7   *Anna* — Queen Anne (1665–1714) younger daughter of James II. She ruled as queen of England from 1702.

105   *board* — table.

106   *berries* — coffee beans.
      mill — coffee grinder.

107   *Altars of Japan* — lacquered tables, i.e., japanned.

110   *China's earth* — china cups.

113   *the Fair* — Belinda.

117   *Coffee . . . wise* — coffee-houses were the haunt of amateur politicians.

119   *the Baron* — Lord Petre, who cut the lock of hair.

122–124   *Scylla . . . hair* — Scylla was the daughter of Nisus, king of the city of Megara. Enamoured of Minos she sacrificed her father and the city by pulling out the hair on which her father's strength depended. However, her love was rejected by Minos, and in attempting to follow him she was changed into a bird.

127   *Clarissa* — there is no record to show whom Clarissa represented in contemporary life.

128   *two-edg'd weapon* — scissors.

134   *fragrant steams* — i.e., from the coffee.

139   *Ariel* — Belinda's guardian spirit.

141   *nosegay* — posy of flowers.

147   *Forfex* — scissors.

150   *fondly* — foolishly.

153   *dissever* — cut.

159   *China vessels* — china cups.

Canto IV

113   *th'inestimable prize* — the lock of hair.

114 *Expos'd thro' crystal*—worn in a ring on the Baron's hand.

117 *Hyde-park Circus* — a place in Hyde Park known as the Ring, where the grass was worn away by constant traffic.

118 *And wits . . . Bow* — the polite and cultured society of the day did not mix with the inhabitants of the City, who lived within the sound of the bells of Bow church.

121 *Sir Plume* — a cousin of Belinda, Sir George Browne, in contemporary life.

124 *nice* — expert.

clouded cane — amber-headed cane.

Canto V

37 *Virago* — female warrior.

47 *Pallas* — daughter of the Greek god Zeus.

Mars — the Roman god of war.

Latona — Greek goddess, mother of Artemis and Apollo.

Hermes — son of Zeus and god of commerce and wealth.

48 *Olympus* — the mountain abode of the gods in ancient Greek legend.

49 *Jove* — Jupiter, supreme Roman deity.

53 *Umbriel* — the evil spirit, the opposite of Ariel. He has just come back from a journey to the underworld, bringing with him a bag of mischievous vapours with which he has caused the battle.

sconce — a bracket or hanging candlestick.

57 *Thalestris* — queen of the Amazons; in contemporary life it refered to Mrs. Morley, sister of Sir Plume.

59–64 *A Beau and Witling* — Dapperwit and Sir Fopling. Dapperwit who 'dy'd in metaphor' was a character in Wycherley's *Love in a Wood*. Sir Fopling, who died 'in song' was the chief character in a popular play *Man of Mode or Sir Fopling Flutter*.

65 *Mæander* — famous winding river in Asia Minor, referred to by Ovid in connection with the legend of the dying swan.

68 *Chloe* — a name used by Pope to refer to Lady Suffolk, mistress of George II.

77 *the Chief* — Lord Petre.

79 *endu'd* — endowed.

83 *Gnomes* — spirits of the earth.

84 *titillating* — tickling.

Tintern Abbey

3 *These waters* — the river Wye.

11 *orchard-tufts* — small orchards.

20   *vagrant dwellers* — wandering gypsies.
38   *burthen of the mystery* — burden of the mystery of life.
42   *affections* — feelings, sensations.
43   *corporeal frame* — body.
58   *half-extinguished thought* — memories which are half-forgotten.
86   *murmur* — complain.
94   *A presence* — an unseen being or influence.
96   *interfused* — imbued.
106–107   *both what . . . perceive* — both what is apprehended by the senses and transfigured by the imagination.
115   *my dearest Friend* — Dorothy Wordsworth, who was very close to her brother and who accompanied him on the walk by Tintern when this poem was composed.

Loud is the Vale

These lines were composed at Grasmere during a walk one evening after a stormy day. The author had just read that the death of Charles James Fox, the famous Whig statesman, was hourly expected.

1   *the Vale* — the vale of the Wye in Monmouthshire.
    the Voice — the noise of the flooded streams after heavy rain.
5   *Depth* — valley.
10   *Importunate and heavy load* — weighed down with depression and worry.
11   *The Comforter* — the Holy Ghost.
17   *A Power* — Fox who was responsible for the abolition of the slave trade.

Surprised by Joy

2   *transport* — i.e., of delight.
3   *Thee* — Catherine, the poet's second daughter who died at the age of four.
4   *vicissitude* — change of circumstance, eventuality.
8   *beguiled* — diverted.

Ode to the West Wind

The poem was written by Shelley in a wood by the river Arno, near Florence, on a wild day when the west wind was blowing.

10   *clarion* — trumpet.

14 *Destroyer* — as destroyer, the wind strips the leaves off the trees.
    preserver — as preserver, the wind carries the seeds to a safe refuge
    to await the spring.
21 *Maenad* — Bacchante or female worshipper of Bacchus, the god of
    wine.
22 *zenith's height* — the highest point (of the sky).
27 *vapours* — mists, clouds.
32 *Baiae's bay* — Baiae, an old Roman town near Naples, which is
    now submerged by the sea. It was a favourite resort of the
    ancient Romans.
51–52 *I would . . . need* — 'I am now striving harder in prayer with
    you than I ever strove in my youth.'
63 *dead* — useless.

Stanzas written in Dejection

4   *transparent might* — the strong light of the sun at midday.
9   *The City's voice* — the sounds of Naples.
40 *untimely* — inopportune.

Ozymandias

Ozymandias — the statue of Rameses II in the desert at Thebes
    was called the tomb of Ozymandias by the Greek historian
    Diodorus Siculus.
1   *antique* — ancient.
8   *The hand . . . fed* — the sculptor's hand which recorded those
    passions, the tyrant's (Ozymandias') heart that fed them.

Ode to a Nightingale

2   *hemlock* — a poison, obtained from the hemlock plant, which may
    be used as a sedative.
3   *opiate* — a sedative drug.
    to the drains — to the dregs.
4   *Lethe-wards* — towards forgetfulness. In Greek legend the river
    Lethe which flows through Hades induces forgetfulness in
    those who drink its waters.
7   *Dryad* — a nymph of the woodlands.
13 *Flora* — Roman goddess of flowers.
14 *Provençal song* — Provence is a province of south-east France.
    Singers from this region, called the trouvères or troubadours,
    won fame for their lyrics during the Middle Ages.

16 *blushful* — blushing.

Hippocrene — a fountain on Mount Helicon which was sacred to the Muses. Keats here calls wine by this name.

26 *Where youth . . . dies* — Keats's brother Tom died of consumption shortly before this poem was written.

30 *Or new Love . . . to-morrow* — even love is inconstant.

32 *Bacchus* — Roman god of wine and revelry.

pards — leopards or panthers. The description here could have been inspired by a picture in the National Gallery in London of Bacchus and Ariadne, where Bacchus is in a chariot drawn by a tiger and a lion.

33 *viewless* — invisible.

36 *Queen-Moon* — Diana, twin sister of Apollo.

37 *Fays* — fairies.

43 *embalmed* — balmy, fragrant.

46 *eglantine* — sweet briar.

51 *Darkling* — in the dark.

60 *To thy high . . . sod* — ' When I am dead I will no longer be able to hear your song.'

66 *Ruth* — After the death of her husband, instead of returning to her own people Ruth accompanied her mother-in-law to Judea (*Ruth* 1 and 2).

72 *sole* — lone.

73 *fancy* — imagination.

Ode on a Grecian Urn

1 *unravish'd* — virginal, untouched.

3 *Sylvan* — rural.

5 *What leaf-fring'd . . . shape* — this is a reference to the story told by the pictures painted on the urn. ' leaf-fring'd ' because leaves were often painted on the edges of the pictures.

7 *Tempe* — a valley in Thessaly which inspired many poets with its beauty.

Arcady — a district in Peloponnesus ; ideal rustic paradise.

8 *loth* — unwilling.

10 *timbrels* — ancient musical instruments like tambourines.

28 *All breathing . . . above* — superior to earthly human love.

29 *cloy'd* — wearied, satiated.

37 *pious* — holy, because it is a day of sacrifice.

41 *Attic* — Grecian.

attitude — disposition, pattern.

brede — braid, narrow band.

44   *tease* — entice.

44–45 *Thou, silent form . . . eternity* — it entices us out of rational thought into imagination. A second meaning might be that it ' teases ' or mocks us with its mystery.

     Cold — lifeless.

La Belle Dame sans Merci

3   *sedge* — flags or coarse grass growing along the banks of rivers or lakes.

9   *lilly* — lily, white, here meaning pale.

13   *meads* — meadows.

18   *zone* — girdle.

29   *grot* — grotto, cave.

40   *in thrall* — enslaved.

Terror of Death

2   *teeming* — fruitful, prolific.

3   *in charact'ry* — in writing, in print.

Bright Star

1   *steadfast* — fixed, constant.

4   *Eremite* — hermit.

10   *ripening* — maturing.

On the Sea

3   *Gluts* — fills.

4   *Hecate* — a Greek goddess who was the protector of witches and enchanters.

5   *temper* — humour.

12   *cloying* — satiating.

14   *quired* — sang.

The Lotos-Eaters

58   *myrrh-bush* — the bush from the resin of which incense and perfumes are made.

60   *Lotos* — a plant which in Greek legend was believed to induce forgetfulness, luxurious dreaminess and a distaste for active life.

87   *pilot-stars* — the stars used in navigation.

88   *amaranth* — a legendary flower which never fades.

     moly — a magic herb given by Hermes to Ulysses as a counter-charm against the spells of the witch Circe.

97   *acanthus* — a plant with splendid leaves, common in Mediter-
     ranean countries.
106 *starboard* — the right side of a ship when looking forward.
     larboard — the port or left side of a ship.
108 *equal mind* — fixed mind.
111 *nectar* — drink of the gods.
     bolts — thunderbolts.
120 *cleave* — plough.
124 *Elysian valleys* — Elysium was the legendary home of the blest.
125 *asphodel* — a mythical undying flower in Elysium.

Because I could not stop for Death

10   *Recess* — play time.
15   *Gossamer* — cobweb-like threads.
16   *Tippet* — a covering for the neck or shoulders worn by women.
     Tulle — a thin silk, rather like chiffon.
20   *Cornice* — an ornamental moulding at the top of a wall or pillar.

The Soul selects her own Society

3   *divine Majority* — death.

Of all the Souls

2   *elected* — selected.
3   *When Sense . . . away* — when body and soul are parted.

At Half past Three

3   *Propounded* — proposed for consideration, voiced.
     term — measure.
7   *Her silver Principle* — her song.
11 *Place* — space, emptiness.
12 *Circumference* — Emily Dickinson said that her task as a poet was
     ' circumference ', meaning the comprehension of essentials.

That Nature is a Heraclitean Fire

Heraclitean—Heraclitus, the Greek philosopher, held that all
    matter was in a state of constant change, and he attributed
    to fire, which is insubstantial and ever-changing, the origin
    of all things.
1   *chevy* — chase.

2   *roysterers* — revellers.
3   *roughcast* — roughcast walls.
4   *Shivelights* — strips of light.
    shadowtackle — the interlocking of shadows.
7   *stanches* — staunches, stops, particularly of a flow of liquid, blood, etc.
11 *firedint* — man's mark on the changing, heraclitean, face of nature must also pass away.
14 *disseveral* — separate, remote.
18 *foundering* — sinking.
20 *residuary* — inheriting; all matter is devoured by the worm which is the universal symbol of death.
23 *Jack* — a common fellow or clown.
    potsherd — a broken piece of earthenware. This image may have been suggested by *Job* 2 : 8 : 'And he took a potsherd with which to scrape himself, and sat among the ashes.'
    patch — can also mean a fool or clown.

The Windhover

Windhover — kestrel, falcon.
1   *minion* — darling, favourite.
2   *dauphin* — prince, heir-apparent (to French throne).
    dapple — mottle, speckle.
4   *rung upon the rein* — this can either refer to a horse being schooled at the end of a rein, or to a falcon held on a lead. In both cases the image is of an animal circling.
    wimpling — pleated, creased.
10 *Buckle* — a third possible meaning might be added to the two mentioned in Exploration 4 : ' clasp, fasten together into a single unity ' all the skills and aspirations.
12 *sillion* — sillon, meaning furrow.
14 *gall* — rub against, hurt.

Felix Randal

1   *farrier* — blacksmith.
4   *Fatal four disorders* — four fatal illnesses.
    contended — attacked.
6   *Being anointed and all* — having received the Sacraments of the Sick.
7   *our sweet reprieve and ransom* — probably confession and penance.
13 *random* — untidy, casual.
14 *fettle* — prepare.

No Worst, there is None

2 *schooled at forepangs* — the greater pangs of griefs yet to come have been prepared for by earlier, lesser sufferings.
3 *Comforter* — the Paraclete, the Holy Spirit.
5 *main* — a crowd, a mass.
8 *fell* — cruel, fierce.
   force — perforce.
12 *Durance* — endurance.
   deal with — cope with.

I wake and feel the Fell of Dark

1 *fell* — a word of rich suggestiveness. It might mean ' fell ' or ' skin ', or ' fall ', or ' threat ' of dark.
7 *dead letters* — letters which cannot be delivered.
9 *gall* — bitterness.

Thou art indeed just, Lord

Translation of the Latin quotation reads as follows :
Righteous art thou, O Lord, when I complain to thee ; yet I would plead my cause before thee. Why does the way of the wicked prosper ? (*Jer.* 12 : 1.)
1 *contend* — dispute, argue.
7 *sots* — drunkards.
   thralls — slaves.
9 *brakes* — thickets.
11 *fretty* — fretted, interlaced.
   chervil — a garden herb.
13 *Time's eunuch* — having renounced human love for the love of God, Hopkins complains in this dark moment that his life seems both spiritually and physically fruitless.

During Wind and Rain

4 *one to play* — one as accompanist.
8 *clear* — clear away.
21 *ript* — torn.
28 *carved names* — names engraved on tombstones.

When I set out for Lyonnesse

1 *Lyonnesse* — a mythical land between Cornwall and the Scilly Isles. The district is traditionally associated with King Arthur and his wizard Merlin. It is also the name of the home of Hardy's first wife, Lavinia.

3 *rime* — frost.

   spray — branch.

15 *surmise* — conjecture.

Afterwards

1 *postern* — a gate or door, usually in the wall of a town or castle.

6 *dewfall* — night-time.

17 *my bell of quittance* — ' the bell which tells of my quittance (leaving) of this life ; my death bell.'

In Time of " The Breaking of Nations "

1 *harrowing clods* — breaking up of lumps of earth with a harrow or clod-crusher.

6 *couch-grass* — long-rooted grass, scutch-grass.

9 *wight* — person, man.

The Love Song of J. Alfred Prufrock

The Italian quotation may be translated as follows :

If I believed that I was giving answer to one who could ever return to the world, this flame should no longer shake, but as no one ever returned alive from this pit, if what I have heard be true, I answer you without fear of shame.

The passage is from Canto XXVII of Dante's *Inferno*. Dante and Virgil, moving through the eighth circle of hell, question the soul of Guido da Montefeltro who on earth had been guilty of fraud through false counsel. Prufrock resembles Guido in as far as his inner thoughts are not in harmony with his outward behaviour. Through timidity, Prufrock is unable to express in action his inner thoughts and desires. He is, therefore, like Guido in a sort of hell, a hell of indecision in which he must practise fraud, in which he must constantly prepare ' a face to meet the faces that you meet '. Unlike Guido, however, he is not evil ; he could hardly be said to injure anyone but himself.

1 *you and I* — It is essential for the understanding of the poem to realise that the ' you ' and ' I ' refer to two aspects of Prufrock's personality. The ' you ' stands for the timid, apologetic, public side of Prufrock ; the ' I ' stands for the inner man with his passionate desire for a more heroic and splendid mode of life. There is a third person in the poem, the woman, who is the object of Prufrock's love. She is consistently referred to as ' one '.

3 *etherised* — anaesthetised.

10 *an overwhelming question* — the precise nature of the ' overwhelming question ' is never defined. It is at least a declaration of love and, perhaps, a proposal of marriage. It certainly involves Prufrock's revealing his inner self to the woman concerned, thereby maybe running the risk of being laughed at.

14 *Michelangelo* — Italian painter and sculptor (1475–1564) whose life and work reflected a heroic imagination. Prufrock, trapped in the triviality of a small world, regards him with admiration and envy.

29 *works and days* — Eliot is an extremely allusive poet. Here he is making an ironic contrast between the *Works and Days* of the Greek epic poet Hesiod and the triviality of Prufrock's own ' works and days '.

56 *in a formulated phrase* — Prufrock, going timidly through the door, knows that the women in the room have already summed him up in a ' formulated ' and probably unflattering phrase.

66 *digress* — for the moment Prufrock forgets the effect created by his public personality and contemplates the physical attractiveness of the woman he loves.

69 Prufrock is on the point of making his proposal, of asking the ' overwhelming question '.

70–72 He wonders confusedly how he should begin and, after an anguished reference to loneliness, he breaks off.

73–74 Prufrock's terrible image of his own failure and self-disgust.

75 The moment has passed, the afternoon relapses into its old dead apathy. In the lines which follow, Prufrock is left to contemplate his failure and make excuses for it.

94 *Lazarus* — If Prufrock had asked the question it would have meant returning, Lazarus-like, from the living death of his public self and revealing the truth about his inner life.

121–124 Prufrock, recognising that he has failed, now wonders what kind of jaunty changes in his dress and manner might mask his inadequacy and cheer him up.

A Song for Simeon

'Now there was a man in Jerusalem, whose name was Simeon, and this man was righteous and devout, looking for the consolation of Israel, and the Holy Spirit was upon him. And it had been revealed to him by the Holy Spirit that he should not see death before he had seen the Lord's Christ. And inspired by the Spirit he came into the temple, and when the parents brought in the child Jesus, to do for him according to the custom of the law, he took him up in his arms and blessed God and said, " Lord, now lettest thou thy servant depart in peace, according to thy word ; for mine eyes have seen thy salvation which thou hast prepared in the presence of all peoples, a light for revelation to the Gentiles, and for glory to thy people Israel." And his father and his mother marvelled at what was said about him ; and Simeon blessed them and said to Mary his mother, " Behold, this child is set for the fall and rising of many in Israel, and for a sign that is spoken against (and a sword will pierce through your own soul also), that thoughts out of many hearts may be revealed." '(*Luke* 2 : 25–35).

Eliot sees Simeon standing at that unique point in time when the pagan world is about to give way to the Christian. Simeon grew up in the old dispensation, he foresees and welcomes the new Christian age but knows that he cannot share in it.

1 *Roman hyacinths* — the hyacinth was a pagan symbol for fertility and for spring.

13–16 *my children's children . . . foreign swords* — The coming of Christianity ushered in a period of great tribulation and persecution for both the Jews and Christians.

19 *stations . . . desolation* — the Way of the Cross, the Crucifixion.

20 *certain . . . sorrow* — see note on Simeon above.

21 *birth . . . decease* — a richly suggestive phrase. Paganism is dying, Christianity is being born. The year is at spring but Simeon is at the end of his life.

23 *Israel's consolation* — the coming of Christ is referred to in St. Luke's gospel as ' the consolation of Israel '. See note on Simeon above.

30 *the ultimate vision* — the full experience of Christian life, i.e., Simeon, an old man caught between the old and the new, is content to have seen his salvation in the figure of the Christ child whom he holds in his arms.

Fern Hill

3 *dingle* — dell, wooded valley.

5 *heydays* — happy days.

14 *means* — ways.
25 *nightjars* — nocturnal birds.
30 *Adam and maiden* — fresh and new like the world in the beginning.
42 *trades* — pastimes.
45 *out of grace* — out of childhood innocence.

A Refusal to Mourn

1–14 An attempt to paraphrase Thomas's poetry is dangerous ; but as the thought of this poem is difficult to grasp, the following reading of these unpunctuated lines is diffidently suggested. ' Never, until that darkness—which created man, fathered bird, beast and flower, and humbled all creation—tells me that my last hour is come and that I must be dissolved again into the inanimate world (of water and corn) to be created again, shall I make any attempt to mourn or do penance for this child's death.'

15–24 In reading these lines it may help to know that Thomas saw death as the central reality of existence : once we are born we begin to die back into the ' darkness ' of God to be reborn again. The world therefore, according to Thomas, is constantly dying, endlessly created—

After the first death, there is no other.

9 *synagogue* — Jewish place of worship.
11 *sow my salt seed* — weep.
16 *stations of the breath* — sighs.

No Second Troy

Troy — also known as Ilium, a ruined city in Asia Minor. Seeing Maud Gonne as one of the fateful women of history Yeats compares her to Helen, whose beauty brought about the conflict between the Greeks and Trojans which resulted in the destruction of Troy.

1 *her* — Maud Gonne, whom the poet loved but who turned from him to devote herself to the cause of Irish freedom. Characteristically, Yeats associates her with Helen of Troy. See note on line 9 *Among School Children* and also note on lines 21 and 22 *The Circus Animals' Desertion*.

September 1913

This poem is one of several that Yeats wrote around the year 1913 expressing his disenchantment with the Dublin merchant class of his time. The sense of disenchantment had two causes. He and his friends had been trying hard to raise money for an art gallery to house the famous Lane pictures. The response was poor and indeed William Martin Murphy, leader of the Catholic merchant class, and owner of *The Irish Independent* had opposed Yeats publicly on the issue. In fact, the poem originally carried the sub-title, ' On reading much of the correspondence against the art gallery'. The second cause related to the first : 1913 was the year of the great strike and lock-out in Dublin. The workers, led by Jim Larkin, had been ruthlessly opposed by the employers, led by W. M. Murphy, who had the backing of the Church. Again Yeats and most of the Irish intellectuals and writers took the workers' side. Consequently, in the phrase ' pray and save ' Yeats expresses his disgust at the manner in which his opponents use religion to justify greed and meanness.

8   *O'Leary* — John O'Leary (1830–1907) one of the founder members of the Fenians and the I.R.B. He was a close friend of Yeats. His respect for art and learning and his sacrifices in the service of his country appealed greatly to the young poet.

10   *The names* — the names of great Irish patriots.

17   *the wild geese* — after the Treaty of Limerick most of the Irish troops under the command of Sarsfield went to France and other European countries.

20   *Edward Fitzgerald* — Lord Edward Fitzgerald, son of the Duke of Leinster and one of the commanders of the United Irishmen.

21   *Robert Emmet* — leader of the rebellion of 1803.
      Wolfe Tone — leader of the United Irishmen.

22   *delirium* — unlike the cautious materialism of those who now ' fumble in a greasy till ', it was emotional fervour and selflessness which inspired these patriots.

25–30   Yeats suggests that people who were incapable of understanding the fervour of the patriotism of these men might be inclined to say that they were motivated by something less spiritual, perhaps by love for a woman.

30   *weighed* — counted, calculated.

The Fisherman

14   *The dead man . . . loved* — probably J. M. Synge.

23–24   This is probably a reference to the Lane picture controversy and the ' Playboy ' riots. See biographical note on Yeats.

Sailing to Byzantium

Byzantium — Constantinople, situated on the Golden Horn in Turkey. Byzantium symbolised for Yeats a perfect form of harmonious life. Yeats wrote ' I think that in early Byzantium, maybe never before or since in recorded history, religious, aesthetic and practical life were one. That architect and artificers . . . spoke to the multitude and few alike.'

1   *That* — Ireland.

5   *commend* — praise, celebrate.

3–14   There is no better way for the soul to rise above the ageing body and rejoice, than through contemplation of immortal works of art.

7–18   The poet now imagines himself standing in front of a Byzantine mosaic which depicts martyrs burning.

19   *perne in a gyre* — to ' pern ' means to move with a spiral motion. The ' gyre ' is a spinning cone which Yeats used as a symbol of time passing. Here he asks the figures in the mosaic to come back to him through time and teach him the perfection of Byzantium and finally ' gather ' his soul back into the eternity of art.

27–31   Yeats wrote ' I have read somewhere that in the Emperor's palace at Byzantium was a tree made of gold and silver, and artificial birds that sang.'

Among School Children

3   *cipher* — to do arithmetic.

9   *Ledaean* — the reference is to Maud Gonne. In Greek mythology Leda was the mother of Helen of Troy and Clytemnaestra. Their father was the god Zeus who descended upon Leda in the form of a swan. Yeats frequently associated his early love, Maud Gonne, with Leda, both because of her beauty and her influence on the history of her country.

15   *Plato's parable* — in his *Symposium* Plato suggests that male and female were twin halves of a complete sphere. It is also possible that Yeats had in mind a book illustration by Maud Gonne which showed two swans intertwined within a sphere symbolising a union through sympathy.

20   *daughters of the swan* — see note on line 9 above.

25   *Her present image* — Maud Gonne in old age.

26   *Quattrocento* — the fifteenth-century period in Italian art when Leonardo da Vinci, Bellini and Botticelli worked.

33–40   The sense of these lines seems to be as follows : ' What young mother would think herself repaid for the agony of childbirth if she were to see her child as an old man ? '

34   *Honey of generation* — Yeats himself explains that this was a drug which was said to destroy the memory of the perfect life enjoyed by the soul before birth. It is referred to again in line 36 in contrast to ' recollection '.

33–36   *a shape . . . drug decide* — these lines describe the struggle of the child to be born, his memory of a former life fighting against the drug which tries to wipe it out.

41   *spume* — light.

41–48   Here Yeats mentions the three philosophers who put forward different answers to the problem of existence. Plato saw this world merely as a shadowy reflection of a perfect and more real existence beyond. Aristotle believed in the existence of matter and bore out this belief in his stern handling of his pupil, Alexander the Great. Pythagoras, the famous mathematician, is seen by Yeats as a great artist because he discovered the relation between the length of strings when vibrating and musical notes. Having briefly referred to the theories of these three men Yeats seems to dismiss them by recalling that, all three, like himself, fell victims to old age.

42   *paradigm* — pattern.

43   *taws* — a leather strap, the end of which is cut in thin stripes, which was used as an instrument of punishment.

44   *king of kings* — Alexander the Great (356–323 B.C.).

45   *golden-thighed Pythagoras* — in Taylor's translation of the *Life of Pythagoras* there is a reference to Pythagoras's golden thighs which are taken to denote his divine origin.

53   *Presences* — the images which are referred to above now take on a supernatural significance.

57   *Labour* — man's work.

62   *bole* — trunk or stem of a tree.

The Circus Animals' Desertion

1   *theme* — subject.

6   *My circus animals* — figures which move through his plays and poems.

7   *Those stilted boys* — the awkward young lovers in his early plays and poems.

    that burnished chariot — the chariot of Cuchulain, Yeats's favourite hero.

8   *Lion and woman* — the Sphinx, who appears in such poems as *The Second Coming.*

10   *Oisin led by the nose* — legendary Irish figure, the subject of Yeats's poem *The Wanderings of Oisin,* who was enchanted by the beauty of Niamh.

11   *three enchanted islands* — the islands visited by Oisin in his wanderings.

15–16   *I that set him . . . faery bride* — ' I who wrote about Oisin's wanderings, was myself starved for love.'

16   *faery bride* — Niamh.

18   *The Countess Cathleen* — a play written by Yeats first produced in 1892. The play is about a famine in Ireland and a countess who sells everything, including her soul, to the demons so that food will be provided for the starving people. She is eventually forgiven because her intention was good.

21   *my dear* — Maud Gonne, who was so passionately devoted to the cause of Irish nationalism.

25   *the Fool and Blind Man* — two characters in Yeats's early tragedy *On Baile's Strand.*

29–30   *Character . . . memory* — Yeatsian tragedy usually culminates in the performance of a deed which in the doing gives definition and meaning to the character of the hero who performs it, his past and his present.

33   *Those . . . images* — the characters and images referred to above and which dominated his early poetry.

33–40   In this final stanza Yeats recognises that the source of all poetry, however pure and high it may be, is the human heart and the common things of life. It is on this ordinary ground that the artistic ladder of creation must be planted.

The Blackbird of Derrycairn

4   *matins* — morning office or, as in this case, the morning song of the birds.

7   *Fionn* — Fionn Mac Cumhaill, the hero of many Irish legends.

12   *gillies* — guides or attendants for sportsmen, especially fishermen.

16   *cashel* — a stone building or church boundary wall.

20   *thong* — fasten ; a strip of leather for holding things together.

The Planter's Daughter

7   *planter* — in Ireland a settler on confiscated land. The poet himself comments ' In barren Donegal, trees around a farmstead still denote an owner of planter stock.'

Stony Grey Soil

7   *Apollo* — Greek god of light and of the sun ; the ideal of male beauty.
11 *mandril, coulter* — parts of a plough.
11–12 Kavanagh remains unconverted to farming life.
12 *lea-field* — fallow field.
23 *the monster's back* — a reference, perhaps, to the small hump-backed hills or drumlins of Monaghan.
29 *Mullahinsha, Drummeril, Black Shanco*—place-names in Monaghan.

Advent

3–4 Advent was formerly strictly observed as a period of penance and fasting.
13 *whins* — furze.
16 *difference . . . burning* — for what allows us to see wisdom in an old saying.
22–23 *please/God we shall . . . payment* — we shall accept without asking for rational explanation.
24 *dreeping* — dripping.

Memory of my Father

5   *Gardner Street* — Gardiner Street, in Dublin.

Inniskeen Road

11 *Alexander Selkirk* — a Scottish sailor (1676–1721) who, after a quarrel with his captain, requested to be put ashore on one of the uninhabited islands of Juan Fernandez in 1704. He was rescued in 1709. Selkirk's adventure was the original of Defoe's *Robinson Crusoe*. William Cowper also wrote a poem entitled *The Solitude of Alexander Selkirk* which includes the lines :

> O Solitude ! where are the charms
> That sages have seen in thy face ?
> Better dwell in the midst of alarms
> Than reign in this horrible place.

Canal Bank Walk

3 *banal* — ordinary, commonplace.

11 *give me ad lib* — give me the gift of spontaneous prayer.

Lines written on a Seat on the Grand Canal

The memorial seat to Mrs. Dermot O'Brien still stands on the canal bank. After Kavanagh's death his friends commemorated him with a canal bank seat according to his wish.

8 *Parnassian* — referring to Mount Parnassus, near Delphi, which was sacred to Apollo and the Muses.

Another September

7 *St. John's* — a farmhouse in County Wexford near where the poet was staying.

all toil — personification. Having toiled in the fields the farming people are now fast asleep.

22–23 *bearing daggers/And balances* — traditional symbols of justice and retribution.

BIOGRAPHICAL NOTES

Geoffrey Chaucer

Geoffrey Chaucer (1340–1400) was the son of a London wine merchant. He spent most of his adult life in the service of England, both as soldier, and what we would now call civil servant. He was with the army of Edward III in France in 1359, was captured and later ransomed. He travelled to France and Italy on diplomatic missions and became acquainted with the works of Petrarch and Boccaccio. He spent the later part of his life in London where he held various official positions.

Chaucer has rightly been called ' the father of English Literature ' ; he was the first major English poet to absorb the Renaissance literature of continental Europe, learn its lessons, and through his own work bring England into the mainstream of European culture. Furthermore, at a time when English was divided into several regional dialects, he gave the language stability by composing his great poems in the East Midland dialect which was already the dialect of London, of the Court and of the two great universities, Oxford and Cambridge. After Chaucer the literary language swiftly took on a more or less standard form.

Though Chaucer's work was influenced by such continental writers as Dante and Boccaccio—the idea of *The Canterbury Tales* is borrowed from the latter—his genius is altogether original and intensely English. The landscape, the people, their dress, trades, customs and beliefs, have been vividly caught in his poetry, especially in the splendid pageant of *The Canterbury Tales*. Living in London Chaucer could see pilgrims making their way to the shrine of Thomas à Becket at Canterbury. It was probably from this that he got the inspiration to write his great ' frame tale ' in which each pilgrim would not only be described, but would also tell a story and join in the conversation as they went along. The pilgrimage was especially useful to his purpose as it was, perhaps, the only occasion in medieval England when all classes were thrown together for an extended period.

William Shakespeare

William Shakespeare (1564–1616) was born at Stratford-on-Avon, the son of a merchant. He has left us no detailed evidence of his early life and education. In his early twenties he left home and by 1589 he was busy both as an actor and a playwright in the London theatres.

During the following twenty-seven years he wrote that massive body of poetic drama—chronicle, comedy, tragedy and romance—which has established him as one of the greatest playwrights, not only in English, but in world literature.

His non-dramatic poetry is equally distinguished. The Sonnets were probably written between 1593 and 1596, but they were not published until 1609. They are certainly the greatest sonnet sequence in English. Taken together they are a profound exploration of a central theme—the passing of youth and beauty and the importance of love and art to, man in his struggle against time. In this sequence he brought to perfection the English or ' Shakespearean ' form of the sonnet which consists of three quatrains and a concluding couplet : abab, cdcd, efef, gg. His non-dramatic poetry also includes *Venus and Adonis* and *The Rape of Lucrece*.

Ben Jonson

Ben Jonson (1572–1637) was born in Westminster and received his education locally. He may have studied at Cambridge, but there is no record of his having taken a degree from the University. He enjoyed a great reputation for learning and collected a famous library.

Jonson was a major dramatist of his age : *Every Man in his Humour*, *Every Man out of his Humour*, *The Alchemist*, *Volpone*, *Sejanus* are recognised classics of the theatre. His comedies, both in popularity and dramatic merit, stand next only to Shakespeare's in the drama of his time. He also wrote a great number of masques for presentation at Court and he was, in fact if not in name, the first Poet Laureate of England, being granted a pension as ' King's Poet ' by James I.

His purely poetic work was less extensive though no less distinguished. *Epigrammes* and *The Forrest* appeared in 1616. *Underwoods* was published after his death. A long narrative poem recounting his adventures on a walking tour to Scotland was never published, being burned in a fire which destroyed his library in 1623.

Though he was on terms of friendship with many of the metaphysical poets of his age, Jonson did not aim at their kind of daring ingenuity in his poetry. He was more in the classical tradition and aimed rather at simplicity, elegance and correctness. He had a great influence on the Cavalier poets of the day—Lovelace, Carew, Suckling and others—who came to be known as ' the tribe of Ben '.

John Donne

John Donne (1572–1631) was born in London and later studied at Oxford and Cambridge. Baptised a Catholic, he became an Anglican in his twenties. He took Orders in 1615 at the persuasion of James I and was then appointed Royal Chaplain. In 1621 he was made Dean of St. Paul's, a position he held till his death. He was considered one of the foremost preachers of his day and his sermons, which have been preserved, are masterpieces, not only of spiritual insight, but of English prose.

He started writing poetry at an early age. The *Satires* appeared in 1593 and in the years that followed he was active both as a soldier in Spain and as an anti-Catholic pamphleteer in England. In 1611 he became seriously ill and underwent the spiritual crisis which led to his conversion. From this date on his poetry became more spiritual and profound. "At the Round Earth's Imagined Corners ", " Batter my Heart " and " O, My Black Soul " are from his *Holy Sonnets* (1618) and "A Hymn to God the Father " comes from the *Divine Poems* of his final period.

With Herbert, Marvell, Vaughan, and the Catholic poet, Crashaw, Donne explored the complex relationships between God and man, lover and beloved, time and eternity. The Metaphysicals used language in a manner as complex as their themes, drawing their comparisons from astronomy, philosophy, theology and natural science, working out their images with a rigorous logic which demands great alertness from the reader. At its worst the metaphysical method of writing resulted in what Dr. Johnson called ' heterogeneous ideas . . . yoked by violence together'. At its best it resulted in the exciting and muscular poetry represented in the present book.

George Herbert

George Herbert (1593–1633) was born at Montgomery, Wales, and educated at Cambridge where he became Public Orator in 1619. He had considerable contact with the Court but, being disappointed in his hopes of preferment, he entered the Church and was ordained in 1630. He was rector of Bemerton near Salisbury from 1630 to 1633. During this time he wrote the series of sacred poems for which he is famous ; these were published posthumously in 1633 in a collection entitled *The Temple*. He also wrote a prose work, *A Priest To The Temple*, which was described as containing ' Plain, prudent, useful rules for the Country Parson '. He was a metaphysical poet who explored in his work the great religious problems of his age, and used language and imagery in that daring, strenuous but extremely logical manner that is so characteristic of Donne and his followers. (See biographical note on John Donne.)

Henry Vaughan

Henry Vaughan (1622–1695) was born in Wales. He studied at Oxford but left without a degree, going on to study law and later medicine in London. About 1645 he began his medical practice in Brecknock in Wales.

His first collection, *Poems with the Tenth Satyre of Juvenal Englished* appeared in 1646. His subsequent poetry became increasingly serious and spiritual. Like many Christian poets and thinkers of his time he was deeply influenced by Platonism : his poem, " The Retreate ", reflects his thoughts on the Platonic belief in pre-existence and there is little doubt that it influenced Wordsworth when he came to write his great *Ode on the Intimations of Immortality*. Vaughan is usually regarded as a metaphysical poet ; he was deeply influenced by Donne and Herbert, both in his poetic methods and in the religious themes which he explored. (See biographical note on John Donne.)

Andrew Marvell

Andrew Marvell (1621–1678) was born in Yorkshire. He was educated at Hull and at Cambridge, travelling extensively in Europe before returning to England in 1646. He lived through a period of great political unrest and was deeply involved with the fortunes of Oliver Cromwell ; he was for a time tutor to Cromwell's ward, William Dutton, and was also tutor to the daughter of the great Puritan soldier, General Fairfax, between the years 1651–53. It was at Fairfax's home, Nun Appleton, with its splendid garden, that he seems to have written his best poetry—notably " Thoughts in a Garden ". A great deal of his energy at this time was given to political writing on the Parliamentarian side, but the only indisputably great poem that came out of this activity was his famous *Horatian Ode on Cromwell's Return from Ireland* (1650). The poetry which has made him famous is a small body of meditative verse in the metaphysical manner : the philosophical poem, *A Dialogue between the Resolved Soul and Created Pleasure*; those exquisite and witty love poems, *To His Coy Mistress* and *The Definition of Love*; his religious poem, *Song of the Emigrants in Bermuda* and such far-ranging meditations on nature as *The Garden* and *Upon Appleton House*.

It is interesting to note that he was for a period secretary to that other great Puritan poet, John Milton, who was in turn Latin or Foreign Secretary to Oliver Cromwell.

John Milton

John Milton (1608–1674) was born in London of cultured well-to-do parents who appear to have given him a good basic education—especially in music and literature. He studied at St. Paul's School and later at Cambridge where he had a brilliant scholastic career. From an early age he seems to have sensed his potential as a writer : he devoted himself ' to labour and intense study ' so that he might ' leave something so written to aftertimes, as they should not willingly let it die '. His studies in the Classics—he is said to have known Homer by heart—in mythology, scripture, theology and contemporary literature were so extensive that towards his death he was regarded by many as the most learned man in Europe.

When Cromwell came to power in 1649, Milton was appointed Foreign Secretary to the Government, chiefly on account of his fluency in Latin, the language of diplomacy at that time. A great deal of his energy at this period went into writing pamphlets on religious and political issues. At the age of forty-four he lost his sight and most of his work from this time on was dictated to his secretaries, one of whom was Andrew Marvell, or to his family.

In 1645 Milton assembled his best poems written before that date into a single volume ; it included *L'Allegro* and *Il Penseroso*, " Lycidas " and his famous masque *Comus*, as well as sonnets in Italian and English. The book demonstrates Milton's characteristic poetic method and approach, which was to take an established form—the elegy, the pastoral, the satire—and adapt it to his own purposes without destroying its outline.

" Lycidas " is a good example of the process. His friend, King, has been drowned and Milton wishes to write a lament. He chooses the pastoral elegy as his form : within the conventions of this form, the poet is presented as a shepherd plucking the ivy and myrtle leaves of his talent before they are ripe ; his companionship with King in the classrooms and the libraries at Cambridge is represented as the friendship of two ' swains ' who drove their flocks to pasture every morning. So far he is strictly within the pastoral elegy. But he goes further ; noting that the word ' pastor ' means both shepherd and clergyman, he reflects that King had been a candidate for Holy Orders and makes the poem an occasion for a commentary on the ' corrupt clergy ' of the day. He also reflects on the unexpectedness of death which so often strikes down the young priest or poet before his maturity. He introduces St. Peter and other Christian figures among his pagan deities and achieves a great complexity of impact.

Similarly, when Milton came to write his great epic " Paradise Lost " (1662) he followed the Homeric and Virgilian convention in invoking the muse and announcing his theme in the first paragraph, in using the epic simile, the roll-call of the chief participants, the extended epic speeches. But he undertakes ' Things unattempted yet in prose or rhyme ', and goes well beyond any of his great predecessors. Homer and Virgil had written tales of heroic human action, Dante had written an epic of little such action but of profound religious insight. Milton's design contains both characteristics ; his devils are presented as great heroic princes and warriors, yet over and above the epic action there is Milton's theological design, to ' justify the ways of God to men '.

In Milton's day the writing of an epic poem was regarded as the greatest human achievement, and in " Paradise Lost ", the immense learning, insight and energy of a dedicated life were combined. The massive music of Milton's ' grand style ' can already be sensed in some passages of " Lycidas " and certain lines of his sonnets ; the mastery of Latin and Greek gives his style a dignity and resonance compatible with his great theme ; his informed spiritual insight made it possible for him to comprehend within his vision the entire sweep of human and divine history as understood by Renaissance man.

John Dryden

John Dryden (1631–1700) was born in Northamptonshire and educated at Cambridge, receiving his B.A. in 1654. He was an admirer of Oliver Cromwell and wrote some early poetry in his praise ; but when the Puritans failed to give England a settled government, Dryden became more royalist in his sentiments and on the accession of Charles II he welcomed the new order with an enthusiastic poem, *Astraea Redux*. There was nothing inconsistent in his political change of heart : he had a passion for order in all areas of life, civic, religious and artistic. His defence of Charles II—especially in his greatest satire, "Absalom and Achitophel" (1681)—and his conversion from Anglicanism to Catholicism were expressions of this desire for stability and order. His other great satire " Mac Flecknoe " similarly shows his impatience with the inferior and shapeless writing that often passed for poetry among the critics of his time. Indeed his integrity was proven when, in the revolution of 1689, he refused to take the necessary oaths and lost his position as Poet Laureate. The remainder of his life was devoted to translations : Virgil, Horace, Ovid, Homer and Theocritus.

Perhaps his greatest contribution to English poetry was the development of the heroic couplet. This had gone out of fashion to a large extent with the rise of blank verse in the Elizabethan and Jacobean theatre ; and the metaphysical poets were inclined to favour stanzaic forms for their meditative lyrics. Dryden brought back the heroic couplet in his satiric writing and it became the most popular metrical form of the eighteenth century, reaching its greatest degree of flexibility and finesse in the work of Alexander Pope.

Alexander Pope

Alexander Pope (1688–1744) was born in London. He was deformed as a result of a childhood illness and was therefore educated at home with the help of literary friends who early recognised his extraordinary gifts.

Pope is the greatest poet of what is known as the Augustan or neo-Classical age of English literature. It was an age that prided itself on its knowledge of the classics, and most of the poetry of the eighteenth century was written in terms of the great classical models, the odes of Horace, the eclogues of Virgil, the satires of Juvenal. Their subject-matter was contemporary life—political, social, moral and philosophical questions—and they adapted the classical models or poetic forms in order to embody their own contemporary insights. It is, therefore, not surprising that Pope's first book of poems, the *Pastorals*, was written on the model of the Virgilian eclogue, that " The Rape of the Lock " took the form of a comic imitation of the epic, that *The Dunciad* was a formal satire, or that he spent many years of his life translating the *Iliad* and the *Odyssey* of Homer.

In the early years of his literary career Pope was friendly with the Whig writers, Addison and Steele, but later he joined the Scriblerus

Club, the stronghold of the Tory writers, which was presided over by such men as Swift, Arbuthnot and Gay. The attacks and counter-attacks of these two groups upon each other and each others' party resulted in some of the finest satirical poetry of the age. In *The Dunciad*, for instance, Pope attacks the dunces among his enemies rather as Dryden had done previously in " Mac Flecknoe ". " The Rape of the Lock ", perhaps Pope's most perfect poem, is remarkable for the extraordinary flexibility and polish of its verse.

William Wordsworth

William Wordsworth (1770–1850) was born in Cumberland, where he spent his youth in the Lake District before going on to study at Cambridge. At the age of twenty he went to France and remained there for two years during which time he became an enthusiast for the ideas of the French Revolution and for republicanism. His early poems, *An Evening Walk* and *Descriptive Sketches* date from this period. When he was twenty-five, Wordsworth received a legacy which enabled him to take a house in Dorset with his sister, Dorothy. His great friend, Coleridge, lived nearby. Together in 1798 the poets published *Lyrical Ballads* which contained among other pieces, Wordsworth's " Tintern Abbey " and Coleridge's *The Ancient Mariner*. It also contained Wordsworth's great *Preface* in which he gave his own views on the nature of poetry and pointed the direction that he believed it ought to take. The book became a major landmark in English poetry and is generally considered as the first important work of the Romantic Movement which was to dominate the first half of the nineteenth century. This same year Wordsworth began to write his long autobiographical poem, *The Prelude or Growth of a Poet's Mind*, which he worked on for the rest of his life and which was not published until after his death. Wordsworth challenged all the assumptions of the Augustan poets. Instead of copying classical models, he believed that the poet ought to strive for freshness and originality. Instead of the ' poetic diction ' which the Augustans deliberately cultivated, Wordsworth recommended ' the real language of men '. For Wordsworth, the source of poetry was in the primary passions of man—' the spontaneous overflow of powerful feeling '. Instead of dealing with the passing issues of political and social life the poet must return to nature for his inspiration. These directions were to a large extent followed by many of the Romantic poets. Perhaps through the influence of Coleridge there was a revived interest in the more remote past, the great mythological stories, the supernatural, the legends of the Middle Ages, tendencies which may be seen in the work of Shelley and Keats in the present collection. Wordsworth also revived the sonnet which had fallen into neglect during the previous century and wrote a considerable number of nature lyrics which appeared in an enlarged edition of *Lyrical Ballads* published in 1800.

In 1813, Wordsworth was given an official position in the County of Westmoreland which he resigned in 1842, receiving a civil list pension. He succeeded Southey as Poet Laureate in 1843.

Percy Bysshe Shelley

Percy Bysshe Shelley (1792–1822) was born in Sussex and educated at Eton and Cambridge. He was an idealistic young man, a hater of injustice and oppression, an adherent of republicanism and the ideals of the French Revolution. He abandoned Christianity at an early age and was sent down from Cambridge in 1811 for publishing his treatise, *The Necessity for Atheism*. At the age of nineteen he married Harriet Westbrook—who was then sixteen—and left her after three years. She committed suicide and soon afterwards he married Mary Godwin, daughter of William Godwin, an influential contemporary thinker whom Shelley admired.

Shelley left England for Italy in 1818. This same year his tragedy *The Cenci* and his long poem *Prometheus Unbound* were published. It was while he lived at Pisa that some of his finest lyrics were written —" Ode to the West Wind ", *Ode to a Skylark* and *The Cloud*.

Shelley's essay, *Defence of Poetry*, ranks with Wordsworth's *Preface* as one of the most eloquent statements of Romantic poetic theory. If it may be said of Pope and most of the Augustan poets, that their work is impersonal, that the man seldom, if ever, appears in his work, it may equally be said that Shelley is rarely absent from his. His lyrics tend to be a constant, passionate assertion, not only of his vision, but of his personality—the skylark has the ' unpremeditated art ' that Shelley as a poet wishes for ; the west wind has the power and force that might scatter his thoughts over the universe. This personal confrontation of reader and poet is a feature of Romantic poetry which inclines to be more subjective and passionate than any previous English verse. And of all the Romantics Shelley was perhaps the most openly self-revealing. Shelley was a friend, both of Keats and Byron. The death of Keats in 1821 moved him to write his great elegy on the dead poet, *Adonais*. In July of the following year Shelley himself was drowned at the age of thirty in a yachting accident.

John Keats

John Keats (1795–1821) was born in London where his father managed a livery stable. He was educated in a good school at Enfield up to the age of fifteen, but after the deaths of his parents, he was removed by guardians from the school and apprenticed first to an apothecary and then to a doctor. He qualified as a surgeon, but determined to devote his life to writing. His development as a poet was packed into a few years. His first really successful poem was the sonnet *On First Looking into Chapman's Homer* which he wrote at the age of twenty. By the time he was twenty-six, when he died of tuberculosis, Keats had produced a body of verse that established him as one of the great poets in English.

With Shelley, Keats belongs to the second generation of the Romantic movement. He was perhaps influenced more by Coleridge than by Wordsworth in that he went for many of his themes to medieval legend—*Isabella*, *The Eve of St. Agnes*, " La Belle Dame sans Merci "—and to the more romantic tales of classical antiquity such as *Lamia* and *Hyperion*.

His letters provide a remarkable account of his aims and exertions as a writer. Keats was a Romantic in all important aspects—his work is deeply personal, passionate and ' imaginative '. Wordsworth had associated poetry with ' the spontaneous overflow of powerful feeling '. Keats asserted that ' if poetry comes not as naturally as the leaves to a tree, it had better come not at all '. But scholarship has shown that he worked strenuously to perfect his poems and to educate his own sensibilities.

Keats's sensuousness has frequently been singled out as his most prominent characteristic. Though the early poems were often shapeless and over-sweet, their vividness in describing the world as experienced through the physical senses was remarkable. In his letters he constantly asserts the importance for the poet of being able to see and feel the outside world without always wishing to put a meaning on it : 'Axioms in philosophy are not axioms until they are proved upon the pulses '. This gift he called ' Negative Capability '—' when a man is capable of being in uncertainties, mysteries, doubts, without any irritable reaching after fact and reason '. This again is Keats's version of Wordsworth's ' wise passiveness ' mentioned in *Expostulation and Reply* where he too condemns ' the meddling intellect '. But while Wordsworth's sensuousness was largely confined to ' the mighty world of eye and ear ', Keats's embraced all the senses.

Keats was not a reformer like Shelley. He applied himself totally to the quest for ' beauty ' ; he even chided Shelley for placing poetry

at the service of human causes in an effort to change the world :
' you might curb your magnanimity, and be more of an artist '. As
he developed, Keats strove for a firmer sense of form and for greater
impersonality in his approach to the natural world. These qualities
he achieved in his great odes, most of which appeared in *Lamia and
Other Poems* published in 1820. By then he had brought his sensuousness
and passion under a splendid discipline : " Ode on a Grecian Urn "
and *To Autumn* are almost classical in their formal perfection
and their objectivity.

Alfred Lord Tennyson

Alfred Lord Tennyson (1809–1892) was born in Lincolnshire. He
was educated by his father, a rector, and was later sent to Cambridge,
where he distinguished himself as a student. From an early age he
wrote and read energetically. His first substantial work *Poems*, which
contained " The Lotos-Eaters " and *The Lady of Shalott*, was published
in 1832. This is a date worth remembering because it was the year
in which the first great Reform Bill was passed in Britain and it
inaugurates what is known as the Victorian Age in English literature.
The most outstanding Victorian poets were Tennyson, Browning,
Arnold and Hopkins—though Hopkins's work was not published until
the present century. Of these, Tennyson was the most popular in
his lifetime. He succeeded Wordsworth as Poet Laureate in 1850
and to crown a career of immense fame and success, he was granted
a peerage in 1884.

Clearly the strongest influence on Tennyson's earlier work was
Keats : *The Lady of Shalott*, for instance, evokes the enchanted world
of the Middle Ages rather as Keats had done in *The Eve of St. Agnes*,
while *Ulysses* and " The Lotos-Eaters " draw similarly on classical
legend. Tennyson had also a sensuousness reminiscent of Keats
and an astonishing skill—with the surface possibilities of language—
to evoke atmosphere, colour, landscape, and, especially, sound. His
status as a poet is still in some doubt. Many regard his skill with
words as too facile to reflect great depth or intensity. Many suspect
the sincerity of the poet who could turn Lord Cardigan's monstrous
blunder at Balaclava into a deed of such thrilling heroism in his
poem, *The Charge of the Light Brigade*. Many see him as one of the
chief perpetrators of ' the great Victorian compromise '. In other
words that he, like many of his contemporaries, kept the mask of
certainty and respectability constantly in place in order to hide the

spiritual and religious doubt that lay behind—doubt caused by rapid social change, the growth of industrialism, urbanisation, utilitarianism and the evolutionary discoveries of Darwin, to mention but a few.

This is why *In Memoriam* is so important. This poem was occasioned by the death of his friend, Arthur Hallam, in 1833 and published in 1850. It is more than a great elegy, it is also a profound questioning of Providence. On the surface it seems a simple Christian poem, but the mood is frequently, indeed disquietingly, pessimistic. T. S. Eliot has praised it not ' for the quality of its faith, but the quality of its doubt. Its faith is a poor thing, but its doubt is a very intense experience.' Yet Tennyson's own generation took *In Memoriam* to be a deeply Christian poem and Queen Victoria ranked it next to the Bible as a source of spiritual consolation. Eliot described Tennyson as ' the saddest of all English poets . . . the most instinctive rebel against the society in which he was the most perfect conformist '.

Emily Elizabeth Dickinson

Emily Dickinson (1830–1886) was born in Amherst, Massachusetts. Her father was a Congressman and in his house she was in constant contact with churchmen, politicians, writers and scholars. It is believed that as a result of an unhappy love affair she became a recluse sometime after 1854. Whatever the reason, she dedicated herself completely to writing and it was only on her death that the extent of that dedication became known. She left behind 1,775 poems which, taken together, add up to a most impressive and individual body of work. All these poems are short, condensed and epigrammatical. Their metre is uneven, the insights fragmentary, the tone varying from the profound to the whimsical. But viewed as a continuing investigation of the human condition, of life, death and love, they add up to such a remarkable achievement that she is acknowledged by many as the greatest woman poet in the English language.

Gerard Manley Hopkins

Gerard Manley Hopkins (1844–1889) was born at Stratford, Essex, and educated at Highgate School and at Oxford, where he became a friend of the poet, Robert Bridges. The famous Oxford Movement was in progress during his time at Oxford and Hopkins was drawn towards Newman and his views on Roman Catholicism. In time he became a Catholic and was ordained a Jesuit priest in 1877. When he joined the Jesuits, Hopkins resolved not to write any poetry—he had already been practising the craft—unless asked to do so by his Superior. This is in fact what eventually happened : his Rector suggested that he should write a poem on a shipwreck in which five nuns had been drowned. The result was his great poem, *The Wreck of the Deutschland* which he completed in 1875. He wrote steadily for the rest of his life, but made no effort to publish, being content with the opinions of Robert Bridges and a few intimate friends. During this period he worked as a priest in the slums of London, Liverpool and Glasgow, eventually coming to Dublin's Catholic University where he was professor of Greek. He died of typhoid in 1889 and is buried in Glasnevin Cemetery, Dublin. His work was first published by Bridges in a selected edition in 1918 and was swiftly recognised for its extraordinary freshness and energy.

While Tennyson was content to develop the language of Keats and the Romantics into subtle and splendid variations, Hopkins made a completely new departure. He abandoned the traditional metres and substituted his 'sprung rhythm' where the stresses responded to the meaning rather than to any mechanical pattern. He replaced the graceful elegance of nineteenth-century syntax with a style that used words in new and startling combinations and frequently dispensed with articles, conjunctions and even verbs. As with all great poets this language was not invented for its own sake, but to embody a deeply personal and passionate response to the world and its Creator. Since 1918 his reputation has risen steadily, and he is now regarded by many as the greatest of the Victorian poets.

Thomas Hardy

Thomas Hardy (1840–1928) was born in Dorsetshire and educated locally. He studied and practised as an architect for a time. While still in his teens he began to write poems and essays. His first real success was the novel *Far from the Madding Crowd* (1874) and until about 1896 his literary output was, for the most part, plays and novels ; on these latter his literary reputation chiefly rests. Thereafter he wrote mainly poetry ; until 1909 he was engaged on the writing of *The Dynasts*, an epic poem based on the wars between Britain and

Napoleon which appeared in three parts. After 1909, Hardy wrote nothing but lyrical poetry : *Time's Laughing-Stocks ; Satires of Circumstance ; Moments of Vision ; Late Lyrics and Earlier ;* a posthumously published volume, *Winter Woods.* In these collections much poetry which had been written earlier in his life was included.

Though Hardy was a fine poet, he was not a great innovator ; his poetry shows little desire to do anything revolutionary with form or language. The traditional forms served him very well in expressing a most intense and individual vision.

Thomas Stearns Eliot

T. S. Eliot (1888–1965) was born in St. Louis, Missouri and educated at Harvard, Oxford and the Sorbonne. He settled in England in 1915 and worked successively in teaching, banking and publishing. Eliot is considered one of the very great poets of the twentieth century and both his poetry and criticism have had a massive influence on modern literature. In 1948 he was awarded the Nobel Prize for Literature.

Looking back at the early years of the century it is now obvious that a new direction had to be found for poetry. The impulse of the Romantic Movement had steadily diluted itself as it had moved down through the previous century—through the Victorians, the Pre-Raphaelites, the Nineties and, at last, the Georgians, Masefield, Drinkwater, W. H. Davies, with their cheery, pastoral optimism. The new direction was supplied by Yeats (cf. note on Yeats), by Ezra Pound, but above all, by T. S. Eliot.

" The Love Song of J. Alfred Prufrock " which was first published in 1915 struck a new note in English poetry : this was the voice of modern urban man, timid, sensitive, unsure, sadly conscious that he may have lost the heroic possibilities of his forefathers. Eliot's early poems are deeply pessimistic and this pessimism finds its greatest expression in his long, difficult poem *The Waste Land* published in 1922. In 1927 Eliot became an Anglican and in that year he wrote *Journey of the Magi* which marked the beginnings of a new mood of Christian optimism in his work. This new mood finds its fullest expression in *Four Quartets*, the greatest poem of his final period. Apart from his poetry and criticism Eliot wrote a series of interesting and influential poetic dramas—*Murder in the Cathedral, The Family Reunion, The Cocktail Party, The Confidential Clerk.*

Dylan Thomas

Dylan Thomas (1914–1953) was born in Swansea and educated at the local grammar school. He began his career as a journalist and went on to become a script-writer for the B.B.C. The best of Thomas's poetry is contained in his *Collected Poems*, published in 1952. In addition to his poetry Dylan Thomas wrote a play for voices, *Under Milk Wood*, completed by the poet a short time before his death, and which has had enormous success both on stage and radio. He also wrote the short stories contained in *The Map of Love* and *Portrait of the Artist as a Young Dog*. His radio scripts were collected and published after his death under the title, *Quite Early One Morning*. Towards the end of his life Thomas undertook a number of lecture tours in the United States and it was in America that he died in 1953.

Dylan Thomas is one of the most truly individual of modern poets. He uses English almost as a new language, using words in new and startling combinations, throwing images together unexpectedly so as to produce complex effects, adapting the language and symbols of the Bible to convey his own curiously sacramental view of the world. In all this there is no one he resembles more than Hopkins. Perhaps the most remarkable quality of his verse is its extraordinary resonance; his poetry is at its best read aloud, and his own recordings of it are quite superb.

William Butler Yeats

W. B. Yeats (1865–1939) was born in Dublin of a Sligo family. The only formal schooling he received in early life was during brief periods at the Godolphin School, London, and the High School, Dublin. Later he studied painting at the Metropolitan School of Art in Dublin. It was here that he met A.E. (George Russell) who shared with him a great interest in mysticism, theosophy and fairy faith. Yeats soon gave up painting and devoted himself to literature. His early masters were the English Romantic and Pre-Raphaelite poets, as well as Blake and Spenser. Slowly he became more and more interested in the Irish tradition, the ancient myths, the history, the folklore. In 1889 he wrote his long narrative poem, *The Wanderings of Oisin*, based on an Irish legend, and from this point on, Ireland figured more and more prominently in his work. With Lady Gregory and J. M. Synge he founded first the Irish Literary Theatre in 1899 and later in 1904, the Abbey Theatre. His first volume of poems, *Crossways* (1889) contained several of his early attempts to adapt the Irish ballad as a literary form—*The Ballad of Father Hart* and *The Ballad of Moll Magee.* His next three volumes, *The Rose* (1893), *The Wind among the Reeds* (1899), *In the Seven Woods* (1904), are usually regarded as his ' early poetry ' : by and large they deal with mystical problems and vague, elusive states of mind, and particularly with his hopeless love for Maud Gonne.

With Maud Gonne's marriage to Major John MacBride in 1903 there comes a change in Yeats's writing. " No Second Troy " which was included in his 1910 volume, *The Green Helmet*, shows a more vigorous and realistic attitude to love, and the entire volume is full of active interest in everyday affairs. All the poems in the present book are from Yeats's middle or final periods ; in one way or another they explore the possibility of perfection in life and perfection in art.

Among the affairs to which Yeats applied himself were the development of drama at the Abbey and the finding of a suitable gallery for the magnificent collection of paintings which Hugh Lane had offered to the nation. On both fronts he was frustrated : the crowds rioted at Synge's *The Playboy of the Western World*, and the citizens of Dublin were niggardly with their subscriptions for the Municipal Gallery. His 1914 volume, *Responsibilities*, contains several satires on the materialism and vulgarity of Dublin's rich. " September 1913 " sets out the problem against its historical background : Ireland has betrayed its heroic past. " The Fisherman " is a variation on the same theme : the ' great art ' is beaten down by the unmannerly scorn of Dublin, and Yeats turns away and tries to build up in words a picture of a Connemara fisherman whose life reflects the values of simplicity, wisdom and quiet dignity. It is only proper to add that in his great poem, *Easter 1916*, he reverses his opinion of Dublinmen, and salutes them for their heroism in the Easter Rising.

All his life Yeats sought for a harmonious way of life as well as a perfect form of art. With the onset of old age he thought of eternity— especially the eternity of art. " Sailing to Byzantium ", in his 1928 collection, makes a contrast between the world of birth and death, between ' Those dying generations ' and the ' artifice of eternity ' which he sees in the perfection of Byzantine art. The same theme is taken up in "Among School Children " : the ' sixty-year-old smiling public man ' looks at the children, reflects on his old age and that of Maud Gonne whom he once loved, considers the attempts of the great philosophers to solve the mystery of time and eternity, and concludes with those two symbols of harmonious life, the ' great-rooted ' chestnut-tree and the dancer lost in the beauty of her dance. " The Circus Animals' Desertion " is one of his last poems. In it he recapitulates his whole life spent in searching for perfect forms as a poet and playwright, forgetting the ' foul rag-and-bone shop of the heart ' from which all inspiration, however high and perfect, must ultimately come. In fact all the poems may be seen in terms of two related themes—the quest for a perfect form of life, and a perfect form of art.

Yeats was made a Senator in 1922 and he was awarded the Nobel Prize for Literature in 1923. He died in France in January 1939, but his body was not brought back to Ireland until after the Second World War. He is buried at Drumcliffe, Co. Sligo.

Austin Clarke

Austin Clarke was born in 1896 in Dublin and educated at Belvedere College and University College, Dublin. He succeeded Thomas MacDonagh as a lecturer in the English Department there in 1917 and continued to work in this position until 1921. He spent the next twelve years in England working as a critic and book reviewer, until his final return to Ireland in the nineteen thirties.

His first poems were short epics based on Irish heroic literature— *The Vengeance of Fionn*, *The Sword of the West*. In 1927 he published his first poetic play, *The Son of Learning*, and in the years following he wrote a distinguished body of poetic drama. He also has written three novels based on medieval Irish life, *The Bright Temptation*, *The Singing Men at Cashel* and *The Sun Dances at Easter*. His most outstanding volumes of poetry have been *Pilgrimage*, *Night and Morning*, *Ancient Lights*, *Too Great a Vine* and *The Horse-Eaters* and his recent satirical volumes, *Flight To Africa* and *Old-Fashioned Pilgrimage*. His remarkable autobiography, *Twice round the Black Church* is not only very interesting in itself, but casts valuable light on many of his poems. The second volume of his autobiography, *A Penny in the Clouds*, was published in 1968.

Regarding his poetry it might usefully be said that Clarke emerged from the matrix of the Irish literary renaissance. His poetry, unlike that of Patrick Kavanagh, is written within the shadow of Ireland's past. His experimentation with Gaelic metres in English has resulted in a most subtle and varied rhythm and cadence in his verse : particularly attractive is his frequent use of assonance or middle rhyme, examples of which can be found in " The Planter's Daughter " and " The Blackbird of Derrycairn ". Clarke's main theme is what he calls ' the drama of racial consciousness ' and in his later poetry he explores the civil and religious tensions of modern Irish society with especial reference to their source in history. His later verse is inclined to be increasingly satirical. He is regarded by many as Ireland's greatest poet since Yeats.

Patrick Kavanagh

Patrick Kavanagh (1906–1968) was born on a small farm in Monaghan and was educated at the local national school. His first volume of poetry, *Ploughman and Other Poems*, was published in 1936 while he was still working on the family farm. Three years later he came to Dublin. His poems can be divided into two main sections : those with a Monaghan background and those with a Dublin background. His first volume and his collection of 1947, *A Soul for Sale*, deal almost exclusively with rural experience, while his later volume, *Come Dance with Kitty Stobling*, has many poems based on the poet's experiences in Dublin.

The most striking aspect of the early poetry was the skill with which Kavanagh could reflect in his verse the common, everyday experiences of Monaghan life. His nature poetry is a constant celebration of such things as the ' heart-breaking strangeness in dreeping hedges ', of ' banks and stones and every blooming thing ', of ' a stick carried down a stream/And the undying difference in the corner of a field '. Side by side with this was his constant sense of the divine in the natural. In "Advent " he writes of ' God's breath in common statement ' and Christ coming ' with a January flower '. While he loved the Monaghan landscape he also resented at times the way it had limited him for so long, had ' burgled ' his ' bank of youth '. This mood finds expression in a poem like " Stony Grey Soil " and even more so in his longest poem, *The Great Hunger*.

The Dublin poems express a new mood of serenity and acceptance. The sacramental view of the world remains and so does his philosophy of the commonplace :

> Leafy-with-love banks and the green waters of the canal
> Pouring redemption for me, that I do
> The will of God, wallow in the habitual, the banal,
> Grow with nature again as before I grew.

Kavanagh was not a prolific poet but in his lifetime he produced a body of poems so remarkable for its freshness of language and individuality of insight as to secure him a place in the front rank of Irish poets. A seat in Kavanagh's memory was erected by his friends on the bank of the Grand Canal near Baggot Street Bridge. It carries the text of his other Dublin sonnet, " O Commemorate me where there is water ". His *Collected Poems* were published in 1964. His novel, *Tarry Flynn*, is not only a fine novel in its own right, but an interesting companion-book to his Monaghan poems. A dramatised version has been staged with great success in the Abbey and Peacock Theatres in Dublin.

Thomas Kinsella

Thomas Kinsella was born in 1928 in Dublin and educated at O'Connell Schools and, later, at University College, Dublin. He worked in the Civil Service between the years 1946 and 1965 when he went to America to lecture in the University of Illinois, where he is now a professor. His first two volumes, *Poems* and *Another September* were published in 1958 and since then his major collections have been *Downstream* (1962), *Wormwood* (1966) and *The Phoenix Park* (1968). He is regarded by many as the leading Irish poet of his generation.

The two poems that represent him in the present book are typical of Kinsella's best work. It can be said of Austin Clarke that he is a poet who sets himself to explore the Irish scene and the Irish state of mind almost to the exclusion of all else. Of Patrick Kavanagh it can be said that he confines himself largely to two areas of Irish life, the small farming community of Monaghan and the Dublin scene. Thomas Kinsella in much of his poetry does deal with specifically Irish experience, but at the same time he strives to go beyond it. "Another September " and " Mirror in February " might have been written by a poet of any nationality. They explore universal states of mind : that moment between sleep and awakening when the individual looks at himself in the ' mirror of his soul ' and thinks about the passing of time, the process of ageing and the coming of death. Both poems aim at great compression of language and of thought. Both are firmly structured so as to contain within their stanzaic form a unified and completed process of thought. In each poem are combined that strong emotional power and intellectual control that characterise Thomas Kinsella's poetry at its best.

ACKNOWLEDGEMENTS

The publishers wish to thank the following for permission to include copyright material in this book :

Macmillan & Co., Ltd., Publishers, and the Trustees of the Hardy Estate, for " During Wind and Rain ", " When I set out for Lyonnesse ", "Afterwards " and " In Time of ' The Breaking of Nations ' " taken from *The Collected Poems of Thomas Hardy*; Macmillan & Co., Ltd., Publishers, and Mr. M. B. Yeats for the following poems from the *Collected Works of W. B. Yeats* : " No Second Troy ", " September 1913 ", " The Fisherman ", " Sailing to Byzantium ", "Among School Children " and " The Circus Animals' Desertion " ; Messrs. Mac-Gibbon & Kee, Ltd., for the following poems from the *Collected Poems of Patrick Kavanagh* : " Stony Grey Soil ", "Advent ", " Memory of my Father ", " Inniskeen Road ", " Canal Bank Walk " and " Lines written on a Seat on the Grand Canal " ; Messrs. Faber & Faber, Ltd., for the following poems by T. S. Eliot : " The Love Song of J. Alfred Prufrock " and "A Song for Simeon " from *Collected Poems 1909–1962* ; Messrs. J. M. Dent & Sons, Ltd., and the Trustees for the copyrights of the late Dylan Thomas for " Fern Hill " and "A Refusal to Mourn ", from *Collected Poems of Dylan Thomas*; The Dolmen Press, Ltd., and the authors concerned for " The Lost Heifer ", " The Blackbird of Derrycairn " and " The Planter's Daughter " by Austin Clarke, and " Mirror in February " and "Another September " by Thomas Kinsella ; Oxford University Press for six poems by Gerard Manley Hopkins from *Poems* ed. W. H. Gardner.